INTEREST GROUPS IN AMERICAN CAMPAIGNS

The New Face of Electioneering

Second Edition

Mark J. Rozell
GEORGE MASON UNIVERSITY

Clyde Wilcox
GEORGETOWN UNIVERSITY

David Madland
GEORGETOWN UNIVERSITY

CQ PRESS

A Division of Congressional Quarterly Inc.
Washington, D.C.

CQ Press
1255 22nd Street, NW, Suite 400
Washington, DC 20037

Phone: 202-729-1900; toll-free, 1-866-427-7737 (1-866-4CQ-PRESS)

Web: www.cqpress.com

Cover design: Circle Graphics

Cover photos: AP Wide World Photos

⊗ The paper used in this publication exceeds the requirements of the American National Standard for Information Sciences—Permanence of Paper for Printed Library Materials, ANSI Z39.48-1992.

Printed and bound in the United States of America

09   08   07   06   05   1   2   3   4   5

Library of Congress Cataloging-in-Publication Data

Rozell, Mark J.
  Interest groups in American campaigns / Mark J. Rozell, Clyde Wilcox, David Madland.— 2nd ed.
      p. cm.
  Includes bibliographical references and index.
  ISBN 1-933116-24-2 (alk. paper)
  1. Pressure groups—United States. 2. Lobbying—United States. 3. Political campaigns—United States. 4. United States—Politics and government—20th century. 5. United States—Politics and government—21st century. I. Wilcox, Clyde. II. Madland, David. III. Title.

  JK1118.R69 2006
    324'.40973—dc22

                                                                2005024950

INTEREST GROUPS
IN AMERICAN CAMPAIGNS

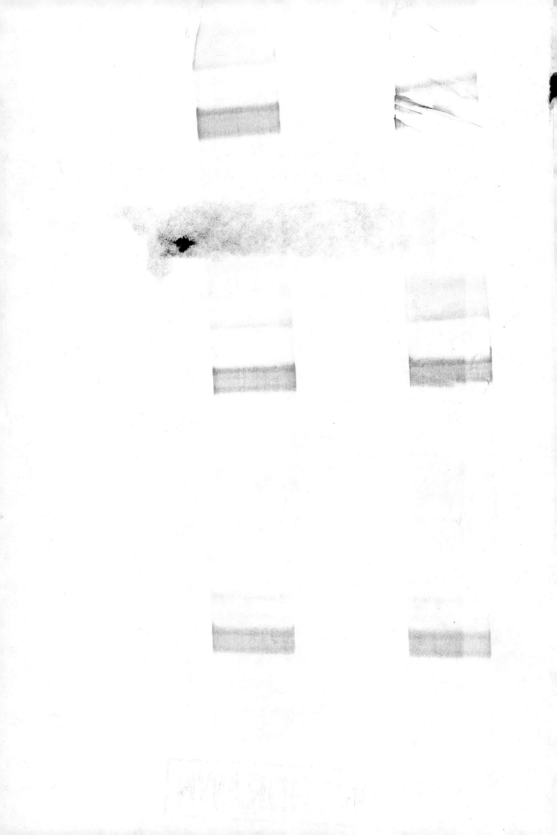

To Renée Kathryn Rozell,
born April 12, 1998
M. J. R.

To the memory of my mother,
Sarah Louise Wilcox
C. W.

To Karin,
D. M.

Contents

Preface

Interest groups have become key players in U.S. electoral politics. Whereas political observers traditionally have referred to campaigns as either party dominated or candidate centered, we believe that the agendas of coalitions of organized groups are increasingly defining the themes and issues on which campaigns are conducted. Groups are more involved in electoral politics than ever before, and oftentimes their activities do more to influence the campaign discourse than do the parties and candidates themselves. For generations, leading scholars have debated the implications for democratic governance when certain groups with the most resources dominate the competitive interest group environment. Most of these critiques focused on how groups try to manipulate the lawmaking process to their own favor. But few have examined what happens when coalitions of groups supplant the traditional roles of parties and candidates in elections. How is democratic accountability affected when the voices of those whose names appear on the ballots are overwhelmed by the steady stream of noise from organized groups?

The first edition of this book appeared in 1999. Since then, the system of financing U.S. federal campaigns has undergone a profound change due to the Bipartisan Campaign Reform Act (BCRA). This new edition describes the role of interest groups through the 2004 election campaign, the first to be conducted after the BCRA rules went into effect. BCRA did not eliminate the role of interest groups in campaigns, but rather it redefined that role to a certain extent and channeled interest group activity.

The focus of this book is on how groups communicate their goals with parties, candidates, and voters. Chapter 1 first describes and analyzes the nature of the U.S. federal election system. It details how U.S. elections differ from those of other Western democracies and thus encourage the active participation of interest groups. Chapter 2 discusses the ways in which groups ally themselves with parties and attempt to influence the candidates whom the parties nominate and the platforms that the parties adopt. Chapter 3 focuses on the methods by which groups communicate with candidates, principally by giving money or goods and services to campaigns. Chapter 4 explores the ways that interest groups communicate with their own members and the broader electorate. The concluding chapter focuses on recent and possible future reforms of laws that channel interest group activities in elections.

A number of individuals assisted with the development and production of this book. We especially thank our colleagues Robert Biersack, John C. Green, and Paul Herrnson as well as the anonymous reviewers who critiqued the book at various stages. Brenda Carter, the director of the college division at CQ Press, provided the early encouragement and support for this project. We thank all of the CQ Press staff who assisted with the production of the manuscript. For the first edition these included production editors Nadine Steffan and Talia Greenberg, copyeditor Sandy Chizinsky, compositor Jessica Forman, and indexer Joyce Teague. For the second edition several individuals assisted as well, including research assistant Debasree Das Gupta, assistant editor Colleen Ganey, production editor Joan Gossett, copyeditor Amy Marks, compositor Jessica Forman, and indexer Enid Zafran.

For both editions of the books we interviewed a number of individuals in the Washington, D.C., community who are active in interest group and party politics. Some of these individuals are quoted in the pages that follow, and many are the sources for important leads and ideas that shaped our own thinking on the role of interest groups in elections. We thank Walter Barbee, Rich Bond, Jeff Butsky, Pat Carpenter, Bob Corolla, Chuck Cunningham, Maggie Duncan, Jeff Eagan, Dylan Glenn, Patricia Goldman, William Greener, William Harris, Heather Herndon, Karen Hincks, Christine La Rocco, Hon. Larry La Rocco, Gregg Lebell, Mitchell Lester, Tanya Metaska, Kim Mills, John Morgan, Rudy Oswald, Trey Richardson, Peter Roff, Bill Samuel, Amy Simon, Ann E. W. Stone, David Voepel, James Wagoner, and Paul Wilson.

CHAPTER 1

Interest Groups and American Politics

In the 2004 elections, interest groups were more active and visible than ever before. They participated in primaries, caucuses, and conventions that nominated Republican and Democratic candidates for various offices—sometimes recruiting candidates, sometimes backing challengers to the party favorite—and also struggled to influence party platforms. In the general election, interest groups supported candidates for the presidency, for Congress, for state legislatures, and for school boards. They held house parties, organized concerts, e-mailed updates, created Web-based videos, distributed voters' guides in shopping malls, union halls, and churches, and called their members to urge them to support specific candidates. In some states, coalitions of interest groups aired television and radio ads attacking presidential and congressional candidates—and these ads were often far more memorable and influential than those aired by the candidates.

Well aware of the potential for gains in votes and contributions, many candidates courted interest groups. These candidates appeared at interest group conventions, met with group leaders and members, and adopted issue positions to appeal to those people. President George W. Bush endorsed a proposed constitutional amendment that would ban gay marriage in an effort to court support from conservative Christian organizations (Cooperman and Edsall 2004). John Kerry, for his part, made special appeals to unions, environmental groups, and women's organizations. Congressional candidates cultivated ties with the National Rifle Association (NRA) and Handgun Control, Inc.; with anti-abortion and pro-choice groups; and with businesses and labor unions.

What leads interest groups to take such an active role in American elections? Interest groups seek to influence governmental policies, and their leaders believe that participation in the electoral process can help achieve this goal. First, by helping to elect candidates who share their views, interest groups can change the personnel of government, thereby increasing the likelihood that the policies they support will be implemented. Second, by aiding policy makers in their campaigns, interest groups can more easily approach these officials to argue their cases.

For example, in March 2005 the *Washington Post* listed benefits that came to business groups that backed Republican congressional candidates and President Bush for reelection. MBNA Corporation, one of President Bush's largest financial backers, won changes in laws making it harder for individuals to claim bankruptcy and cancel credit card debt. Exxon Mobil Corporation and other oil companies that had channeled large sums to Republican candidates were close to winning the right to drill for oil in the Arctic National Wildlife Refuge in Alaska, and Wal-Mart won protection from certain class-action suits. It is unlikely that any of these bills would have passed had Democrats controlled either chamber of Congress or the presidency. Clearly these companies had reason to be involved in elections, and the trial lawyers, labor unions, and environmental groups that opposed these measures had reason to be active as well (VandeHei 2005).

Interest group strategies and tactics depend on two sets of factors: the legal regulations and common practices that govern electoral activity, and the goals and resources of the group. The combination of legal regulations and common practices creates an *opportunity structure*—the framework within which interest groups can conduct their electoral activities. The interaction of the opportunity structure with goals and resources creates the *strategic context* of elections. Interest groups choose broad strategies on the basis of their goals and resources and then choose among the tactics that are available under the rules.

Why are more interest groups active in elections in more ways than ever before? To begin with, there are simply more interest groups than there were in the past, and they are pursuing more diverse policy goals. Early in the twentieth century, most interest groups were economic organizations, such as corporations and labor unions, with fairly narrow goals—to maximize profits or wages and benefits, for example. Although these groups sought to influence government policy, political action was not their primary activity. In contrast, the principal goal of the newer interest groups—often referred to as *citizens' groups*—is to influence public policy, and the leaders of many of these groups view political action as the primary means of achieving policy goals. Although the goals of any one group may be narrow, collectively these new groups have taken on an extraordinary array of domestic and foreign policy issues, from banning abortions to limiting product liability lawsuits, and from expanding trade with China to expanding the U.S. space program.

The vast majority of citizens' groups currently active in Washington were created since the 1960s (Walker 1983). The wave of interest group formation that began in that decade—and continues, more moderately, today—springs largely from major social movements—principally the civil rights, feminist, gay and lesbian rights, and Christian Right movements, although there are also a number of interest groups that focus on single issues such as abortion or gun control. However, both single-issue groups and those that have sprung from social movements are highly active in electoral politics.

A second factor driving growth in interest group activity is the expansion of government involvement in everyday life. Legislation in the 1960s protecting citizens from discrimination on the basis of race or sex spurred the development of interest groups among minorities and women. The creation of Medicare in 1965 had a similar effect among older Americans. Growth among environmental groups occurred both before and after the passage of legislation to guarantee clean air and water, to protect endangered species, and to protect wetlands. Government regulations of the past four decades have spurred corporations to be more active in politics than they were before the 1960s.

Third, technology has made it much easier for interest groups to participate in electoral politics. Consider, for example, what would once have been a virtually impossible task: producing and mailing thousands of specially targeted materials two weeks before an election. Today, all any group needs is a moderately sophisticated computer, a good color printer, a minimum of expertise, and a few days of time. Technology has made it possible to identify the twenty closest congressional races, to match the zip codes of interest group members against congressional districts, and to produce targeted mailings just in time to sway members' votes.

Finally, George W. Bush's narrow electoral college victory in November 2000 and the policies that his administration enacted with the help of slim Republican majorities in the House and Senate mobilized all kinds of political groups in the early years of the new century. Business and environmental groups alike understood that the relaxation of environmental regulations might be reversed with a few more votes in the 2004 presidential election, or a few more Democratic victories in the House or Senate. Pro-life and pro-choice groups understood that the next president might replace several Supreme Court justices, which might alter abortion policy for a generation. A closely divided nation gave strong incentive for both sides to try harder to convince and mobilize voters in 2004, for the lesson of Bush's narrow 2000 victory was that every vote can matter. And the 2004 election certainly confirmed that lesson, as Bush won reelection by a one-state margin in the electoral college and analysts credited the successful mobilization of various groups—most notably, religious conservatives, gun enthusiasts, and small business advocates—as critical to the outcome.

A Brief History of Interest Groups in Elections

Although interest groups are indeed more active in American elections than at any time in U.S. history, their participation in electoral politics is as old as the nation itself. In 1757, local merchants donated liquor to bribe voters in George Washington's run for election to the Virginia House of Burgesses (Sabato 1984). Religious groups were deeply involved in the party cleavages of the nineteenth century (Howe 1980; Swierenga 1980), in debates over removing Native Americans from their territory, and in controversies over slavery.

The election of 1896 was a watershed for interest group involvement in electoral politics. Mark Hanna, a Cleveland industrialist, contributed $100,000 (equivalent to more than $1 million today) to Republican William McKinley's presidential campaign; more important, however, Hanna *organized* the campaign. While McKinley sat greeting visitors on his front porch in Canton, Ohio, Hanna recruited and sent off on tour an army of some 1,400 pro-McKinley speakers. Hanna also raised record amounts for McKinley—between $35 million and $100 million in current dollars— by assessing banks and corporations a fee based on their assets. Standard Oil and J. P. Morgan gave $250,000 each (Baida 1992). While Democratic nominee William Jennings Bryan mobilized farmers, workers, and evangelical Christians, the Grand Old Party tapped the deep pockets of corporate America, outspending the Democrats by perhaps as much as twenty to one. By the early twentieth century, interest groups had become increasingly involved in elections, spurring efforts to regulate their activities. In 1907 the Tilman Act banned direct corporate and bank contributions to campaigns, but business found other ways of channeling money to candidates.

As interest groups increased in number and influence, they made their presence felt in both the Democratic and Republican Parties. Populist and progressive groups made their way into the Democratic Party, especially in states such as Wisconsin and Iowa. Newly formed labor unions allied themselves with the Democrats, and small and large businesses became core groups in the Republican base. Immigrants became part of the Democratic Party machine, while nativist groups were active in Republican politics. Eventually the New Deal coalition defined the Democratic Party as a collection of diverse groups—including labor, Catholics and Jews, racial minorities, and southerners—while the GOP established a strong constituency among both large and small businesses.

Although party organizations remained strong and party leaders continued to control nominations, interest groups were increasingly active and visible members of party coalitions. By midcentury the two dominant political parties had established comfortable relations with interest groups: parties chose candidates and developed platforms, and interest groups backed the party nominees. But in the 1960s the landscape changed abruptly.

There was an explosion in the formation of groups that represented not just economic interests but other policy issues as well. In 1986 Kay Lehman Schlozman and John Tierney reported that a majority of civil rights groups and more than three-fourths of citizens' groups, social welfare groups, and poor people's organizations had been founded since 1960 (Schlozman and Tierney 1986, 75). In the years since this study, the growth of policy-oriented groups has slowed somewhat, but the overall trend has continued.

Citizens committed to the broad social movements of the 1960s and early 1970s—in particular, the civil rights, antiwar, and feminist movements—surged into the Democratic Party, demanding representation and a voice in party policy. During the 1968 Democratic National Convention, the party establishment kept the newcomers out, and they marched by the thousands in the streets of Chicago. By 1972 the party had changed its regulations to allow interest groups greater influence on party nominations. At about the same time, changes in campaign finance laws led corporations and ideological groups to become involved in financing electoral campaigns. From the 1970s onward, interest groups were actively engaged in all stages and aspects of electoral contests.

During the 1990s, the two parties moved farther apart on key issues. The Republican victories of 1994 brought a new cohort of very conservative Republicans to Congress, often replacing moderate Democrats whose departures left a more liberal Democratic party. The narrow GOP majority meant that many interest groups that had once supported candidates from both parties would now focus their efforts to aid candidates from a single party. Changes in campaign finance rules led coalitions of interest groups to mount their own independent campaigns on behalf of candidates in specially targeted House races, spending millions of dollars on advertising that defined candidates' positions on issues and attacked their opponents' records and even their character.

By 2004, coalitions of interest groups faced off in contested congressional races and in the presidential election. Business groups became more solidly Republican, environmental groups became more solidly Democratic, and many groups had greatly increased their political activity. Interest group coalitions and newly formed interest groups spent millions in television ads, in voter contact, and in new forms of electioneering.

To explore fully the role of interest groups in America, first we describe the diversity of interest groups and the nature of their political goals. Next we examine varying views of the role of interest groups in American politics. Then we consider the ways in which the unique characteristics of the American electoral system create opportunities for electoral involvement by interest groups. Finally we explore the laws and regulations that govern interest group activity in elections.

DIVERSE GROUPS, DIVERSE GOALS

Rhetoric about "special interests" has succeeded in persuading many citizens that interest groups play a devious and damaging role in American democracy. Candidates inevitably attack the "special interests" that support their opponents while welcoming contributions and endorsements from the "organized citizens" who are members of their own coalitions. In 1984 President Ronald Reagan enjoyed the support of much of corporate America and of citizens' groups that included the Veterans of Foreign Wars, the NRA, and the Moral Majority. Nonetheless, because Democratic challenger Walter Mondale had the support of unions, environmental groups, feminists, and civil rights organizations, Reagan successfully attacked Mondale as the "candidate of special interests." In the 2004 presidential campaign, John Kerry attacked George W. Bush for receiving support from corporate interests, especially energy companies, while Bush attacked Kerry for receiving support from trial lawyers.

Surveys show that a majority of Americans believe that both parties are beholden to special interests. According to a 2003 *Newsweek* survey, 70 percent of respondents agreed with the statement "this country's political system is so controlled by special interests and partisanship that it cannot respond to the country's real needs" (*Newsweek* 2003). For many years, the National Election Studies have asked citizens whether they believe that "the government is pretty much run by a few big interests looking out for themselves or that it is run for the benefit of all the people." In 2004 nearly 60 percent of respondents replied that the government is run by a few big interests.

Ironically, many Americans who fear the power of interest groups are themselves members or supporters of such groups. Interest groups are simply collections of individuals who seek to influence public policy. Many small local organizations are interest groups. Consider, for example, two groups organized in Fairfax County, Virginia. Citizens United to Preserve Huntley Meadow was organized to protect a small wetlands park—home to herons, bitterns, beaver, and raccoons and the site of beautiful sunsets—from a proposed road that the group believes will drain oil into the watershed. The Family Friendly Libraries group was formed to protest the inclusion of a gay newspaper among other community publications distributed free of charge at public libraries. Both organizations have attracted a number of committed activists, along with a somewhat larger group of less involved members, and have succeeded in drawing public attention to their causes.

Interest groups also include large organizations. Environmental groups such as the Sierra Club and Friends of the Earth are interest groups, and so are anti-abortion and pro-choice groups such as Operation Rescue and the National Abortion and Reproductive Rights Action League (NARAL

Pro-Choice America—hereafter, NARAL). The NRA and Handgun Control, Inc., are interest groups, as are the National Organization for Women, Concerned Women for America, the Children's Defense Fund, the National Council of Churches, and the National Association for the Advancement of Colored People (NAACP).

Interest groups focused primarily on economic policy include corporations both large and small, from Microsoft to the thousands of small companies with only a handful of employees; umbrella business organizations, such as the U.S. Chamber of Commerce and the National Federation of Independent Businesses (NFIB); trade associations, such as the National Petroleum Institute, that represent entire sectors of the corporate economy; large national labor unions and small local unions; and professional organizations, such as the American Bar Association (ABA), the American Medical Association (AMA), and the American Political Science Association.

Whether an organization constitutes an interest group according to our definition depends critically on whether it seeks to influence government policy. An Elvis fan club is not an interest group, but if the members approach government officials to support an Elvis stamp, it becomes an interest group. Similarly, churches become interest groups when they lobby government or seek to influence elections. Many churches confine their activities to the religious arena, but some endorse candidates, others mount voter registration drives, and still others collect petitions against abortion or urge their members to write letters to Congress in support of national health insurance. Entire religious denominations constitute interest groups when they lobby government—as many often do (Hertzke 1988).

Some political groups do not have individual members. Rather, their members are other groups. The American Federation of Labor–Congress of Industrial Organizations (AFL-CIO), for example, has as its members individual labor unions. The members of trade associations are not primarily individuals but companies. In recent years, the boundaries of what constitutes a political group have blurred. In the 2004 campaign, liberal groups formed a number of formal coalitions, including Americans Coming Together, America Votes, and the Progressive Network. These organizations were primarily structures through which other organizations could cooperatively plan electoral activity. Other groups appear to be primarily political amplifiers for the voices of single wealthy individuals.

Let Freedom Ring, a multi-issue conservative group, was funded primarily by a single donor at first and later primarily by him and his friends. The group aired Internet advertising and distributed in churches in Ohio and Pennsylvania a video designed to increase support for George W. Bush. By channeling his money through an organization with an attractive and broad name, this individual hoped to be more successful than he would have been had he simply spent the money under his own name. In this book we treat these organizations as though they were interest groups, although it is important to understand that they are very different from membership organizations such as the NRA or Sierra Club.

It is useful to think of four distinct types of groups: business groups, professional associations, labor unions, and citizens' groups. Business groups include corporations, trade associations, and larger business organizations. Corporations often approach government for assistance with particular problems—to obtain relief from regulatory controls, to obtain protection from product liability suits or from foreign or domestic competition, or to seek government contracts. Note that the goals of one corporation are often in conflict with those of another, as they compete for markets and resources. Although the resources of large corporations enable them to get involved in elections, many corporations are too small to play significant roles in electoral politics. Trade associations, which represent entire industries, seek policies that will benefit a particular type of business—construction, oil, or tobacco, for example. Business associations, such as the U.S. Chamber of Commerce and the NFIB, seek to influence economic policy: to lower taxes, reduce regulation, protect American patents and copyrights, and keep labor costs low.

Professional associations vary widely in their goals. Most seek some protection from competition through licensing and control over professional credentials. Teachers' associations, for example, want to ensure that only those with education degrees can teach in public schools; lawyers' groups want to ensure that certain services can be provided only by lawyers. Professional associations also promote policies that will benefit their members economically, such as when the AMA promotes certain policies regarding government health insurance programs. Professional associations also support broader policy changes, however. For example, the ABA proposes model legal codes for the states and rates presidential nominees for federal court, and the AMA lobbies for antismoking legislation.

Labor unions generally support policies that promote job creation, protect union workers from economic loss during recessions, protect union workers from job loss when factories move overseas, regulate employer-worker relations, and require employers to provide health insurance benefits. Unions also favor policies that benefit retired workers, such as funding for Medicare and Social Security. At times, unions have joined larger coalitions to promote civil rights.

Citizens' groups represent an almost bewildering array of causes: legal protection for African American, Hispanic, gay, lesbian, and disabled citizens; policies that make it easier (or harder) for women to work outside the home; policies for or against gun control; policies that provide greater environmental protection or less government regulation; funding for abortion or for child welfare; or the abolition or the use of capital punishment.

Some citizens' groups are part of broad, decentralized social movements that hope to shape society according to their particular visions. In their early stages, social movements are usually intensely ideological, spawning a number of competing organizations, each of which seeks to define an ideology and an agenda for the movement. Although activist leaders may be reluctant to compromise during this stage, the intensity associated with the early development of a social movement subsides eventually, usually leaving behind a large, fairly moderate organization and several smaller, more radical groups. The civil rights and feminist movements are examples of relatively successful movements that have become more moderate with time and that now work within the system as mainstream interest groups. Activists from the Christian Right, a social movement in its more ideological phase, are often unwilling to compromise with GOP moderates over policy or politics.

Social movements are not themselves interest groups. Rather, a social movement often leads to the formation of interest groups that compete with one another to attract resources and to define the movement's goals. Within the Christian Right are organizations that focus entirely on a single issue such as abortion and gay marriage and others that have broad agendas that encompass many issues. Some Christian Right groups are committed to working within the Republican party; others threaten to leave the party if it does not promote their key policy initiatives. Members of a social movement such as the Christian Right may be members of many interest groups within the movement, of a single group, or they may not be a member of any group. Nonetheless they may be influenced by the stances of groups and their leaders.

It is also important to understand the distinction between an interest group and a political party. One textbook defines political parties as "organizations that seek to control government by recruiting, nominating, and electing their members to public office" and interest groups as "organizations that try to achieve at least some of their goals with government assistance" (Welch et al. 1998). These definitions are useful in distinguishing between the Republican National Committee and the U.S. Chamber of Commerce, but many organizations fall into a gray zone between political parties and interest groups.

Consider, for example, EMILY's List, which recruits pro-choice Democratic women to run for office and helps to train them and to fund their campaigns. Although EMILY's List might seem to fit the definition of a political party, it is more accurately viewed as an interest group that is closely but informally associated with one faction within the Democratic Party. Similarly, Americans for Tax Reform, founded by a longtime Republican activist, mobilizes voters to support Republican candidates. Or consider the role of a political action committee (PAC), an organization that contributes funds and campaign services to federal candidates. The PAC 21st Century Democrats seeks to help build the Democratic Party by electing progressive candidates. EMILY's List and Americans for Tax Reform will be defined as interest groups because they seek to promote specific policies by electing and influencing members of one political party. Organizations such as 21st Century Democrats and the Democratic Leadership Council, in contrast, will be defined as quasi–party organizations—first, because they are composed almost entirely of party activists and, second, because their primary goal is to promote the party, not specific policies.

THE ONE, THE FEW, OR THE MANY: INTEREST GROUPS AND AMERICAN POLITICS

The framers of the Constitution anticipated and welcomed a vigorous role for interest groups in electoral politics and governing. When James Madison, our chief constitutional architect, warned of the "mischief of factions," he meant that the greatest threat of factions—or what we commonly call interest groups—was the potential for one or a few of them to become too large and powerful—to the point of being able to control the levers of government and destroy the rights and liberties of others. Madison's cure was the creation of a large federal republic in which numerous diverse interests would flourish and in which no one group could become so overwhelmingly powerful as to threaten the rights and liberties of numerically smaller or less powerful groups. In a competitive policy environment, numerous groups would counter each other, and public policy, in the ideal, would represent compromises among competing interests and reflect "the public good."

Scholars have debated for generations whether the Madisonian solution has succeeded in preventing one or a few groups from dominating American politics. Some social scientists see corporate interests as forming a single dominant coalition that routinely triumphs in political struggles. Others see an evolving two-party system of interest groups allied with the two major political parties. And pluralists suggest that a multitude of groups, representing many Americans, compete with one another to define the public agenda and that no one group or coalition dominates politics.

Is the universe of American interest groups dominated by a single coalition of business interests, or is it characterized by thousands of competing groups? Social scientists have long argued the point. Studies have shown that business groups are numerically dominant in lobbying government, and they have many important financial advantages (Schlozman and Tierney 1986; but see Berry 2000 for a contrasting view). Studies of those who contribute significant sums to congressional candidates show that most of these contributors are members of business groups (Francia et al. 2003).

However, it is also true that many Americans are members of interest groups. One comprehensive study showed that 79 percent of Americans are members of some kind of voluntary association, including hobby and sports groups (Verba, Schlozman, and Brady 1995). Sixty-one percent are associated with a group that they described as taking a stand on politics. Such broad citizen involvement would seem to support a pluralist view of interest groups.

Although Verba and colleagues (1995) report that interest group membership and activism are more prevalent among those with greater resources (such as income and education), they also found that involvement in interest groups and other voluntary associations builds civic skills that lead to more effective citizenship. Some institutions—most notably churches—build these skills among those who may initially be at a substantial disadvantage in relation to the political process, and some issues— particularly abortion—mobilize citizens who would otherwise be unlikely to join or form groups.

Empirical research thus supports some of the claims of the critics of interest groups and some of the claims of their supporters. The interest group universe is dominated by business interests, which along with professional associations and labor unions generally seek economic benefits for their members. But some interest groups do represent disadvantaged segments of the population, and by encouraging their members to get involved in politics, to become educated about issues and candidates, to volunteer in campaigns, and to develop the kinds of skills that make them more effective citizens, these groups may strengthen democratic representation.

We have seen that many types of interest groups are active in American elections, representing myriad causes. The nature of interest group involvement in electoral activity is constrained by the political system and by the laws, regulations, and practices that create opportunity structures. We turn next to a discussion of the political system and the opportunities it creates for interest group involvement in elections.

INTEREST GROUPS AND THE AMERICAN POLITICAL SYSTEM

Interest groups' high level of involvement in American elections stems, in part, from distinctive characteristics of American government, political parties, and elections. First, governmental decision making offers multiple incentives and opportunities for influencing policy. Second, the major U.S. parties are permeable to outside interests, enabling interest group activists to obtain powerful positions within local, state, and national party organizations. Third, American elections are unique: they are much more frequent than those of most other Western democracies, and far smaller percentages of citizens vote. Moreover, American elections are candidate centered: candidates must decide to run, raise their own funds, assemble their own coalitions, and reach voters with carefully targeted messages—all of which occurs outside the formal party structure. The next three sections consider each of these characteristics in more detail.

Characteristics of American Government

At the same time that our federal system creates incentives for interest group involvement, it also places demands on interest groups, which must work within the system to successfully influence policy. First, because policy can be made at the national, state, and local levels, interest groups are generally called upon to be active at all three levels. Consider, for example, gun control policy. The NRA and Handgun Control, Inc., are committed to influencing gun control legislation in Congress, in state legislatures, and in county commissions and local councils. To do so, these organizations must have friends at each level of government, and being active in elections at all levels is one way to ensure this. Sometimes a victory at one level of government can be overturned at another level. For example, Handgun Control, Inc., has won a number of victories at the city level, and the NRA has therefore successfully lobbied state governments to overturn such laws (Bruce and Wilcox 1998). Business groups are currently seeking to pass comprehensive national legislation limiting their liability from damages caused by their products, but they are also seeking to change state laws, and even to elect state judges who might interpret existing liability laws differently.

Second, interest groups are well aware that local councils and state legislatures constitute a pipeline of potential candidates for the House of Representatives. Thus they often participate in state and local races with the intention of cultivating and training potential candidates for national office.

Third, the division of powers between the executive and legislative branches means that interest groups must try to cultivate access to both the president and Congress. Given that the executive and legislative branches have different constituencies, timetables, and interests, this is a difficult enough task, but it has been made even more complex since the 1960s because the two branches have often been under the control of different parties. During the late 1990s, interest groups with access to the Republicans in the House and Senate needed the signature of a Democratic president before their bills could become law. The House is a predominantly urban and suburban body in which the majority party can generally pass what it pleases, but the Senate has a disproportionately rural slant and has rules that allow any senator—including members of the minority party— to delay voting on a measure indefinitely.

Fourth, because members of Congress are not bound to vote for the policies of party leaders but are independent actors, even those of the minority party are in a position to help or hurt an interest group's policy agenda. Any member of the House or Senate can introduce a bill drafted in consultation with an interest group and offer amendments in committee or on the floor to make the bill more palatable to interest groups. When a bill is up for a vote, members of Congress may vote however they choose. In the Senate, any member can put a "hold" on a bill, delaying a vote perhaps indefinitely.

Interest groups often bolster their lobbying efforts by engaging in electoral activities. By helping members of Congress in elections, interest groups hope to establish relationships with senators and representatives—and to get some return on their investment in the form of public policy actions. On occasion, relationships cultivated through electoral activity enable interest groups to build coalitions in support of their policy positions, even over the objections of party leaders.

Finally, the U.S. government is perhaps more willing than those of many other countries to distribute particularistic economic benefits to interest groups. Appropriations, tax, and even substantive bills such as highway bills are generally filled with specific language benefiting one or more companies or interest groups. Corporations get government contracts, special tax provisions, and exemptions from regulations (or, more commonly, delays in implementing regulations), all of which can affect their profits. In addition, members of Congress and occasionally even presidents intercede with the bureaucracy in an attempt to win favorable treatment for particular groups. The opportunity to obtain specific economic benefits offers yet another incentive for interest groups to develop close relationships with policy makers—and one important way to do so is through electoral politics.

Characteristics of American Parties

Like the American government, American political parties differ from their counterparts in other democracies. In many countries, parties are closely linked with one or a few interests that they can be said to represent. In Europe, labor unions are represented by Labor or Social Democratic parties, the Catholic Church speaks through Christian Democratic parties, environmentalists have formed "Green" parties, and very conservative citizens are represented by "new radical right" parties. In Israel, orthodox religious groups have their own political parties. In some countries, interest groups are represented by distinct sectors of a party. In Mexico, for example, the Partido Revolucionario Institucional has separate sectors representing farmers, other workers, and students.

In the United States, however, the parties have established relationships with a variety of interest groups that make up their core constituencies, but they also interact with groups that are nonpartisan or that are willing to back candidates of either party. Democratic Party activists include members of labor unions, civil rights organizations, feminist organizations, environmental groups, and consumer protection organizations. Republican

Party activists include small business owners, conservative Christians, and advocates of gun rights. Although large businesses tend to support Republicans, they also give to Democratic candidates, and although the executives of most large companies prefer Republican lawmakers, they are usually willing to do business with whoever controls the governmental agenda. The loose coalitions of interest groups that make up American parties often pull parties in different directions: within the Democratic Party, unions and environmental groups may clash over clean air standards for industry; within the Republican Party, conservative Christians and the business community may differ over policies enabling women to participate more fully in the paid workforce or over the teaching of evolution in high school biology classes.

Interest groups have resources—mailing lists, newsletters, conventions, and volunteers—that can help political parties reach out to group members and other voters. Thus, parties often rely on interest groups to help them communicate with voters, often working closely with particular groups to develop and distribute distinctive messages targeting group members. Republican leaders have relied on interest groups to help them convince Christian conservatives that the GOP is the party of moral conservatism. As mentioned earlier, in 2004 Let Freedom Ring distributed a video on George W. Bush's personal religious faith to conservative churches in Pennsylvania and Ohio. Similarly, Democratic officials rely on unions to reach workers, on feminist organizations to reach working women, and on environmental groups to reach voters who are concerned about pollution.

Perhaps the most distinctive feature of American parties and elections is that party leaders play only a small role in selecting candidates. Through party primaries, caucuses, and conventions, interest groups can help to determine which candidates win nomination and can even work to nominate activists and members from their own groups. Although party officials are usually neutral in intraparty contests, interest groups—both individually and in coalition with others—are extremely active in aiding one candidate over another.

On rare occasions, party leaders may personally endorse candidates in primaries or even conventions, only to see their favorite defeated by a candidate who has the backing of powerful interest groups. For example, in a 1996 party primary for the seat he had vacated to run for the presidency, Bob Dole backed incumbent U.S. senator Sheila Frahm, a pro-choice but fiscally conservative former state senate majority leader who had been appointed by the governor to complete Dole's term. Largely because of efforts by Christian Right activists, the election went to social conservative Sam Brownback, a one-term representative. In 2004 the conservative group Club for Growth targeted incumbent senator Arlen Specter in the Pennsylvania GOP primary. President Bush endorsed Specter, who then narrowly won the primary.

Finally, unlike many European parties, which receive most or all of their campaign money from the government, American parties must raise their own money from individual and group contributions. Interest groups provide much of the money for parties through a variety of legal mechanisms. Money from interest groups helps fund party electoral activities, as well as buildings, computers, and party workers' salaries. Interest groups also contribute to party foundations and think tanks that develop policy proposals for party leaders.

Characteristics of American Elections

Elections are a necessary component of democracy, but democracies implement elections in very different ways. In most countries, elections are held at regular intervals and generally occur at the same time, both for national executive and legislative offices and for regional and local government posts. Moreover, campaigns in most countries are relatively short: in Britain, for example, the 2001 campaign lasted thirty days and included all the seats in the national legislature and most local races.

In the United States, by contrast, elections are held almost continuously. Consider, for example, the electoral calendar in Virginia, where in 2004 there were nominating primaries and general elections for U.S. House seats, and in 2005 there will be party conventions, primaries, and general elections for the state legislature and three statewide offices (governor, lieutenant governor, and attorney general). In addition, local governments will hold hundreds of contests to elect members of county boards, local councils, and school boards as well as other important officials. A diligent voter in Virginia might cast ballots at least twice a year and frequently more often.

Because members of the House of Representatives stand for election every two years, representatives are constantly campaigning—raising money, addressing voters, and refining their images and their messages. And their challengers sometimes begin campaigning more than a year before the election. Senators, who are elected for six-year terms, generally campaign for at least two years, and some senators focus on fund-raising throughout their terms. Even before a new president is sworn into office, prospective candidates from the other major party may drop in on the early presidential caucus and primary states of Iowa and New Hampshire to "test the political waters." In January 2005, as Bush was sworn in for a second term, there was considerable activity by potential candidates in both parties, because the president cannot seek reelection.

Another distinctive characteristic of American elections is that they are candidate centered. In most democracies, parties run against each other with the help of their candidates; in the United States, candidates run against each other with the support of their parties. Indeed, some candidates do not even use party labels during their campaigns and attempt to distance themselves from other candidates of their party. In 2001 Vermont senator Jim Jeffords, just months after running for reelection as a member of the Republican Party, announced he was leaving the party to become an independent. Jeffords's decision temporarily made Republicans the minority party in the Senate. In a parliamentary system, where voters elect parties and not individuals, Jeffords would have had to resign his position. In the American system, he was able to keep his position, and many Republican voters in his state continued to support him.

Although American elections provide opportunities for individual candidates to adopt distinctive campaign themes, they also place significant burdens on candidates. In most other democracies, party leaders choose the candidates. The party finances the elections, chooses the issues to frame the campaign, and appeals to voters through party organizations and mass media. The party platform includes pledges for all party members, and once elected, a legislator is expected to vote the party line on all or most issues.

In the United States, candidates must declare their intention to run and seek their party's nomination in a primary election, caucus, or convention. Their campaigns are financed with little help from the party, often with significant amounts of their own money in their first run for office. They must assemble their own electoral coalition—including and going beyond party loyalists in their state or district—and they must reach well-defined groups of voters with precisely targeted messages. They must take positions on a variety of issues—positions that may differ greatly from those of other party candidates or even from the official party platform.

The difficulties of running a candidate-centered campaign render interest groups obvious allies. Interest groups can recruit candidates and encourage them to run, help finance their campaigns, and assist them in selecting campaign themes. By providing access to special communication channels such as newsletters and group gatherings, interest groups can also help candidates reach interest group members effectively and inexpensively. When interest groups work closely with candidates during campaigns, they have opportunities to "encourage" them to adopt certain positions on issues of concern to the group—from abortion to the flat tax to trade with China. Interest groups that succeed in recruiting and assisting sufficient numbers of candidates from outside the party mainstream may be able to redefine the philosophy, goals, or agenda of the party as a whole.

A third unique characteristic of American elections is the low rate of voter turnout. In most Western democracies, substantial majorities of eligible voters cast ballots in national elections; turnout in national elections is over 80 percent in most European countries, and only in Switzerland do fewer than two-thirds of eligible voters cast ballots. By contrast, in recent presidential elections in the United States, only about half of those eligible to vote did so. Even in 2004, when there was the highest level of participation since 1968, only 60 percent of those eligible voted. In the 2002 congressional elections, the figure was just 39 percent.

Low levels of voter turnout create opportunities for organized groups to greatly influence election outcomes. In the 1994 elections that transferred control of Congress to the Republicans, for example, most candidates were elected by the votes of fewer than one-third of all eligible voters, and in many states, fewer than one-fifth of eligible voters supported the average winning candidate (Center for Voting and Democracy, 1995). With such slim margins, interest groups that can successfully mobilize their members to support a particular candidate may well be able to swing an election outcome. Voter mobilization efforts by unions, African American churches, and the Christian Right are vital to the success of many candidates. Indeed, parties sometimes provide money to interest groups to help them mobilize voters, as the Republicans did in 1996 when they gave over $4 million to the conservative group Americans for Tax Reform.

Finally, American elections are nearly always winner-take-all contests in single-member districts. To see why this creates an incentive for interest groups to participate in elections, consider the consequences of a 2-percent shift under two different systems: if German labor unions succeeded in increasing by 2 percent the vote share of the German Social Democratic Party, that party would gain approximately 2 percent of the seats in the Bundestag, the German parliament, because a party's share of seats in the legislature is proportional to its percentage of the popular vote. In the United States, where representation is not proportional but is based on single-member districts, a 2-percent increase in the Democratic Party's share of the vote for the U.S. House would likely enable Democrats to regain control of that body, because the increase would allow a number of Democratic candidates in close races to win the seats. Thus a modest aggregate swing in votes may allow one party to capture most of the close contests in the United States, resulting in a much larger shift in seats. In 1994 the Republicans won control of the House by a net swing of less than 2 percent of the popular vote. In 2004 a shift of 2 percent of the popular vote would have given the Democrats control of the presidency, the House, and the Senate.

REGULATIONS, GOALS, AND RESOURCES

Taken together, the distinctive features of American government, parties, and elections give interest groups many opportunities and incentives to participate in election campaigns. Yet the precise form of their electoral involvement is channeled by government regulations that affect the ways in which interest groups use their resources to achieve their goals. These regulations are discussed in detail in the chapters that follow, but we look briefly in this section at the laws and regulations that influence how interest groups interact with parties, with candidates, and with voters.

The U.S. Constitution does not mention political parties, and relatively few federal regulations affect parties. Although state governments do regulate parties, the Supreme Court has limited the ability of the states to interfere with the parties' internal affairs. However, the rules of the national, state, and local parties, which are sometimes influenced by state and local law, do have a profound impact on the opportunity structures that interest groups encounter.

Most important is the structure of the nomination process. Parties can choose among various types of primary elections, caucuses, and conventions to nominate their candidates, and rules pertaining to the nomination process influence the ability of interest groups to sway the outcome. Party primaries, for example, generally attract a sizable minority of eligible voters, making it more difficult for interest groups to dominate the process. Because conventions and caucuses often involve only a small minority of party supporters, they provide interest groups with much greater opportunities for influence. Thus interest groups are often more active in recruitment and nomination politics in states with caucuses and conventions than in states with primary elections.

In Minnesota, in 1994, for example, conservative Christians mobilized their followers to help nominate former Republican legislator Allan Quist instead of incumbent Republican governor Arne Carlson. It is unusual for a major constituency group in a political party to work to deny the nomination to a popular incumbent, but Quist's long opposition to abortion had won the support of anti-abortion groups. Party moderates considered Quist an extremist, and many of his statements and policy positions had lent credibility to the charge. At the party convention, Quist defeated Carlson by two to one, winning the party's endorsement; but in the primary election, which actually selected the nominee, Carlson prevailed by the same margin. Carlson went on to win the general election in a landslide. Similarly, the Democratic Farm Labor Party (the name of the Minnesota Democratic party) in 2000 endorsed one candidate at the convention, but a more moderate candidate later won the primary election.

National party rules also affect interest groups' strategies. Both parties have rules governing participation on committees and make it relatively easy for interest groups to influence the platform process. The power of grassroots organizations to influence the GOP platform has been most evident on abortion, where pro-life groups have worked hard to make sure that moderates do not weaken the platform language or insert a clause that calls for tolerance of diverse views on abortion. The most visible fight was in 1996, when GOP nominee Bob Dole (himself a strong pro-life senator) pushed for a tolerance plank but lost. Public and private polls show that there are more pro-choice than pro-life GOP voters, but pro-life groups dominate convention politics and platform committees.

Other rules that affect interest groups' strategies are portions of the tax code that determine which groups can receive tax-deductible contributions from members. Organizations that do not lobby Congress but that advocate positions to executive agencies and provide information to Congress can qualify for 501(c)(3) status, which exempts them from income tax and allows contributors to deduct donations from their taxes. Such organizations cannot take part in partisan electoral activity, although they may provide citizens with nonpartisan information about issues and can encourage citizens to vote.

Organizations find 501(c)(3) status highly advantageous because it allows them not only to receive large contributions from wealthy donors in search of tax breaks but also to receive money from tax-exempt foundations, which are legally prohibited from giving to lobbying groups. When the Sierra Club was stripped of its 501(c)(3) status in the 1960s because of lobbying activities, it established the Sierra Club Foundation, a separate organization that does not lobby or engage in campaign activity and therefore qualifies for 501(c)(3) status. The Sierra Club continues to lobby from within the main organization and runs an affiliated PAC that raises money from club members and contributes to candidates' campaigns. In the 2004 campaign, 501(c)(3) organizations were more involved in campaigns than in the past, developing lists of individuals who could be contacted by campaigns and parties, and providing "nonpartisan" electoral messages in paid advertisements. Other types of groups are active in campaigns under the tax code, including 501(c)(4), 501(c)(6), and 527 committees.

Finally, electoral activity is regulated by the Federal Election Campaign Act, as amended in 1974 and again in 1979; by the Bipartisan Campaign Reform Act of 2002; and by Supreme Court interpretations of the free speech provisions of the First Amendment. Campaign finance regulations are quite complex and are discussed more fully in Chapters 3 and 4.

Interest groups can form PACs, which can raise funds from members to be spent in any of a number of ways. The money can be given to candidates directly; or it can be spent by the PAC itself, in the form of independent expenditures, to advocate the election or defeat of particular candidates. PAC activities must be disclosed to the Federal Election Commission, and the funds involved must fit within certain contribution limits.

Some interest groups create byzantine organizational structures to deal with the various provisions of campaign finance laws. For example, organizations engaged in "independent expenditures" cannot coordinate their actions with the candidates on whose behalf they are spending the money. To avoid being accused of coordinating expenditures, interest groups that provide advice to candidates as an in-kind contribution may go so far as to establish a separate organizational unit (sometimes even setting it up in a different city) to provide this advice. Interest groups can also spend treasury money to run advertisements that help or hurt a candidate's electoral chances, although the precise language of these advertisements is subject to regulation.

Characteristics of the American political system and applicable regulations combine to establish an opportunity structure for interest group involvement in elections. Faced with a set of opportunities and constraints, interest groups decide—largely on the basis of their goals and resources—whether and how to become involved in electoral politics.

Interest groups vary widely in the types of policies they seek to influence and in the frequency with which they attempt to do so. Many groups seek policies that provide a direct economic benefit such as higher wages, higher corporate profits, or the power to issue professional licenses. When firms or professional or trade associations seek special treatment from government—a contract, a tax break, or regulatory relief—they need access to incumbents. Although Republicans are generally more willing than Democrats to support corporations, incumbents of both parties routinely try to help firms and professional and trade associations in their states and districts. Because a tax break from a Democrat is worth as much as a tax break from a Republican, many interest groups seek access to incumbents of either party, as long as officeholders have the power to insert into legislation special language that will help the groups to meet their goals. Such goals generally lead to strategies that focus on financial contributions from PACs and from corporate executives and their families.

Labor unions and business associations tend to be interested in broader policies affecting the entire economy. Because clear distinctions exist between the parties on a number of economic issues—levels of taxation and regulation, for example—interest groups tend to form close ties with one party or the other. Organized labor is more than a constituency group within the Democratic Party; it also performs many traditional party functions—organizing, fund-raising, conducting issues research, and sending campaign professionals into the field. Other groups provide some of these functions for the Republicans as well. The precise boundaries between such organizations and party committees are unclear, and campaign professionals often work first for one group and then for the other. Indeed, party activists may encourage the formation of a group and encourage donors to provide some or all of its funding.

Other organizations seek noneconomic benefits from a variety of policies, from those that affect the quality of the environment to reproductive choice to the types of books and magazines sold in bookstores. Some of these organizations seek access to both parties, helping candidates who support their position. Indeed, primarily so that it can maintain its bipartisan stance, the Sierra Club practices "affirmative action" for

Republicans, endorsing GOP incumbents with acceptable environmental records even when they are opposed by Democratic challengers with "greener" policy views (Cantor 1999). NARAL and the NRA back candidates from both parties, although the widening differences between the parties' positions on abortion and gun control mean that these groups increasingly support candidates of one party (Patterson and Eakins 1998; Thomas 1999).

Still other ideological groups are closely linked with a single party. GOP committees have helped fund voter mobilization efforts conducted by the National Right to Life Committee. In some cases, the same ideological position may be represented by different groups associated with different parties. EMILY's List and WISH List (Women in the Senate and House) are two pro-choice PACs dedicated to electing more women to Congress, but as mentioned earlier, the first group supports only pro-choice Democratic women, whereas the second backs GOP women candidates.

Interest groups' strategies are also influenced by their resources: groups with substantial financial assets may make sizable contributions to parties and spend significant amounts to help elect candidates. The tobacco industry, for example, includes two firms that ranked among the highest donors of soft money (contributions to political parties unregulated by the Federal Election Commission) to both parties when such contributions were legal. The National Association of Realtors gives in almost every congressional race in the nation, and in many state and local races as well. Groups with large memberships—such as the AFL-CIO and the NRA—work hard to communicate endorsements to their members and get them to the polls.

Interest groups that are well respected may strive to communicate their views to the wider electorate: one Sierra Club official refers to that organization's endorsement as the environmental version of the "Good Housekeeping Seal of Approval" (Cantor 1999). Interest groups that are part of large, enthusiastic social movements may channel activists into volunteer efforts for campaigns and recruit members to run for office. Conservative Christian organizations fielded thousands of activists in the 2004 campaigns. These individuals helped to distribute information in churches, canvas districts, and distribute absentee ballots. Finally, groups with considerable electoral skills often send professionals into campaigns and may mount independent campaigns on behalf of candidates. In the 2004 elections, labor unions and environmental groups had field staff assisting candidates in specially targeted races, and many of these organizations produced their own advertisements to help elect or defeat candidates.

STRATEGIES AND TACTICS

Interest groups are involved in all aspects of American elections, and many begin their work on the next campaign the day after election results are announced. Many of the tactics they use in their electoral activities center on offering candidates access to their groups' resources: money, advice, volunteer labor, and votes. In addition, interest groups work to influence the two major parties—partly by maintaining ongoing relationships with the parties but sometimes more aggressively, by attempting to dominate party committees or to rewrite party rules and platforms. Interest groups also recruit and train candidates who seek nomination in the major parties. In general elections, they invest funds in communicating their endorsements to members and in targeting particular candidates for defeat.

Consider the range of activities undertaken by interest groups in the 2004 elections. Women's groups, including the National Women's Political Caucus (www.nwpc.org), recruited women to run for local, state, and national office, often in coalition with other feminist organizations. Similarly, the AFL-CIO encouraged its members to run for state legislatures and Congress; it was also involved in discussions with potential presidential candidates as they considered the decision to run.

Organizations such as GOPAC provided training for candidates, and Human Rights Campaign trained young activists, offering advice on topics that ranged from how to assemble electoral coalitions to dealing with the media. Anti-abortion groups distributed pamphlets to sympathetic candidates on how to finesse the abortion issue in public discussions. Advice to candidates was sometimes continuous; the Sierra Club placed its staff and volunteers directly into some campaigns, affording candidates ongoing access to their expertise.

Interest groups provided candidates with resources throughout the nomination process. Organizations such as EMILY's List contributed money to pro-choice women running in Democratic primaries; more important, these organizations encouraged their members to contribute as well. Such gifts are almost always welcomed, although they can occasionally create problems: although George W. Bush raised large sums from drug and energy companies, he also faced criticism that his policies benefited these contributors.

Interest groups gave more than cash. Some provided services such as polls or information on targeting campaign communications to voters, and others encouraged their members to volunteer for campaigns. Interest groups also provided candidates with forums to address their members: all six prospective Democratic presidential candidates addressed the annual NARAL Pro-Choice America gathering in Washington, D.C., in 2003, and most candidates campaigned by traveling from one group-sponsored event to another. Overall, these efforts helped interest groups influence candidates fielded by both parties in the 2004 general elections.

Interest groups also worked closely with the parties, often in the context of long-established relationships. The National Committee on an Effective Congress (www.ncec.org) provided the Democratic Party with information to help the party better target its communication and voter mobilization efforts (Herrnson 1994), while major corporate interests gave record sums to Republican incumbent candidates and helped to finance other interest groups that advocated the election of Republicans. Labor unions exchanged tips on strategy with Democratic Party committees and launched voter contact drives to encourage their members to support Democratic candidates, while the Christian Coalition distributed voters' guides containing flattering photos and descriptions of Republican candidates and unflattering photos and descriptions of Democrats.

Perhaps more important, interest groups worked within both political parties to influence party rules and nominations. Interest group members ran for party office at the precinct, county, state, and national levels. In 2004, conservative Christian groups encouraged their members to serve on the GOP platform committee, in an effort to ensure that the platform remained pro-life and supported a constitutional amendment banning same-sex marriage. The Democratic convention was attended by large numbers of feminist and civil rights activists, union members, and trial lawyers—groups that traditionally work to influence the Democratic Party platform.

Many interest groups endorsed candidates in both primary and general elections. Labor union endorsements sent to all union members served as the basis for later voter mobilization efforts. Sierra Club endorsements of both Democrats and Republicans were communicated to members and the media, while the League of Conservation Voters (LCV) publicized the names of the "Dirty Dozen"—the twelve candidates with the worst environmental records—and another list of environmental heroes.

During the general election, interest groups continued to provide candidates with access to the same kinds of resources they had made available during primary elections and caucuses: advice, services, volunteers, cash, and forums in which to address interest group members. They communicated messages directly to voters through television, radio, mail, and the Internet, and they provided volunteers to help mobilize voters on election day.

Despite the apparent diversity of tactics, interest groups generally pursue a mix of two basic strategies: an *electoral strategy,* which is designed to change the personnel of government, and an *access,* or *legislative strategy,* which uses electoral activity as an adjunct to lobbying efforts. The electoral strategy is an attempt to increase the number of policy makers who share the group's policy views. When the leaders of the Business-Industry Political Action Committee (BIPAC) endorse a challenger in a House race, they are telling the business community that they are confident the candidate, if elected, will vote for pro-business policies. When the leaders of the LCV refer to certain members of Congress as the Dirty Dozen, they are hoping to replace those members with others more sympathetic to environmental causes.

Groups most likely to use an electoral strategy are labor unions, citizens' groups, and social movement organizations. Such groups often attempt to influence party nominations by recruiting and supporting candidates in primary elections, sending delegates to party conventions to influence the platform, spending large sums in a few closely contested races where candidates take opposing stands on issues of special importance to the group, and mobilizing voters to help sway close contests. They make use of their special resources—their members, their activist core, their reputations, and any media support they can muster.

Often, however, interest groups assist candidates who are not involved in close races: PACs give money to committee chairs who face no serious competition; interest groups endorse candidates who are running unopposed or mount voter mobilization efforts for candidates whose victory is assured. Why bother? As noted earlier, interest groups seek not only to change the personnel of government but also to secure access to those who have the power to make or influence decisions—a cabinet member, a party leader, a committee chair. There are many ways to gain access to policy makers, but one important way is to develop an ongoing relationship through campaign contributions. When interest groups pursue a legislative or access strategy—helping candidates and parties in order to secure time to make their argument before policy makers—whether the policy maker needs electoral help is of little concern. For example, Rep. Bill Thomas, R-Calif., chair of the House Ways and Means Committee, hosted $5,000-a-plate breakfasts during the 2004 election cycle, providing interest group representatives with an opportunity to contribute to his reelection campaign and meet with him to discuss issues of concern (National Republican Congressional Committee, www.nrcc.org). Thomas ran unopposed in 2004, but the groups that chose to contribute were assured of his ear, at least during the breakfast, and those that chose not to contribute were less likely to be able to meet privately with the congressman to discuss tax matters. In fact, interest groups that pursue access strategies often prefer to contribute to candidates who are sure winners.

Corporations, trade associations, and professional associations are the groups most likely to emphasize an access strategy. Groups seeking access rarely participate in primary elections and do not usually undertake voter mobilization efforts. Their preferred tactics are, instead, to give substantial sums to party committees (often to both parties), to help finance party conventions, and to form PACs to give money to incumbents.

How This Book Is Organized

Interest group involvement in American elections takes myriad forms, and an examination of that involvement can be structured in a number of ways. This book focuses on communication: with whom are interest groups communicating, and to what end? Some of the activities of interest groups are aimed primarily at communicating with political parties, in order to influence the policies that the parties pursue. Recruiting and training candidates, working to elect candidates in primary elections and caucuses, working at party conventions, and placing group members in party office are all ways of influencing political parties, as are direct contributions to party committees. Other activities are meant to communicate with candidates, for example, by direct contributions of cash or goods and services. Finally, some activities are meant to communicate with interest group members and voters at large: newsletters, voter mobilization efforts, Web pages, endorsements (and hit lists), independent expenditures, and issue advocacy campaigns.

Because the purposes of communication are often complex and the same communication may be directed to multiple audiences, not all electoral activity will fit this framework. For example, voter mobilization comes under the heading of communicating with the electorate, but it also serves as an indication of an interest group's party loyalty and as a reminder of its importance to the party coalition—measured by the number of voters the group is capable of delivering to the polls.

Recognizing that communication often has more than one purpose and more than one audience, we structure our examination of interest groups around communication as a general theme. Chapter 2 focuses on the efforts of interest groups to influence the policy direction of political parties: recruiting and training candidates, sending delegations to party conventions, working to shape party platforms, and attempting to gain admission to the party apparatus. Chapter 3 describes the ways in which interest groups help candidates directly: by providing money, services, volunteers, and advice. Chapter 4 investigates interest groups' efforts to influence voters: by endorsing candidates or advocating their defeat, by undertaking independent expenditures and issue advocacy campaigns, and by attempting to mobilize their members and others to participate in politics. Each of these chapters begins by exploring the strategic context—the interaction of laws, regulations, and practices with interest groups' goals and resources—that shapes the selection of strategies and tactics. Each chapter then describes in detail the specific activities of interest groups. The concluding chapter evaluates the role of interest groups in electoral politics and considers a variety of proposals for reform.

CHAPTER 2

Interest Groups and Political Parties

In January 1998, the Republican National Committee (RNC) met in Indian Wells, California, to consider a resolution that would cut off party support for GOP candidates who did not oppose banning a late-term abortion procedure referred to by anti-abortion forces as "partial-birth abortion." Party chair Jim Nicholson, who had won his job in part because of Christian Coalition support, opposed the resolution, while GOP presidential hopeful Steve Forbes and Christian Coalition chair Randy Tate urged committee members to support it. Although the resolution ultimately failed, it created a firestorm within the GOP and attracted national headlines for days. The debate over the resolution divided even social conservatives, some of whom urged support for it on the basis of principle, while others—concerned about setting a precedent—argued that a national party should not apply a litmus test to identify candidates eligible for party support.

Seven years later, in early 2005, Democratic Senatorial Campaign Committee chair Charles Schumer, D-N.Y., sought to recruit some anti-abortion candidates such as Pennsylvania state treasurer Robert P. Casey Jr. to run in the 2006 Senate elections in states where public opinion might give such candidates an edge. In response, EMILY's List political director Karen White posted a statement on the group's Web site that said, "We fought like mad to beat back the Republicans. Little did we know that we would have just as much to fear from some within the Democratic Party who seem to be using choice as a scapegoat for our top-of-the-ticket losses." EMILY's List promised to back a different candidate in the primary, seeking to defeat Casey, who early polls showed held a considerable lead over incumbent Republican Rick Santorum.

The internal party controversies about recruiting and funding candidates with diverse positions on abortion are a vivid demonstration of the power of interest group politics in the internal life of American political parties. Parties do have the right to withhold funding from candidates, and they have done so in a few cases. In Louisiana, the GOP denied funding to David Duke, a former Ku Klux Klan member and leader of the American Nazi Party who had won the GOP gubernatorial primary; in Illinois, the Democratic Party withheld money from two followers of extremist Lyndon LaRouche who had won Democratic nominations for lieutenant governor and attorney general. But even in these cases the party could not deny the candidate access to the ballot under the party label. Duke ran as a Republican in the gubernatorial election, although many prominent Republicans in the state and outside it worked to make sure that he was defeated.

Relationships between interest groups and political parties are complex and tend to vary with time and circumstance. In some cases, the connection is symbiotic, with both the party and the interest group benefiting; in other cases, the relations can be tense, with occasional open conflict. Today, labor unions and the Democratic Party maintain a strong, mutually supportive link, with unions providing significant assistance to party candidates and performing many of the functions of the party itself, while the party supports labor on many important issues. Business groups have a similar relationship with the GOP: party leaders support reductions in business taxes and in environmental, consumer, and safety regulations, while business groups provide money and services to the party.

Although relations between the civil rights movement and the Democrats and between the anti-abortion movement and the Republicans are generally supportive, they have been marked by occasional conflict. In the 1990s, civil rights groups pressured the Democratic Party to oppose welfare reform, threatening to bolt if Democrats moved too quickly to dismantle programs to assist low-income Americans. Similarly, in 1996, anti-abortion activists threatened to withdraw their support for the Republican ticket if presidential nominee Bob Dole selected a pro-choice running mate. And in 2004, religious conservatives heavily lobbied GOP senators and the White House to oppose moderate senator Arlen Specter, R-Pa., in his bid to become the Judiciary Committee chairman. Specter's rise to that post was in doubt until he made repeated public statements and pledges to assure the Christian Right that he would be fair to anti-abortion judicial nominees. Religious conservatives had unsuccessfully led an effort to defeat Specter in the GOP nomination contest earlier that year. In some states, moderate Republicans and the Christian Right are engaged in virtual party warfare, whereas in others the two sides have formed successful coalitions. For example, in Georgia, many GOP moderates and social conservatives have worked together to support former Christian Coalition executive director Ralph Reed's 2006 candidacy for lieutenant governor.

Chapter 1 noted that an interest group's choice of strategies and tactics depends on the interaction of two sets of factors: (1) the opportunity structures created by the political system, with its laws, regulations, and common practices, and (2) the goals and resources of the group. The interaction of the political system on the one hand and a group's goals and resources on the other creates the strategic context for interest group involvement in electoral activity. This chapter first describes the strategic context that leads some interest groups to communicate with, to influence the internal politics of, and in some cases even to "take over" political parties. The chapter then examines in some detail the various tactics used to achieve such goals.

The Strategic Context: Regulations, Goals, and Resources

The Constitution does not even mention political parties, and few federal regulations affect them. In addition, the Supreme Court has ruled in recent years that political parties have free speech rights that can be regulated in various ways but not significantly curtailed. For interest groups, much of the regulation that affects the opportunity structure comes from state governments. States retain considerable authority to regulate how political parties select their candidates and how they structure internal party committees; states may even regulate parties' internal rules and activities.

In all states, candidates are selected through some type of electoral process that allows voters to choose candidates. This process varies widely across states, across parties, and sometimes even within parties, primarily along two dimensions. First, states and parties choose among primary elections, caucuses, and conventions. Primary elections require little commitment from voters—other than showing up at the ballot box—and therefore generate higher turnout. Caucuses sometimes require voters to spend time in a public meeting and vote publicly, which helps explain why turnout is lower. State conventions are even more demanding, requiring that voters travel to the convention hall and sometimes dedicate the weekend to political activity. Because turnout is generally lower for caucuses and conventions than for primaries, it is much easier for interest groups to dominate caucuses and conventions than primary elections.

Second, state regulations determine who is allowed to vote in internal party elections. Some states restrict participation to voters who have registered a preference for a particular party (for example, only registered Democrats can vote in a Democratic primary). Other states allow independents to vote in either party's contest but forbid cross-party voting (for example, both registered Republicans and independents could vote in a Republican caucus). Still other states have open selection processes limiting voters to one internal election per year. Thus any voters who wish to can attend the Democratic Party convention, but this would bar them from attending the GOP convention. Open rules for primary elections dilute the influence of interest groups, while open rules for conventions may actually strengthen their influence.

Compared with the political systems of other nations and with patterns prevalent earlier in U.S. history, however, all of these nomination procedures are unusually open to interest group involvement. In other Western democracies, party leaders select candidates, rewarding loyal party workers and promoting promising young party loyalists. A few interest groups with strong ties to a party may have some say in the nomination process, but in the United States, interest groups can independently recruit candidates and help them to win intraparty contests, even against candidates favored by party leaders.

States and parties determine the kinds of party committees that are allowed as well as the selection process for committee members. Both parties have national committees, state committees, and a variety of local committees (most commonly county committees and congressional district committees). Members of these committees are usually selected at open party meetings, which give interest groups the opportunity to influence—and, on occasion, "take over"—party committees. If, for example, interest group members show up in large numbers, without warning, at a party meeting designed to elect the county party officers, they can sometimes ensure the election of their own activists to important posts, including party chair.

Unlike their counterparts in other Western democracies, American political parties are often deeply divided. In the 1960s and 1970s, the Democrats were divided between a progressive wing that included activists from civil rights, antiwar, and feminist groups and a moderate wing that included members of labor unions and business groups. Today, the GOP is split into a conservative wing that includes members of Christian Right groups and a moderate wing that includes representatives of the business community. Such internal divisions may be more or less severe at times, but there is always debate about where the party should stand on economic, social, and foreign policy issues.

Disagreement within American parties provides an opening for interest group involvement and influence. In most other Western democracies, in contrast, political parties have enduring platforms that lay out the basic values and goals of the party and specify policies that the party will enact should it gain control of the legislature. Party leaders determine which candidates will represent the party on the ballot, and all candidates are required to subscribe to the party platform and to pledge to support party legislation if they are elected. Candidates who do not pledge to vote the party line on all issues are routinely denied access to the ballot.

In the United States, although general ideological differences exist between the two major parties, candidates are free to adopt their own positions on all political issues. In party primaries, candidates within the same party disagree on taxes, abortion, environmental regulations, and education policies. Within each party, contending factions with strong interest group support vie to define the values that the party should support and the policies that it should pursue. They also struggle to influence the party platforms—which, in practice, often embody nothing more than the momentary sentiments of a majority of party activists.

Why would interest groups try to gain influence over political parties that cannot impose discipline on their members? First, by helping to determine which candidates receive party nominations, interest groups can indirectly influence who sits in Congress and the positions the party takes on crucial legislation. If a significant number of legislators are members or supporters of a particular interest group, they can often persuade their colleagues to pass or support legislation that enacts the policy preferences of that group; they can also try to obtain the support of their party caucus.

The large number of Christian conservatives among GOP members of the House and Senate, for example, is one reason that Congress passed the partial-birth abortion ban. Similarly, the Congressional Black Caucus, a significant voting bloc among House Democrats, has on occasion swayed Democratic colleagues to support policies that aid cities or increase assistance for low-income citizens.

Second, by influencing the nomination process, interest group activists can pressure candidates to adopt particular positions. As anti-abortion activists moved into the Republican Party and pro-choice groups formed alliances with the Democrats, the abortion issue became a litmus test for presidential candidates, and pro-choice Republicans and anti-abortion Democrats were forced to change their public positions on the issue (Cook, Jelen, and Wilcox 1992). In the Republican Party the strong presence of anti-abortion activists in the nomination process is undoubtedly one of the reasons that businessman Steve Forbes—who had sought the GOP presidential nomination in 1996 as a social moderate—switched to an anti-abortion stance in his nomination campaign in 2000. Forbes's switch, in turn, echoed that of George H. W. Bush in 1980. Among Democrats, Al Gore, Richard Gephardt, and Jesse Jackson all moved to support a pro-choice position when they sought the presidency in the 1980s. As anti-abortion and pro-choice groups became active in recruiting and supporting candidates in party primaries, they succeeded in changing the composition of the parties' delegations to Congress and in creating genuine party differences on abortion at a time when the issue did not cleave the general public along partisan lines (Adams 1996). Similarly, in the 2004 Democratic presidential primary campaign, Massachusetts senator John Kerry began moderating his position on trade to be more in line with the view of the American Federation of Labor–Congress of Industrial Organizations (AFL-CIO), and he called for workers' rights in future trade agreements, even though he had previously supported trade agreements without such worker protections.

Interest groups with broad public policy goals are most likely to work within political parties to nominate candidates and to influence party platforms. In general these tactics are more likely to be used by social movement organizations, groups that succeed in mobilizing citizens previously outside of the party: for example, feminists and African Americans in the Democratic Party in the 1960s and 1970s and Christian conservatives in the Republican Party since the 1980s. Yet even professional associations such as the National Association of Realtors and the American Medical

Association become involved in internal party politics on occasion. Similarly, business groups played an important role in shaping the 1994 Republican Contract with America. Generally, however, groups with more narrow goals are more likely to approach incumbents directly than to work within political parties.

Although most interest group activity within parties is aimed at influencing public policy on controversial issues, at the national conventions, corporations often find the occasion to cozy up to party leaders—helping, for example, to finance the convention, receptions, and other events, and providing goods and services. The corporations are not seeking to influence party positions on controversial issues but are instead seeking access to policy makers who can help promote corporate economic interests.

One resource is central to effective intraparty electoral activity: membership. Social movement organizations have the best pool of resources: dedicated activists, a large membership base, and an even larger pool of sympathizers who might support movement candidates in primary elections. Interest groups with fewer members are less able to compete with other party factions.

Recruiting and Training Candidates

Candidate recruitment and training are important tactics in interest groups' efforts to achieve their policy goals. In American politics, citizens who want to run for office must declare their candidacy and are often required to assemble petitions before they can get their names on the ballot for a primary election or caucus. Although a number of potential candidates may consider running, most ultimately decide against mounting a campaign (Fowler and McClure 1989). By reaching out to potential candidates and offering encouragement and support, interest groups can influence who decides to run. By offering training, interest groups can influence who wins.

Approaches to Recruitment

Many interest groups find that the most reliable and loyal candidates can be drawn from the activist and leadership bases of their own organizations. Historically, only a few interest groups have recruited candidates from within their ranks, and these candidates have constituted only a small percentage of all candidates in congressional elections. But in recent years feminist and Christian Right groups have increased their efforts to recruit members to run for office, and the AFL-CIO has a long-term project to encourage union members to seek public office. The AFL-CIO decided that it could best promote its goals by recruiting its own members rather than by recruiting and training candidates outside the movement who may agree with some—but not all—of the labor agenda. Although most of the AFL-CIO's efforts focus on local offices, long-term gains are potentially substantial, including not only more policies that are sympathetic to labor but also a pool of strong candidates for federal office. In 2000, 2,141 union members held or ran for public office. The AFL-CIO's latest goal—Target 5000—is an initiative to bring five thousand union members into public service (American Federation of Labor–Congress of Industrial Organizations 2005).

Although interest groups may look first to their own members, many recruit nonmembers as well, identifying individuals with good political skills who appear to share their policy goals and encouraging them to seek higher office. Interest groups looking to recruit candidates for the U.S. House usually begin by encouraging citizens to run for local or state office—city council, county commission, or state legislature. Because many candidates for the House first serve in local government, interest groups have ample opportunity to work closely with many members of the candidate pool and assess their support for the group's priorities.

Recruitment is especially important for interest groups that wish to increase the number of policy makers from previously underrepresented groups, such as women, racial and ethnic minorities, and Christian conservatives. Without the encouragement and assistance of interest groups, many talented citizens who are members of such demographic groups would not otherwise consider running for political office; interest groups thus play an important role in increasing the diversity of demographic representation among officeholders.

The National Women's Political Caucus (NWPC) has mounted a large coordinated effort to recruit women to run for public office. Since 1994 the caucus has held a series of training events to teach state and local activists how to identify candidates and campaign managers, generally for state legislative and county offices but also for U.S. House and Senate seats. Democratic pollster Celinda Lake has advised the caucus to seek out women who have their own businesses, who are important members of community organizations, or who serve on local school boards or other appointed or elected bodies. In a number of states, the caucus has mounted sophisticated efforts, first determining which state legislative and congressional districts might be open seats (where new candidates stand the best chance of winning), and then identifying potential women candidates to run for those offices (Duerst-Lahti 1998).

The NWPC has state and local caucuses throughout the country, and recruitment is most likely to occur when activists identify potential candidates in their own communities. The national organization facilitates the recruitment process by providing local caucuses with a recruitment manual. The manual tells recruiters how to find women candidates who fit the profile of the district, provides guidelines on how to take candidates through the process, and offers tips on how to help candidates overcome any fears they may have about running. In addition, the manual covers the technicalities that might seem overwhelming to a new candidate, such as how to get started and how to file. For caucus leaders, the manual provides advice on how to instruct candidates on a number of other aspects of campaigning—researching the district, assessing opponents, identifying sympathetic interest groups, conducting media interviews, and raising money (National Women's Political Caucus 1997b).

Civil rights organizations have played an active role in recruiting black candidates. Within the African American community, churches have historically recruited and trained candidates for all levels of public office, providing them with opportunities to develop leadership and organizational skills, to cultivate a constituency of supporters, and to emerge as activists and leaders. Even today, many black elected officials are ministers who periodically return to their districts to preach to a congregation.

Similarly, Christian conservative organizations recruit activists who have developed their political skills in white evangelical churches. The Christian Right has been quite active in encouraging Christian conservatives to run for county office, for school boards, and even for Congress. Christian Right groups provide training sessions on campaign mechanics (how to form a campaign committee, how to set up a campaign account) as well as on matters of presentation (how to address issues such as abortion and health care).

Although many organizations are eager to increase the number of elected officials who fit a particular demographic profile, most will support only those candidates who favor a specific policy agenda and have a credible chance of winning. Candidate recruitment and training are clearly a means toward achieving policy ends. Candidates seeking campaign assistance must favor the policy views of the group in order to receive its assistance in running for office.

Although agreement on policy may be the first and most important criterion for recruitment, it is not necessarily enough: interest groups want candidates who can win elections. For example, a leadership manual developed by the Christian Coalition in the 1990s asks, "What kind of people make the best candidates for public office, and where do you find them?" The manual then notes that although surface impressions—"poise, good looks, brains"—are not irrelevant, they can be misleading. Christian Right leaders are advised to also take the following into account: background, achievement, other personal characteristics such as the ability to balance the ticket, and competence for office. The manual notes that recruitment involves the "unpleasant task" of "digging out . . . intimate details"— including whether a potential candidate has a bad credit rating, a poor professional reputation, questionable moral character, or an unpublicized divorce (Fisher, Reed, and Weinhold 1990).

Recruitment by interest groups is usually most important for state and local office and to a lesser extent for the U.S. House. Most senatorial and presidential races involve ambitious and established politicians who have long considered making a bid for higher office. Yet even here, recruitment efforts can be important. A potential candidate may be mulling over a race for the Senate or the presidency, weighing the costs in time, money, and wear and tear on family life, and commitments of support from interest groups may help determine whether—and for what office—the candidate runs. For example, in 2004, some labor union officials urged former representative Richard Gephardt, D-Mo., to seek the presidency, which may have influenced his decision to run. As mentioned earlier, in the 2006 election cycle, EMILY's List sought to recruit a pro-choice candidate to run in the Pennsylvania Democratic primary to choose a challenger for Rick Santorum's U.S. Senate seat.

Training Methods

Once they have identified and encouraged good candidates to enter a campaign, interest groups provide various forms of training: seminars, manuals, and video and audiotapes, along with other sources of advice. Training is most common for U.S. House and state legislative races; few candidates for the Senate or the presidency believe that they need training to improve their candidacy, although a few could probably use some advice.

Political parties and quasi-party organizations also offer training to candi-dates, and interest groups often refer candidates they have recruited to party-run training sessions.

Interest groups that offer training vary in their approaches; some are content to mail helpful materials to candidates, whereas others send staff throughout the country to conduct training seminars. Training focuses on two principal concerns: (1) issues presentation, the art of framing issues in a way that is favorable to the interest group; and (2) campaign techniques, the basic tasks of running a campaign.

Many interest groups help educate candidates in how to best defend their issue agenda to unfriendly audiences. Anti-abortion groups in the 1990s circulated documents to candidates advising them to avoid debates over banning all abortions, and to instead focus on more popular limita-tions on abortion rights such as waiting periods, parental consent, and partial-birth abortion. In the mid 1990s, the National Rifle Association (NRA) faced a declining membership base and a public perception that the organization's issue positions were extreme. The NRA mailed to can-didates a multimedia package entitled *The Politics of Crime: Winning Strate-gies for Your Campaign* (National Rifle Association 1994). The centerpiece was a video short course in how to respond to gun control advocates and develop a winning campaign message on crime and guns. The training package contained an audiotape, an NRA report on criminal justice reform, a booklet to supplement the video and audiotapes, and reprints of articles from journals and popular magazines. The overall goal was to con-vince candidates that adopting the NRA view would put them on the winning side—as long as they controlled the message by focusing on crime, not gun control (see Box 2-1).

The NRA Institute for Legislative Action presently has a Grassroots Division that hosts election training seminars throughout the country for activists and candidates. Another technique is to identify one election vol-unteer coordinator for each congressional district to help organize grass-roots activities and also to serve as the liaison between local gun owners and candidates for public office. Perhaps no organized group has been more successful in the past decade at convincing candidates for office that its views will put politicians on the winning side of elections. In the 1990s, political observers commonly referred to NRA support and pro-gun posi-tions as dangerous to aspiring politicians. A decade later, many Democrat-ic candidates—including once strong gun-control Democrats such as Sen-ator John Kerry and Virginia governor Mark Warner—have gone to great

---

BOX 2-1

FROM *THE POLITICS OF CRIME*

Violent crime is one of the single most important issues in America today. It will be a key factor in virtually every campaign in 1994.

Members of the media and "liberal scholars" are telling us that guns, not criminals, are the problem. Big guns, small guns, ugly guns, whatever. And they're telling us that the answer is to ban them, tax them, register them, control them. Some of them, all of them, you name it. But gun control doesn't reduce crime. It never has and it never will. The statistics prove it and the public knows it.

The real issue is crime control, not gun control, and there are votes for candidates who are willing to be tough on crime, tough on criminals, and who propose workable, long-term solutions. To make this issue work for your campaign, you must stake out a position early and clearly; make the commitment of resources necessary to communicate your position; organize your supporters; and work to keep the anti-gun, pro-criminal lobby on the defensive, discussing crime on *your terms*, not theirs.

Source: Excerpted from National Rifle Association, "Summary," *The Politics of Crime: Winning Strategies for Your Campaign* (Fairfax, Va.: National Rifle Association, 1994), 11. Used with permission of the National Rifle Association of America Institute for Legislative Action.

---

lengths to assure gun owners that they do not want to take away their guns. In the 2004 presidential campaign, Kerry took time to hunt pheasants in Iowa, where he demonstrated good marksmanship that came from a lifetime of hunting.

The National Federation of Independent Businesses (NFIB) also uses a packet of educational materials to focus on issues presentation. The intent is to show candidates how to present a pro–small business message in a campaign and to convince them that such a message is a formula for success. Vice President for Political Development David Voepel also invites prospective candidates to visit the NFIB for one-on-one interviews to "talk about small-business issues and how to incorporate them into a campaign."

> We will then mail out a letter to our members in that district asking them to volunteer their time with that candidate. Then we have regional political directors and they go out and meet with our members and instruct the members on how to become involved politically. The members then develop liaisons with the candidate informing him or her of their concerns on small-business issues and in turn offering their volunteer services to the campaign. In addition to asking our members to volunteer with the candidate we take it one step further and ask them to become an NFIB activist or a member of our Political Action Team (PAT). As a PAT member, we try to work one-on-one with each member to get them more involved politically, as their time allows.

In addition to distributing multimedia educational materials, other interest groups provide formal training in campaign techniques. The NWPC holds numerous training schools for candidates each year, in conjunction with the organization's regional caucus meetings. The organization claimed that by 2005 its training programs will have been attended by thousands of candidates who were eventually successful in seeking public offices such as boards of education, city councils, state legislatures, statewide offices, and even Congress. Rep. Loretta Sanchez, D-Calif., was one such successful candidate who said that she began her campaign for Congress by attending an NWPC training program (National Women's Political Caucus 2005).

The NWPC gives its candidates and campaign workers a training manual entitled *Campaigning to Win: The NWPC Guide to Running a Winning Campaign* (National Women's Political Caucus 1997a). The highly detailed manual covers, among other topics, hiring campaign staff and structuring a campaign organization; budgeting and fund-raising; developing a public image; targeting and contacting voters; and dealing with the media. Some of the advice is quite specific and deals with ordinary details of campaigning; sections with titles such as "TV Clothing Tips" and "Special Speaking Tips for Women Candidates" include advice such as the following:

> Always have an extra pair of nylons handy in case of runs. On a hot day, a candidate may want to take along an extra blouse as well. Some candidates prepare for the unexpected by leaving a spare set of clothes at campaign headquarters or in the car.

The manual explains that because of a societal double standard, women are more likely than men to be judged on the basis of appearance. In addition to offering candidates guidance on what colors and patterns to wear and what fabrics to avoid, the manual advises them not to change their hairstyle or the design of their eyeglasses during a campaign, not to wear "bold earrings" or too much makeup, and to dress in business attire but to "avoid wearing designer outfits that cost more than the average voter's monthly salary." In a series of detailed tips on television "body language," the manual explains the importance of looking animated rather than too serious, describes how to make eye contact with the news anchor or reporter, and offers guidelines on the use of hand gestures: "Keep all gestures within an imaginary box the size of a twenty-one-inch television screen from your chin down to your chest, between the shoulder blades, and six to eight inches out" (National Women's Political Caucus 1997a) (see Box 2-2).

The level and type of instruction are keyed to the candidates' backgrounds and interests. For example, the NWPC offered an advanced training program for incumbents looking to move to higher positions and for field workers seeking to learn campaign management. The training seminars open with general sessions for all participants, and then the candidates and campaign workers split up to focus on their particular needs.

Some training programs are focused on particular groups of candidates such as one in April 2005 entitled "Political Training for Women of Color." At this program, prospective candidates attended sessions on topics such as "Making the Decision to Run for Office," "Campaign Planning, Budgeting and Fundraising," "Strategy, Message and Using the Web," and "Targeting Voters and Getting Out the Vote."

EMILY's List, the largest political action committee in the nation, also offers a combination of training and support. EMILY's List recruits, trains, and supports pro-choice Democratic women running for federal, state, and local offices. Its training programs prepare candidates and campaign staff on how to organize a campaign, raise money, and communicate messages to voters. The training programs teach campaign professionals how to be campaign managers, researchers, field operatives, and fund-raisers. In the 2003–2004 election cycle alone, EMILY's List held 34 training sessions in 25 states, attended by 1,274 candidates and staff.

After his failed 2004 presidential campaign, former Vermont governor Howard Dean formed an organization called Democracy for America and teamed with Progressive Majority to sponsor candidate training schools for

---

BOX 2-2

SPECIAL SPEAKING TIPS FOR WOMEN CANDIDATES

Candidates must have a strong ego, but many women are afraid to blow their own horn. Go ahead and brag about your strong points.

Control your emotions, especially anger or tears. Avoid tilting your head or using other body language which suggests a lack of confidence.

Recognize that some voters question a woman's leadership skills. Highlight any experience that shows you leading others or making tough decisions.

Be prepared to speak on all issues that the winner will have to face. Some voters still link female candidates only with "family" issues such as health care and education.

Voters may pay more attention to your family status than that of your male opponent(s). If you're single, be prepared for curiosity about your sex life or speculation about your sexual preference. You may want to find an appropriate escort for some events. If you have children, find a good, reliable baby-sitter, preferably a relative.

Prepare answers for stupid questions. For example, "What does your husband think about your candidacy?" Possible response: "He supports me and recognizes that my background and work in our community make me the best candidate for this office."

Avoid drinking alcohol or smoking cigarettes in public.

Source: Excerpted from National Women's Political Caucus (NWPC), "Special Speaking Tips for Women Candidates," *Campaigning to Win: The NWPC Guide to Running a Winning Campaign* (Washington, D.C.: NWPC, 1994), 7–10. Used with permission.

---

aspiring progressive candidates in a number of states. The training schools focused on campaign techniques and deliberately borrowed ideas from conservative-leaning groups that had been so successful in building a core of candidates for local offices around the country over the past generation. Progressive Majority also helped raise seed money for various progressive candidates who had attended the training schools. Dean's organization also teamed with other progressive groups such as 21st Century Democrats and Latinos for America to cosponsor candidate training programs at which participants learned media skills, campaign staff selection, fund-raising, and constituency outreach. Participants paid a nominal fee, with most of the cost offset by Democracy for America, and received a detailed training manual and a certificate signed by Dean.

One of the most prominent party-related groups conducting candidate training is GOPAC. Although not officially a part of the formal party structure, GOPAC exclusively promotes the fortunes of conservative Republican candidates at all levels. GOPAC's current chairman is former Republican representative J. C. Watts Jr. Former House Speaker Newt Gingrich headed the organization previously. Watts offers inspirational audio messages to potential GOP candidates on the group's Web site.

GOPAC offers candidates both training seminars and a multimedia package, but several of its training services go far beyond those offered by groups focused on specific issues. GOPAC has five different training programs, each geared toward a particular purpose, and a number of GOPAC trainers travel throughout the country conducting seminars. The program for elected legislators teaches them how to use their incumbency for future electoral advantage. Another program teaches candidates how to communicate effectively in different contexts—speeches, debates, media interviews, and television advertisements. Another program focuses on campaign strategies and tactics and yet another on fund-raising. Finally, GOPAC offers financially strapped challengers a seminar on how to run a grassroots, volunteer-based campaign.

Training sessions can be especially helpful, because they offer personal feedback and role playing. Some training sessions by interest groups train candidates on how to shake hands, a seemingly silly topic until you consider that shaking five thousand hands in a day can take a real toll. But GOPAC and other groups also offer documents online for candidates who cannot attend these sessions. For example, "Precinct Leader Get Out the Vote Handbook" offers advice on how to train precinct leaders to mobilize voters for a campaign. In "Money: A Step-by-Step Guide to Raise the Necessary Capital for Your Winning Campaign," the group advises

> If this is your first time running for office and you have not had the opportunity to adequately introduce yourself to the local donor community, third party letters can be the better vehicle for gaining credibility and acceptance

in these circles. . . . When preparing your third party solicitation, target your fundraising letters to individuals who will respond positively not only to your candidacy, but to the person or group that is sending out the letter on your behalf. . . . Often the most effective way to utilize the recognition and popularity of the people or groups who will be signing the letter is to send the fundraising request to _their_ donor list(s). State legislators or members of congress who support your campaign may offer to solicit their donor base on your behalf. In some cases, the law may require your campaign to reimburse the third party for the use of their list and for all mailing costs, but the potential financial rewards will likely far outweigh any costs. . . . On the following page, you will find a sample third party solicitation letter from a member of the United States Congress in support of a candidate for the state legislature. (GOPAC, 2004, p. 16)

Other conservative groups often request permission to review and adapt GOPAC's training materials for their own purposes. Even unsympathetic groups have learned from the opposing forces: EMILY's List seeks to emulate some of the tactics mastered by GOPAC, and a state Democratic legislative caucus director acknowledged that in developing training booklets for candidates and activists, he borrowed freely from the Christian Coalition's training manual, which he believed to be the most sophisticated at that time (Rozell and Wilcox 1996, 85).

The Nomination Process

In addition to recruiting and training candidates, a number of interest groups provide direct assistance to candidates seeking their party's nomination. Interest groups may endorse candidates, provide voters' guides to their members and other voters, contribute money or services directly to the candidate, engage in voter mobilization efforts, and even pay for television advertising. Many of these tactics are discussed more fully in Chapters 3 and 4. For the purposes of this chapter, it is worth noting that interest groups can change the character of political parties by changing the identity of those who represent the parties in office. This influence then gives them the opportunity to influence the policies that the parties espouse.

Again, such tactics are most common among social movement organizations. Feminist, civil rights, and Christian Right groups all support candidates in primaries, sometimes marshaling significant resources on their behalf. Such groups can play an important role in determining party nominations, especially in states that nominate through conventions or caucuses rather than through primaries.

As noted earlier, turnout is lower in states with caucuses or conventions, enabling a well-organized and dedicated minority of voters to significantly influence party nominations. Nevertheless, interest groups can play an important role even in primary elections. In Pennsylvania in 2004, interest groups poured millions of dollars into a party primary pitting Arlen Specter, the moderate incumbent senator, against Representative Patrick Toomey, a social conservative. Both candidates raised money from corporate committees, but pro-choice groups helped Specter, while anti-abortion and especially very conservative business groups rallied behind Toomey. Specter won the Republican nomination as well as the Senate seat.

PRESIDENTIAL NOMINATIONS

Many interest groups focus their greatest efforts on influencing presidential nominations. Because the positions of candidates within the same party often differ greatly, interest groups may have much at stake. Consider, for example, some of the Democratic candidates for president in 2004. Some candidates strongly supported the Bush administration's decision to go to war in Iraq, whereas others (notably Howard Dean and Dennis Kucinich) made opposition to the war the centerpiece of their campaigns. Several candidates strongly favored gun control legislation, whereas Dean and eventual nominee John Kerry stressed their firm support for gun owners' rights. Kucinich, John Edwards, and Richard Gephardt supported various forms of protectionist legislation, whereas Dean emphasized his support for free trade. With the candidates at odds on so many important issues, the battle for the Democratic nomination was an important one.

The rules by which the parties choose their nominees have changed over time, and these rules have important implications for the way that interest groups are active in campaigns, and their effectiveness in helping a candidate win the nomination. Moreover, parties are free to change the rules for presidential nominations in the future, and the rules are not neutral in their effect: whatever form they take, they create part of the opportunity structure for interest groups that wish to influence internal party affairs.

In the 1960s, both political parties had rules that allowed party leaders to dominate the candidate selection process. In 1968 Senators Eugene McCarthy and George McGovern won many state primaries and caucuses, but the Democratic nominee was Vice President Hubert H. Humphrey, who had not campaigned in a single state primary or caucus. In frustration over the nomination and in protest against the Johnson-Humphrey administration's policies on Vietnam, thousands of activists took to the streets outside the convention while others remained in the hall, repeatedly disrupting the proceedings.

The next year, McGovern helped direct a reform commission that increased the role of primary elections in the Democratic selection process. In 1972 McGovern used those rules to win his party's nomination by successfully defeating his opponents in a lengthy series of open primary contests that chose delegates to the national convention. These rules increased the role of primary elections—almost 61 percent of the 1972 delegates were selected by primaries—and imposed a complex formula to ensure that the delegates had the same proportion of women, minorities, and young people as in the general population.

By 1976, with further changes in the rules, thirty presidential primaries selected 73 percent of delegates to the Democratic conventions. More important, party rules were changed to prohibit "winner-take-all" primaries, in which the winning candidate receives all the delegates. In 1972 McGovern's narrow victory in California gave him all of the delegates from that state's huge delegation. After 1972, candidates received delegates in rough proportion to their strength in the primary.

The Republican Party also opened its nomination process during the early 1970s, although it added fewer primaries and retained winner-take-all rules. Both parties have continued to change the nomination process during the past several decades. Indeed, the Democratic Party makes minor modifications after almost every election cycle. But since 1972, both parties' nominations have been determined through a system of state primaries and caucuses over a period of several months.

Changes in rules governing nominations have profoundly affected interest group participation in conventions. Under the old rules, convention delegates were chosen at state conventions and caucuses where party insiders ran the show. This system favored groups with long-established ties to party elites (for example, labor unions and the Democratic Party, business interests and the GOP). Under more open nominating systems, delegates are allotted according to the popular vote. Interest groups that successfully mobilize activists in primary elections and caucuses can thus play an important role in nominations, including sending members as delegates to the nominating conventions.

The contrast between the 1968 and 1972 Democratic convention delegates shows the impact of changes in party rules. In the 1968 Democratic convention, interest groups with close ties to party leaders influenced the nomination, while activists from ideological groups demonstrated outside the convention hall. In 1972, under a different set of rules, grassroots activists dominated the selection of the party standard-bearer, while some representatives of established interests failed to be selected as delegates. Outside the convention hall, future Speaker of the House Thomas P. O'Neil quipped that he had been defeated for a slot as a party delegate by "the cast of *Hair*."

Modern national conventions formally nominate presidential candidates. The nominees are chosen by delegates who are in turn selected at state party primaries and caucuses leading up to the conventions. The parties have complex and sometimes changing formulas for allocating delegates to each state. In general, however, both Democrats and Republicans award extra delegates to states that have supported the party's nominee in recent presidential elections; the GOP also favors less populous states (Wayne 1996).

The number of delegates from a state who support each candidate is based on the popular primary or caucus votes. Each party has a different formula for determining the precise number of delegates for each candidate, but in general, the Democrats assign delegates on the basis of the percentage vote for each candidate (with a bonus for the primary or caucus winner), and the Republicans have a winner-take-all system in which the candidate with the most votes gets all the delegates from a state. In the Democrats' modified proportional system, somewhat smaller groups that might be shut out in a winner-take-all system have the opportunity to send delegates to conventions and to have a voice in the proceedings. The Democrats also have a special category of "superdelegates"—elected officials, members of the party national committee, and other party leaders. But the vast majority of delegates are pledged to vote for the winner of a primary election or caucus in their state or district.

Studies show that participation rates in party primaries and caucuses are relatively low and that those who do participate are unrepresentative of voters in general elections (Ceaser 1979, 1982; Ladd 1978). Interest groups that can mobilize their members can thus have a strong influence on primary elections and especially on caucuses. Consider, for example, the success of Pat Robertson, a Christian conservative candidate who ran for the GOP nomination in 1988, and Jesse Jackson, an African American civil rights leader who sought the Democratic nomination in 1984 and 1988. Christian conservatives and African Americans each constitute between 10 and 20 percent of the general public, but if members of either group turn out in force to vote in a primary or caucus, their strength is increased significantly. In the Iowa caucuses, Robertson finished ahead of then–vice president George H.W. Bush simply because Robertson's supporters turned out to vote. (Bush joked lamely that his supporters had all been at their daughters' debutante balls on caucus night.) In 1988, civil rights groups and black churches helped Jesse Jackson win several primaries in southern states.

Indeed, because participants in caucuses and some party primaries disproportionately represent interest groups, many scholars argue that the current presidential nomination process is heavily skewed in favor of ideological and issue-oriented candidates capable of appealing to interest group activists (Banfield 1980; Ceaser 1979, 1982; Ladd 1978; Wilson 1962). Nevertheless, party moderates often defeat more extreme candidates: both George H. W. Bush and Bob Dole defeated Patrick Buchanan for the GOP nomination in 1992 and 1996, and Bill Clinton defeated Jesse Jackson and Paul Simon in 1992. In 2000 George W. Bush defeated several far more conservative opponents by running as a "compassionate conservative." In 2004 John Kerry successfully ran from the middle for the Democratic nomination and thus defeated several candidates perceived by voters to be more liberal, including Kucinich and Dean.

Ideological groups do not, in fact, always support ideological candidates. Many conservative groups supported Bush in 2000, and similarly many liberal groups backed Kerry in 2004, because of the belief that these candidates were electable, whereas the more ideologically pure alternatives were not. In 2000, for example, Pat Robertson and former Christian Coalition executive director Ralph Reed worked behind the scenes to improve Bush's chances with Christian conservative voters, despite the presence of more socially conservative candidates such as Alan Keyes, Gary Bauer, and Steve Forbes. In 2004 many liberal leaders and activists lined up behind Kerry's campaign because they believed that he had a better chance to win a general election than did the less experienced Dean.

DELEGATE SELECTION

Once primary elections and caucuses have been held, delegates are pledged by state law and party rules to support the winning candidates. Yet the actual selection of convention delegates occurs later, often in a series of local caucuses and regional conventions that sometimes culminate in a state convention. Many interest groups encourage their members to participate in the selection of delegates and try to send large blocs of their members to national conventions. Some interest group blocs actually meet together during the convention, and a few even have sophisticated "whip" systems to help deliver the votes on party platforms and rules (Schlozman and Tierney 1986). In 2004, 25 percent of the Republican convention delegates were members of the NRA, whereas 33 percent of Democratic delegates (but only 4 percent of Republican delegates) were members of labor unions (Rosenbaum and Elder 2004; Seelye and Connelly 2004).

In the GOP, although delegates from a state are all pledged to vote for the candidate who received the most votes in that state, not all the delegates necessarily support that candidate. Historically, winning candidates have dominated the delegate selection process, although they have often allowed the strongest supporters of losing candidates to serve as delegates to the national convention. In 1988, however, Pat Robertson contested the delegate selection process in states where he had lost primary elections, and members of conservative Christian groups sent many more delegates to the convention than they might have otherwise. In Virginia, for example, Robertson's supporters, who were mostly members of conservative Christian groups, worked hard (at local caucuses, congressional district conventions, and the state convention) to get selected as delegates to the national convention. Eventually a majority of Virginia's delegates were Robertson supporters who were pledged to support Bush at the convention. By ensuring that a majority of delegates were Robertson supporters, the Christian Right gained control of the Republican Party apparatus in Virginia (Rozell and Wilcox 1996). A similar approach was used in other states as well (Herztke 1993).

Interest groups often send substantial delegations to the parties' national conventions. In 1984 Walter Mondale had 2,076 pledged delegates at the San Francisco convention, of whom 563 were members of unions of the AFL–CIO, 220 were members of the National Education Association (NEA), and 280 were members of the National Organization for Women

(Schlozman and Tierney 1986). In 1996, 28 percent of the delegates to the Democratic National Convention were members of either the AFL-CIO or the NEA (Sack 1996), and over 1,000 Democratic convention delegates overall were labor union members, of whom 405 delegates and alternates were NEA members (Wolf 1996).

In 1996 the Christian Coalition spent over $2 million to get its members and sympathizers elected as delegates to the Republican National Convention (Jackson 1996b). The effort paid off: about five hundred delegates—one out of every four—were registered members of the Christian Coalition, and two-thirds of all delegates were either members or supporters. The group then spent an additional $750,000 at the convention itself. In all, expenditures came to about $6,000 per member or supporter elected as a GOP delegate—a good measure of the importance that some groups attach to convention politics.

Occasionally the selection of delegates to the presidential convention sparks visible and divisive fights within state parties. In Texas in 1996, many delegates on the slate proposed by the Dole campaign were defeated in the congressional district caucuses, including former party chair Fred Meyer, U.S. House members Henry Bonilla and Mac Thornberry, and the co-chair of Dole's Texas campaign. The greatest controversy surrounded the defeat of U.S. senator Kay Bailey Hutchison, who was later seated as an at-large delegate after the intervention of the governor, the party chair, Dole, and Sen. Phil Gramm (Bruce 1997).

THE NATIONAL CONVENTIONS

Why do groups such as labor unions and Christian conservatives work so hard to send delegates to the parties' national conventions? First, a strong and visible presence at a national convention signals to party leaders that an interest group is an important constituency that cannot be ignored in policy making. Second, conventions ratify the party platform, which embodies the official policy preferences of the party. Third, rules for delegate selection may be altered at conventions, which may affect candidates' chances in the next election. At the 1988 Democratic convention, Jesse Jackson's delegates successfully pressured the party to make its rules more favorable to "outsider" candidates. In addition, conventions provide interest group members with the opportunity to rub shoulders with party leaders and elected officials, perhaps doing a bit of unofficial lobbying in the process. And perhaps most important, group members who attend national conventions are often inspired to become more active, not only within their own interest group but also in the broader realm of electoral politics.

Conventions also provide interest groups with an opportunity to publicize their issues by inviting speakers and using the media to reach delegates and the larger electorate. At the 2004 Democratic National Convention in Boston, youth activists sponsored numerous meetings and receptions, including a concert by Wyclef Jean (Democratic National Convention Committee 2004a). In the days leading up to the convention, MTV's Choose or Lose and 20 Million Loud! held a press conference announcing the winner of the "Speak Out for the Future" essay contest, as part of its efforts to encourage young people to vote. Because television broadcasts of the conventions draw large numbers of viewers and convention halls are filled with reporters looking for a story, rallies and presentations can help publicize and promote interest groups' positions on crucial issues.

Many interest groups also use conventions as an opportunity to protest party policies. During the 2004 Republican convention in New York, hundreds of thousands of people demonstrated in the streets to protest President Bush's policies, especially the war in Iraq and tax cuts favoring the wealthy. Groups such as United for Peace and Justice, Billionaires for Bush, and the A31 Coalition marched in the streets during the convention. Over 1,800 protesters, most of them nonviolent, were arrested, more than double the number arrested during the tumultuous Democratic convention in 1968 (Powell and Garcia 2004). New York City police have come under scrutiny for their mass arrests.

The calendar of official events at the 2004 Democratic convention in Boston included the following: "Boston Tea/She Party," sponsored by the National Organization for Women and Feminist Majority; a "Unity Celebration," sponsored by Human Rights Campaign; a public policy forum sponsored by the American Jewish Committee; and live music sponsored by Rock the Vote (Democratic National Convention Committee 2004b).

Inside the convention hall, some interest groups try to coordinate the actions of their members. At the 1996 GOP convention, the Christian Coalition made what was perhaps the most extensive coordination effort by any group in history. The group had 102 whips, 8 regional whips, 40 runners on the convention floor, and a war room to map out strategy. It provided each of its delegates with a new digital communication system—in essence, hand-held computers—using a new wireless frequency that had just been approved by the Federal Communications Commission.

According to Ralph Reed, the communication system would afford his group a tremendous advantage in any potential floor debate and would also enable him, for example, to signal to delegates when to cheer during speeches (Drew 1997, 120; Goldberg 1996a; Jackson 1996b).

This activity perhaps seemed especially important to religious conservatives because the party was nominating a more moderate candidate, Bob Dole, for the presidency. The Christian Coalition did not have such influence in the 2000 and 2004 conventions, partly because the organization fell on hard times but also because the GOP was united behind a socially conservative nominee, George W. Bush. Thus, in these more recent conventions, the Christian Coalition was a quiet presence, and in 2004 its director, Pat Robertson, was not even offered a speaking role. The differences in these roles highlight an important limitation to group activity at conventions: in 1996 the religious conservatives dominated the platform committees, but the party nominated a moderate who immediately dismissed the platform as irrelevant. In 2000 and 2004, social conservative groups placed less emphasis on dominating the platform, but ultimately the party nominated a candidate who supported their agenda.

Influencing Party Platforms

Because candidates are not bound by party platforms, many analysts are quick to dismiss these platforms as irrelevant. Many interest groups, however, take a different view and have made strong efforts—particularly in recent years—to influence the platforms of both political parties. Interest groups assign symbolic importance to the creation of platforms that reflect their policy preferences, and they believe that candidates do ultimately heed platforms to some degree. Moreover, interest groups are aware that because platforms receive considerable media coverage, they become important documents in the "battle of ideas."

Interest groups are probably correct in assigning importance to platforms. In the words of William Greener, the 1996 GOP convention manager, "I challenge or defy people to identify a better indicator of what a party will do during a campaign—much less what they will do in office—than the party platform." There is, moreover, empirical evidence that presidents do make an effort to fulfill many of the promises in their platforms. Political scientist Gerald Pomper reported that presidents prior to Reagan had fulfilled approximately 75 percent of the specific pledges in their platforms (Pomper with Lederman 1980), and the *Washington Times*—surely no friend to Bill Clinton—credited him with having fulfilled 47 percent of his campaign and platform promises during the first ten months of his presidency (Moss 1994).

Party platforms are drafted by a platform committee, which may hold one or more hearings to allow interest groups to testify. Groups sometimes arrive with long lists of platform planks. In 1984, for example, labor unions, feminists, and other groups succeeded in inserting lengthy and detailed provisions into the Democratic platform, allowing Ronald Reagan to attack Democratic nominee Walter Mondale as a candidate of special interests. Subsequent Democratic platforms have been far less detailed and occasioned far less open conflict.

In 1992 and again in 1996, Clinton supporters dominated the Democratic Platform Committee. Because party rules allowed the nominee a great deal of ultimate control over the platform, issue activists had no opportunity to take over the convention proceedings and write the platform (Maisel 1996, 80–87). Although, for example, representatives from diverse groups in the party coalition made up the 1992 drafting committee, Democratic National Committee chair Ron Brown allowed the Clinton campaign to choose about one-half of the members of the committee (Maisel 1996, 81–82). The group most influential in drafting the platform language was Clinton's Democratic Leadership Council, an organization of moderate party leaders committed to moving the party toward the ideological center and away from the perception of being dominated by special interests on the left.

In 1996 the Democratic Platform Committee held a marathon one-day hearing in Cleveland at which representatives from the Sierra Club, Americans for Democratic Action, Veterans of Foreign Wars, the America-Israel Public Affairs Committee (AIPAC), and the American Petroleum Institute, among many others, testified (Maisel 1996, 82–83). Political scientist Sandy Maisel reported that some groups were more effective than others at both getting their viewpoint heard and influencing the convention. He noted that AIPAC was particularly effective: the group not only testified at the Cleveland hearing but also succeeded in getting strongly pro-Israel activists selected to both the drafting and platform committees. Ultimately the wording of some sections of the platform document reflected AIPAC's influence (Maisel 1996, 84).

Union activists also played a major role in drafting the party platform, which included a section entitled "Standing Up for Working Americans." The platform staked out such pro-labor stances as pension protection, job training legislation, and a ban on replacing strikers. Yet overall, the platform was clearly controlled by Clinton supporters who wanted a moderate document from which to wage the presidential campaign.

In contrast, the GOP platform has in recent years provoked highly visible conflict between party moderates and anti-abortion Christian conservatives, and nominees have not always succeeded in controlling the language of the document. The chair of the RNC, in consultation with the party nominee, selects the chair and vice chairs of the platform committee, and each state delegation sends one man and one woman to the committee. Interest group members run for slots on the platform committee. Thus, to ensure the selection of platform committee members who hold particular views, interest groups vie to obtain a majority within the state delegation. In 1996, pro-choice Republican groups worked closely with Massachusetts governor William Weld in an unsuccessful effort to create a pro-choice majority among the state's delegates who would, in turn, send pro-choice delegates to the platform committee.

In 1992 former RNC chair Rich Bond selected a committee that traveled across the country, holding hearings and taking testimony from various groups on policy issues. The information gathered at these events was turned over to the convention platform committee to assist in deliberations on format and content. According to Bond, although President George H. W. Bush wanted to retain control of the platform document and his campaign pressured the head of each state delegation to do everything possible to get sympathetic people selected to the platform committee, the platform was ultimately a highly conservative document that seemed ill-suited to Bush's moderate Republicanism. Maisel has argued, however, that the Bush campaign appointed conservative chairs and vice chairs in an effort to appease interest groups and activists on the party's right wing (Maisel 1996).

In 1996 GOP nominee Bob Dole lost a highly publicized battle on language addressing the abortion issue. The platform committee adopted a strongly anti-abortion plank, and pro-choice advocates failed to get the full platform committee even to approve a supplemental official minority report in the document, even though they needed only 27 of 107 member votes (Republicans for Choice Report 1996). Although Dole was personally anti-abortion, his campaign managers believed that it would be advantageous to have a "tolerance plank" stating that the GOP respected the right to hold different views on some controversial issues such as abortion. Dole tried to forge language for a tolerance plank that would be acceptable to both sides and made personal appeals to some of the interest group leaders and platform committee members. But as one conservative leader commented, "Dole thinks it's '68, when the candidate could pick up the phone and dictate the platform." The members of the platform committee had been elected in their states with grassroots support from conservative groups, and their agenda for the convention simply differed from that of the party's presidential nominee. Many of the delegates, at the urging of leaders of conservative groups, had signed on with Dole merely because they knew that their chances of being elected to the convention and influencing the platform would be improved by siding with the likely winner (Drew 1997, 108).

When Dole quipped at the end of the convention that the platform was irrelevant to his campaign and that he had no intention of even reading the document, his statements appeared calculated to signal to more moderate voters that he did not plan to run on the hard-right positions of his own party's platform. Ralph Reed, however, considered it a major victory that the anti-abortion plank in the party platform had been forged by grassroots activists elected as delegates rather than by the party nominee (Drew 1997, 109).

In 2004 George W. Bush had endorsed a moderate version of a constitutional amendment that would ban same-sex marriage in the states but that would permit states to offer certain legal protections to same-sex couples in the form of civil unions. But Vice President Dick Cheney, whose daughter is a lesbian, had announced that he opposed the effort. Social conservatives responded angrily, strengthening the language in the GOP platform to endorse a constitutional amendment that would ban same-sex marriage *and* civil unions. Tony Perkins, president of the socially conservative group Family Research Council, acknowledged that strengthening the platform's opposition to same-sex civil unions was partly a response to the vice president's statement that he personally favored leaving the issue up to the states.

The language of the Republican Party platform on same-sex marriage is shown in Box 2-3. The platform takes the unusual step of urging Congress to pass a law that would forbid the courts from examining the constitutionality of the Defense of Marriage Act. Congress has never used this power on major legislation.

Financing Convention Activities

Although the two national conventions are partially financed by public funding, costs are increasingly likely to exceed the public grant. Each of the

---

BOX 2-3

LANGUAGE USED IN GOP PLATFORM
ON SAME-SEX MARRIAGE

The material in italics was inserted by Christian conservatives after Vice President Cheney made a public statement that he did not support the Marriage Amendment.

> We strongly support President Bush's call for a Constitutional amendment that fully protects marriage, *and we believe that neither federal nor state judges nor bureaucrats should force states to recognize other living arrangements as equivalent to marriage. We believe, and the social science confirms, that the well-being of children is best accomplished in the environment of the home, nurtured by their mother and father anchored by the bonds of marriage. We further believe that legal recognition and the accompanying benefits afforded couples should be preserved for that unique and special union of one man and one woman which has historically been called marriage.* After more than two centuries of American jurisprudence, and millennia of human experience, a few judges and local authorities are presuming to change the most fundamental institution of civilization, the union of a man and a woman in marriage. Attempts to redefine marriage in a single state or city could have serious conse-

---

2004 national conventions was extremely costly, with much of the funding coming from the private sector. The Republican convention was estimated to cost over $160 million, with $64 million of the cost coming from private sources. The Democratic convention cost nearly $100 million, with almost $40 million coming from private sources (Campaign Finance Institute 2004a).

Corporations donated large sums of money to help defray costs, sponsored events for the parties and their candidates, and most important, contributed many of the goods and services that make conventions work. For

quences throughout the country, and anything less than a Constitutional amendment, passed by the Congress and ratified by the states, is vulnerable to being overturned by activist judges. On a matter of such importance, the voice of the people must be heard. The Constitutional amendment process guarantees that the final decision will rest with the American people and their elected representatives. President Bush will also vigorously defend the Defense of Marriage Act, which was supported by both parties and passed by 85 votes in the Senate. This common sense law reaffirms the right of states not to recognize same-sex marriages licensed in other states. *President Bush said, "We will not stand for judges who undermine democracy by legislating from the bench and try to remake America by court order." The Republican House of Representatives has responded to this challenge by passing H.R. 3313, a bill to withdraw jurisdiction from the federal courts over the Defense of Marriage Act. We urge Congress to use its Article III power to enact this into law, so that activist federal judges cannot force 49 other states to approve and recognize Massachusetts' attempt to redefine marriage.*

the 2004 conventions, over seventy organizations donated more than $100,000, and several gave over $1 million (Campaign Finance Institute 2004b). Many of the small and large corporations that provide funding for the conventions do so to retain the goodwill of party leaders, but there are sound business reasons as well. Approximately one-fifth of the 1996 GOP convention delegates were millionaires, and another one-fifth were worth at least $500,000—making the convention a good occasion for entrepreneurs to show off their wares.

At the 1992 party conventions, the first ones at which cellular phones were in widespread use, delegates' cellular phones were constantly busy and subject to eavesdropping. For the 1996 GOP convention, Ericsson Corporation, the pioneer in secure digital communications, donated three hundred of its phones (which also allow for paging, faxing, and call waiting and have a caller-identification feature) for delegates to use. Not only did the company make an impression on a lot of well-heeled Republican delegates, but it also captured the attention of policy makers and the media. News reports of the advantages of the Ericsson technology brought the company more publicity than almost any paid advertising campaign could have (Goldberg 1996b).

In 1996 AT&T gave about $1.5 million to the GOP convention to help supply computers and cable wiring for online broadcasting. The company spokesman cited business incentives for the donation, which provided "the opportunity for us to showcase our technology and to help the Republican National Convention or the party put on a very expensive event" (Jackson 1996a). Subsequently the GOP designated AT&T the official long-distance carrier at the convention. General Motors donated the official car, and United Airlines was the official airline. Gerald R. Parsky, chairman of the San Diego host committee, claimed that politics had absolutely nothing to do with any of the corporate contributions: "Our sponsors' motivations for contributing to the host committee are nonpartisan in nature. . . . Their primary focus is a combination of a desire to contribute to the community and a desire to showcase their company in a commercial way" (Labaton 1996).

In 2004 General Motors supplied three hundred vehicles to both the Democratic and Republican conventions. Panasonic donated video and audio products to both conventions, giving more than one hundred Panasonic Viera high-definition plasma monitors. These kinds of freebies have become so routine that convention officials now write up formal proposals asking for donations. For its 2004 convention, Republicans asked for housing for a year for designated GOP convention staff, new computer equipment, Blackberry wireless devices, three hundred air-conditioned buses, sedan car services for GOP officials, gasoline and drivers for all vehicles donated to the host committee, and more than $1 million in office supplies (Center for Public Integrity 2004).

Much of the impetus for public funding of party conventions came from the ITT scandal of 1972. During the Nixon administration, the Justice Department investigated the ITT Corporation for antitrust violations. The Nixon campaign solicited a donation from ITT, and the corporation ultimately donated $400,000 to the Republican National Convention in Miami.

Although the Federal Election Campaign Act amendments of 1974 mandated public rather than private funding for conventions, the law allowed local businesses in host cities to provide special convention discounts. The Federal Election Commission (FEC) significantly softened this regulation in 1994, with a new interpretation that permitted local businesses to donate products to conventions for "promotional purposes" (Labaton 1996). Companies showered delegates to the 1996 conventions with free disposable cameras, Frisbees, and many other gifts with brand names advertised on the products. These freebies seemed benign enough and attracted little criticism, if any.

But Stephen Labaton of the *New York Times* reported that despite claims of nonpartisan, civically oriented motivations for giving, the largest donations to the two major party conventions did, in fact, come from industries with substantial stakes in current legislation and federal regulations. The vice president of Anheuser-Busch, a large brewing company, admitted that although his company's donations to the two party conventions were in the spirit of promoting civic life, the corporation did plan to lobby delegates about the elimination of a 1991 federal tax increase on beer (Labaton 1996).

Similarly, in 2004, Altria, the owner of the tobacco company Philip Morris, donated over $100,000 to the Democratic convention, as well as a substantial sum to the Republican convention. At the time of the conventions, Congress was considering bills with major implications for the tobacco industry, including provisions that would regulate tobacco and a multibillion-dollar buyout for tobacco farmers (Toedtman 2004).

Local companies often provide important services for the conventions, in part to show the convention city in a good light to the rest of the country. The law allows local businesses to donate money to host committees as a form of civic boosterism. In the following exchange, a CNN reporter and William Grebe, chair of the 1996 GOP Convention Arrangements Committee in San Diego, discussed contributions made to the host committee by Philip Morris. The conversation illustrates just how tenuous the connections have become:

CNN: Philip Morris has a strong business connection to San Diego?

Grebe: Sure they do.

CNN: What's the connection?

Grebe: Kraft Foods. I assume people here buy Kraft Foods products. I know they think a lot of Miller beer. So sure, they have a connection here. And maybe some San Diegans actually smoke. (Jackson 1996a)

Political parties used to use conventions to raise soft money contributions from corporate executives, generally offering access to party leaders at special events in exchange for contributions. At the 1996 GOP convention, the party offered each contributor donating $15,000 a chance to meet personally with Speaker of the House Newt Gingrich and to play in an exclusive golf tournament. For $25,000, donors could attend a horse race and reception at the Del Mar racetrack—events that, according to the *New York Times*, attracted twenty-five contributors of $25,000 and another fifty contributors of at least $100,000. One contributor of $250,000, the vice president of a large corporation, beamed that he and other contributors had been "surrounded by governors" and by "other GOP leaders" (Goldberg 1996b). The GOP gave contributors of at least $250,000 "season tickets"—invitations to all the major party events leading up to and during the convention, skybox seats at the convention, and the opportunity to have their photos taken with Dole and his running mate Jack Kemp (Drew 1997, 117).

Since 2002, direct contributions to parties by corporations, trade associations, and labor unions have been banned. Yet the costs of conventions have gone up dramatically, nearly doubling from 2000 to 2004. Thus the one way to spend money on behalf of the parties while not running afoul of the ban on soft money contributions is to help finance the nominating conventions. Public interest organizations have charged that the sharp increases in such spending at political party conventions have violated the spirit of campaign finance regulations. Jeffrey Birnbaum and Thomas Edsall of the *Washington Post* reported from the 2004 Democratic National Convention in Boston,

And the money has poured in. Every day, from 7 A.M. to 2 A.M., breakfasts, brunches, luncheons, cocktail parties, dinners and post-convention fetes are convened to honor senior Democratic officials. These events range from a simple breakfast meeting with coffee, fruit and bagels in a downtown hotel to the rental of a cruise ship docked at Boston Harbor or a golf tournament on the outskirts of Boston.

Over a week's time, at least 265 such events are listed on public and private schedules handed around by lobbyists and major contributors to the party. But that is clearly an understatement. There are so many parties here that even high-profile lobbyists . . . can't attend every one to which they are invited." (Birnbaum and Edsall 2004)

Conspicuous at both 2004 national conventions were the many lavish events sponsored by lobbyists, trade associations, unions, and corporations. Although Senate ethics rules prohibit a member from accepting a dinner costing more than $49.99 from a lobbyist, that same member is permitted to accept a meal and even be honored at a widely attended event. This distinction is based on the assumption that a member accepting a private dinner or a gift from a lobbyist who has business before the government would be indebted to the lobbyist, whereas at a widely attended event, there is no one person to whom the member might potentially feel gratitude. Senate rules allow a senator "free attendance at a widely attended event that is officially related to Senate duties." At the 2004 Democratic National Convention, the Chicago Board Options Exchange, the Chicago Board of Trade, and the Chicago Mercantile Exchange honored Sen. Richard Durbin, D-Ill., at a $19,000 luncheon. Durbin, an original sponsor of the McCain-Feingold campaign finance reform, saw no contradiction in his participation in such a lavish event sponsored by these groups with a direct interest in government policy, and he defended his participation as an extension of his duties as a U.S. senator (Birnbaum and Edsall 2004).

For both businesses and members of Congress, the benefits of a widely attended event are substantial. Businesses do not have to report their expenses to the FEC but may report the events as business expenses for tax purposes. Members of Congress, even those designated as the guests of honor, do not have to report these events as in-kind political contributions. "With all the restrictions on campaign finance, the conventions are a place companies can still spend legally and make their positions felt," said Rep. Peter King, R-N.Y., noting the influence of money at the national conventions (Toedtman 2004).

The 2004 national conventions were ideal occasions for groups with an interest in government policy to sponsor well-attended events. At the GOP convention in New York, Rep. Joe Barton, R-Texas, chairman of the House Committee on Energy and Commerce, was feted at a party sponsored by energy industry leaders such as Edison Electric Institute, the American Gas Association, the National Mining Association, and the Nuclear Energy Institute. At the party, Barton was put on center stage with country singer Clint Black, the main entertainment for the invite-only event. New York governor George Pataki and the New York delegation were entertained at another event sponsored by a different group of energy companies where female acrobats hung from the ceiling.

The American Gas Association sponsored a trap shoot tournament honoring Oklahoma senator James M. Inhofe, chairman of the Environment and Public Works Committee, and a late-night concert to honor California representative Richard Pombo, chair of the House Resources Committee. PepsiCo Inc. sponsored a party for Sen. Bill Frist of Tennessee, the majority leader, at the Metropolitan Museum. General Motors hosted an event for Rep. J. Dennis Hastert of Illinois, the House Speaker, at the famous restaurant Tavern on the Green (Getter 2004; Justice and Burros 2004).

One of the more innovative approaches was taken at the 2004 GOP convention, where major industry lobbyists were assigned various roles in actually running the convention. Birnbaum and Edsall reported that about one hundred industry lobbyists performed various functions at the convention:

> These men and women make sure speakers get on and off the podium on schedule. They escort elected officials and their families to the convention floor. They run the floor whip operation, directing delegates through all their duties, from waving placards to attending platform committee meetings. They also served as senior staffers for the committee that wrote the party platform. Anne Phelps, for example, is executive director of the Platform Committee. Her lobbying clients include the Ho-Chunk Nation Indian tribe of Wisconsin and FMC Technology Inc. (Birnbaum and Edsall, August 31, 2004)

This participation offered the lobbyists a unique access to lawmakers not afforded other citizens. It also provided them an ideal opportunity to impress corporate clients with visible evidence of their access. Although the GOP for years has had close ties with corporate interests, the extent to which industry lobbyists were directly involved in the convention and its activities worries many public interest advocates.

STATE PARTY CONVENTIONS

Although the national conventions attract the most attention, many state parties hold conventions as well. In a few cases, candidates are actually selected or endorsed at conventions; more commonly, conventions provide an opportunity for the party to rally behind the nominee chosen through primary elections or caucuses. State conventions also perform other important functions: they adopt state party platforms, which sometimes differ significantly from those of the national party; they create and modify party rules for the distribution of resources and the selection of nominees; and they are often the forum for the selection of the state party chair, state committee members, and state representatives to the national party committee. In presidential election years, the state conventions sometimes make the final selection of delegates to the national conventions.

Generally, delegates to state conventions are chosen through a multistage process that includes local caucuses, congressional district conventions, and sometimes regional conventions. In most states, it is not especially difficult to become a state convention delegate, and in some states almost anyone who wants to attend can do so. Indeed, party leaders sometimes have to "beat the bushes" to find enough delegates to represent their geographic area at the state convention.

Interest groups play an active role in state conventions. Table 2-1 shows the percentage of attendees at GOP conventions in five states in the 1990s who indicated that they were members of various interest groups. Few delegates were members of labor unions or environmental, feminist, or pro-choice groups. The percentage who were members of business and professional groups varied across the states: in Virginia, more than 50 percent of the delegates were members of professional groups, whereas in Florida, more than 60 percent of the delegates were members of business groups. The percentage who were members of pro-family, conservative Christian, and anti-abortion groups also ranged widely: more than half of Minnesota delegates were members of anti-abortion groups, versus less than one-third in Virginia. Nearly half the Florida delegates were members of pro–gun rights organizations (Green, Rozell, and Wilcox 1995).

At the huge (14,000-delegate) GOP nominating convention in Virginia in 1993, Christian Right delegates threw the nomination for lieutenant governor to Michael Farris—former Washington state chair of the Moral Majority and former attorney for Concerned Women for America—despite the fact that he had never held elected office. In 1994, at an equally large Virginia convention, Christian Right and NRA delegates helped to nominate Oliver North, a former White House aide and participant in the Iran-contra scandal, as a candidate for the U.S. Senate. North was perhaps the only Republican in the state who could not defeat incumbent Democratic senator Charles Robb, who indeed was easily defeated in his

TABLE 2-1

Attendees at State Republican Party Conventions Who Identified
Themselves as Members of Interest Groups, 1993–1995

	Virginia	Washington	Florida	Minnesota	Texas
Business	36%	43%	61%	47%	39%
Professional	53	44	58	51	46
Labor	2	n.a.	n.a.	n.a.	n.a.
Civic	41	37	73	54	46
Fraternal	17	15	27	19	15
Community	50	34	45	43	34
Education	23	26	37	28	26
Environmentalist	9	6	14	9	5
Pro-choice	7	4	5	5	6
Feminist	1	n.a.	n.a.	n.a.	n.a.
Women	n.a.	17	20	15	16
Church	n.a.	74	76	88	86
Conservative Christian	28	38	39	31	45
Pro-family	n.a.	37	28	42	43
Religious	63	37	25	53	40
Pro–gun rights	28	36	45	30	39
Anti-abortion	30	44	38	53	50
Taxpayer	n.a.	15	23	15	12
Conservative	n.a.	48	48	47	48

Source: Survey data collected by the authors and by John C. Green.

Note: Entries are the percentages of all attendees at state party conventions who indicated membership in each type of group. Each respondent could claim membership in multiple groups.

n.a. Not asked.

next reelection bid in 2000. Many observers saw these choices as examples of ideological groups taking control of nominations and then consigning their party to general election defeat (Rozell and Wilcox 1996).

Ideological activists at conventions also succeed frequently at commanding state party platforms. Thus the party positions on platforms oftentimes reflect the viewpoints of deeply committed activists, such as religious conservatives in the GOP. For example, the 2004 Oklahoma Republican Party platform includes the following language:

We believe that homosexuality is not a genetic trait, but a chosen lifestyle.

We oppose no fault divorce.

We support the right of parents to rear, educate, discipline, nurture and spiritually train their children without government interference.

We affirm the State's recognition that marriage between one man and one woman is a covenant relationship, instituted by God, not to be entered into casually.

We believe that in order to encourage and protect family values, those promoting homosexuality or other aberrant lifestyles should not be allowed to hold responsible positions over children or other vulnerable persons.

We oppose abortion (including the use of RU-486).

We support retaining the religious significance of national holidays, and we support the privately funded display of religious symbols in public places.

We strongly support federal and state legislation to encourage and pre-serve inscriptions, in or on, public buildings, and on our currency, that have reference to God; such as "In God we Trust."

We strongly support retaining the phrase "One Nation under God" in the Pledge of Allegiance.

We encourage rigorous enforcement of all anti-pornography laws. Government agencies or tax-supported institutions, especially libraries and public schools, should not provide access to pornography.

We believe that organizations, such as the Boy Scouts of America, have the right to carry out their mission without interference by special interest groups. (Oklahoma Republican Party 2004)

The platform also emphasizes a particular view of religion's role in education. The platform's education section begins: "We acknowledge our dependence upon Almighty God and ask His blessings upon our students and their parents, teachers and nation." The section goes on: "The primary goal of public schools should be to teach proficiency in the basic subjects of phonics-based reading, written and oral communication, mathematics, sciences, traditional history, founding documents and Godly heritage of our nation. The traditional family unit, consisting of a husband (man), wife (woman) and child(ren), is the foundation of our social structure. We believe that the Oklahoma Department of Education should uphold and teach this definition of family at all levels of public education" (Oklahoma Republican Party 2004).

The 2004 Mississippi GOP platform is strongly anti-abortion, affirming the Republican Party's "support for a human life amendment to the Constitution," as well as calling for judges to oppose abortion. "We reaffirm our support of the election of judges who respect traditional family values and the sanctity of innocent human life," the platform reads (Mississippi Republican Party 2004). The Washington state GOP platform in 2004 opposed the acceptance of homosexuality in schools. The platform reads: "We support: A policy that public schools not promote or identify homosexuality as a healthy, morally acceptable, or alternative lifestyle" (Washington State Republican Party 2004).

Democratic Party state platforms have in recent years also adopted controversial positions on issues such as affirmative action, parental notification on abortion, and welfare reform. In the 1960s and 1970s, state Democratic political parties were often deeply divided over civil rights issues. Today, social, cultural, and defense issues are among those that divide the party. The 2004 Alaska Democratic Party platform, for example, defends both gun owners' rights as well as the freedom of all citizens to make their own decisions about "marriage and life partners" (Alaska Democratic Party 2004). The Connecticut Democratic platform the same year says nothing about gun rights or gun control but advocates full legal recognition for same-sex unions (Connecticut Democrats 2004). The Idaho Democratic platform strongly advocates for gun owners' constitutional rights but says nothing about same-sex marriage or civil unions (Idaho Democratic Party 2004). The Maine Democratic platform defends gun owners' rights as well and then also states, "We support extending to Gay and Lesbian couples and their families all the same legal and social rights and protection as other couples receive by civil marriages" (Maine Democratic Party 2004). The Virginia Democratic platform by contrast supports gun owners' rights but then merely takes a stand against discrimination on the basis of sexual orientation and advocates laws to provide domestic partner benefits (Virginia Democratic Party 2004).

State conventions often select state party chairs and committee members as well. Because the policy preferences of party officeholders can have profound effects on party policy, interest groups offer encouragement, support, and training to help their members and supporters secure election to party office. In Texas in the 1990s, for example, the Christian Coalition held at least twenty-five training sessions for members planning to run for the important position of party precinct chair. Precinct chairs select the delegates to state senatorial-district party conventions; at those conventions, chairs for the state senatorial districts are chosen, and delegates are selected for the state convention. The Christian Coalition fielded candidates for 80 percent of precinct chair positions, winning many of them (Bruce

1997). In 1994 nearly two-thirds of state party convention delegates were conservative Christians, more than half of whom had never attended a party meeting before. These activists drove the sitting party chair from office, and the convention defeated several referenda that would have officially proclaimed that the party included members with a range of views (Bruce 1997).

In recent years, efforts on the part of the Christian Right to influence—and even control—state Republican Party committees have been highly successful. In 1994 *Campaigns and Elections*, a Washington, D.C., political magazine, reported that the Christian Right was the dominant force in GOP politics in nineteen states and had substantial influence in another twelve. Reacting to this news, Christian Coalition founder Pat Robertson told a coalition gathering in 1995, "I'm glad to see all this they say about thirty-one, but that leaves . . . a lot more. We've got more work to do. Because I like 100 percent, not 60 or 70" (Edsall 1995). By 2002 *Campaigns and Elections* could report that Robertson had moved significantly closer to his goal. In that survey, nearly a decade later, the Christian right had dominance in eighteen states and substantial influence in another twenty-six. In many states, Christian Right activists control a substantial number of precinct, county, and other party committees, enabling group members to channel party resources for the benefit of candidates that they support, to schedule official meetings to discuss policy, and to adopt party rules that make it easier for Christian Right candidates to win nomination (Conger and Green 2002).

Although the Christian Right is the most visible and active set of interest groups in internal, state-level party politics, labor unions, civil rights groups, farmers' groups, and others have been active in Democratic politics; and in some states, members of one or another of these groups are the dominant faction in the Democratic Party. Nevertheless, the efforts of the Christian Right to control the GOP are unique in American history and may indicate a profound change in the relationship between social movement organizations and political parties.

SUMMARY

Changes in party rules over time have created an opportunity structure that allows interest groups to be active players in intraparty politics. Involvement in political parties is attractive to groups with broad policy goals, especially social movement organizations that seek to transform social relationships or "moral policy."

Specific tactics include recruiting interest group members and sympathizers as candidates; training candidates to run in party primaries; and providing endorsements, financial support, and volunteer labor to assist candidates in their quest for nomination. Interest groups also work to send delegates to state and national party conventions and to change the language of party platforms to include explicit endorsement of their policy goals.

Finally, interest groups sometimes seek to change the personnel not only of government but also of the party itself. They may encourage their activists to become members of party committees or even to run for the position of local or state party chair. Obtaining such positions sometimes enables interest group activists to rewrite party rules in ways that are favorable to candidates who share their policy preferences and to direct party resources toward the goals of their particular group.

Groups with more narrow goals also participate in party politics, but in very different ways. Corporations have become major sponsors of conventions, hosting lavish parties and receptions for party leaders. Such groups are often neutral in intraparty contests but show general support for the party as part of an access strategy, seeking to cultivate ongoing relationships with party leaders to further their lobbying goals.

Once parties select their nominees and approve their platforms, candidates move on to the general election. American elections are costly affairs, and candidates must raise hundreds of thousands of dollars for House races and millions of dollars for senatorial and presidential contests. Interest groups work closely with candidates as well as with parties, communicating their views and their support. Chapter 3 explores the relationship between parties and candidates.

CHAPTER 3

Interest Groups and Candidates

On any evening during an election campaign, the nation is alive with fund-raising activities, and interest groups are likely to be involved in virtually every one. At a political action committee (PAC) fund-raiser in Washington, D.C., PAC officials present their checks, shake the hand of the host—an incumbent member of the House—have a drink, eat a bite, and swap political gossip. In her home state, an incumbent senator holds a fund-raising dinner, arranged with the help of an interest group, at which several tables were "purchased" by other groups. At campaign headquarters, a presidential candidate telephones corporate executives, asking for contributions to the party or the campaign. At a direct-mail fund-raising firm, staff members are preparing solicitations to send to interest group members on a list the firm has rented for a candidate. In the solicitations, the candidate makes a special pitch on issues of concern to the group's leaders.

As noted in Chapter 1, one of the organizing principles for our exploration of interest groups and American political life is the communication between interest groups and candidates. What do groups want to "say" to candidates, and how do they get their message across? Financial or in-kind contributions facilitate much of the communication between interest groups and candidates. Interest groups donate money directly to candidates;

channel money through PACs to candidates; and provide a wealth of goods and services for candidates, parties, and campaigns.

We begin the chapter by looking at the strategic context: how is communication between interest groups and candidates shaped by laws, regulations, and common practice on the one hand and by the groups' goals and resources on the other? Next, we examine one of the primary vehicles for both raising and channeling the financial contributions of interest groups and their members: the PAC. The chapter looks in detail at the history and resources of PACs, as well as at how they determine their contribution strategies. We then examine the various ways in which interest groups manage to "give beyond the limit"—to make contributions that exceed what regulations allow. Next, the chapter explores interest groups' contributions to political parties and to other organizations such as 527 committees. Finally, we discuss contributions of goods and services, an uncommon but effective way for interest groups to gain greater control of the use of their money and to maximize the impact of their contributions.

THE STRATEGIC CONTEXT: REGULATIONS, GOALS, AND RESOURCES

In this section of the chapter, we first consider how funds from interest groups make their way into the electoral process. Like the state regulations and party rules that shape interest groups' involvement in party politics, campaign finance laws—and judicial interpretations of them—create an opportunity structure within which interest groups must work. Given that opportunity structure, interest groups select various strategies and tactics, which are shaped by the goals the groups are pursuing and the resources they have available.

The Evolution of Campaign Finance Regulation

Interest groups have made direct cash contributions to candidates throughout American history. In the latter part of the nineteenth century, corporations helped finance national elections—and also bribed some members of Congress and the executive branch. Mark Hanna, an industrialist who raised funds for Republican William McKinley's 1896 presidential campaign, approached many major corporations and suggested donations based on the firms' revenues, warning that the administration would not do business with companies that failed to contribute. The excesses of the McKinley fund-raising efforts made the role of interest groups in financing elections more visible than ever before, and in 1907 the Tilman Act banned banks and corporations from making contributions to federal candidates. By the 1930s, organized labor had become involved in campaign finance: through labor's Nonpartisan League, unions gave more than $1 million to federal campaigns (Wright 1996). During World War II, direct contributions from union treasuries were banned by passage of the Smith-Connally Act in 1943—a change made permanent by passage of the Taft-Hartley Act in 1947.

Although corporations and unions could not make political contributions from their treasury funds, they found ways to channel money to candidates nonetheless. Corporations often gave their executives "bonuses" and then directed them to pass the extra money along to specific candidates. Labor chose another route: in 1943 the Congress of Industrial Organizations (CIO) formed a PAC that collected voluntary contributions from union members and contributed it to candidates. Because the PAC was not technically a labor union and the contributions were voluntary (although union treasury funds did pay the operating expenses of the PAC), unions believed that their PAC was not subject to the ban on union contributions. In 1955 the American Federation of Labor and the CIO merged, and the combined AFL-CIO created COPE, the Committee on Political Education, which quickly became the most important political arm of organized labor (Gerber 1999). By the 1960s, other unions had formed PACs, as had professional associations such as the American Medical Association (AMA). Business groups were represented by the Business-Industry Political Action Committee (BIPAC), which encouraged corporate involvement in elections. But in the 1960s, unions were by far the best represented in the PAC universe.

Although the legality of PACs was questioned almost from the beginning, the Supreme Court did not rule on the issue. In 1968, however, a federal trial court and a court of appeals ruled that labor PACs violated the Taft-Hartley Act and sentenced officials from a labor union to fines and jail terms. Many labor activists feared that the Supreme Court would uphold the convictions and order the dismantling of COPE. In 1971, as Congress was drafting the Federal Election Campaign Act (FECA), unions pressured their congressional allies to include language that would legalize PACs. An amendment drafted by AFL-CIO lobbyists and introduced by Rep. Orval Hansen, R-Idaho, allowed both corporations and labor unions to form

PACs. Labor strategists believed that the benefit of retaining COPE out-weighed the potential danger that corporations would form PACs; indeed, by the early 1970s, few had done so (Epstein 1980). However, urged on by BIPAC, corporations mobilized quickly to form PACs.

In the 1972 presidential campaign, despite the fact that corporate con-tributions were illegal, Richard Nixon's Committee to Reelect the Presi-dent chose to follow the McKinley model, recommending contribution targets for corporations—a tactic that worked especially well when the company had business before the White House. The campaign solicited a contribution from the ITT Corporation at a time when the company badly wanted antitrust relief, and the committee received donations from milk producers before the president raised supports on milk prices. The campaign laundered many corporate gifts through Grand Cayman Island, and the campaign official in charge of corporate contributions eventually went to jail (Sorauf 1988).

Information uncovered during investigations of Nixon's reelection cam-paign led Congress, in response to public and media pressure, to create an entirely new regulatory regime. In 1974 Congress amended the language of the FECA. The amendments established a campaign finance system with four main elements: limits on contributions, limits on spending, public funding, and disclosure.

LIMITS ON CONTRIBUTIONS. The law permitted private individuals to give $1,000 to each candidate for national office for each election in which that candidate was involved. Because most candidates run in primary as well as general elections, individuals could ordinarily give $2,000 to any candidate.[1] Interest groups were permitted to form PACs that could col-lect voluntary donations of up to $5,000 per year from each of their mem-bers and contribute up to $5,000 to candidates in any federal election.

The law limited the amounts that party committees could give to can-didates or spend on their behalf. Individual contributions to all kinds of political committees—parties, PACs, and candidates—were limited to $25,000 per year. There were also limits on the amounts that candidates could contribute to their own campaigns. Contribution limits were not indexed to inflation, and the 1974 values remained unchanged until 2002.

LIMITS ON SPENDING. The amendments limited spending by candidates for Congress and the presidency and also limited what individuals and PACs could spend independently to urge the election or defeat of candidates. Moreover, the law held that independent expenditures could not be made in coordination with campaign officials.

PUBLIC FUNDING. The amendments provided public funding for presidential elections, but provisions for funding congressional elections were dropped from the final bill. The law established a public fund created by checkoffs on federal income tax returns; today, taxpayers can designate $3 of their taxes to be diverted to that fund. The Federal Election Commission (FEC) uses this money to provide matching funds for presidential candidates during primary campaigns, to help pay for the major-party conventions, and to provide a public grant for major candidates during the general election. During the primary election and caucuses, the fund is used to match the first $250 given by any individual to qualified presidential primary candidates. Under this system, a donation of $1,000 to Richard Gephardt in 2004 would thus have been worth $1,250 to the campaign because the federal government matched only the first $250, whereas a contribution of $25 to Dennis Kucinich was worth $50 because the entire amount was matched. During the general election, public grants in equal amounts are given to the nominees of the two major parties, and under some circumstances to candidates of minor parties.[2] In 2004 the Bush and Kerry campaigns received roughly $75 million each from the government to finance their campaigns. Minor parties that received at least 5 percent of the vote in the previous election qualify for partial funding. In 1996 Ross Perot received approximately $29 million, compared with approximately $62 million for the major-party candidates. In 2000 Ralph Nader did not receive 5 percent of the popular vote and thus did not qualify for funding in 2004. (Public funding is discussed further in Chapter 5.)

DISCLOSURE. The amendments established a single agency, the FEC, to enforce the law and to collect and disseminate information about the financing of national elections. The commission creates rules and brings action against violators, but there are six commissioners—three Democrats and three Republicans—and it takes four votes to make policy. As a consequence the FEC is not an aggressive regulatory agency, but it does play an important role as the repository of campaign finance data. All candidates, PACs, and party committees that participate in federal elections are required to file regular reports with the FEC, which then makes this information available to the public in a variety of formats.[3]

The 1974 FECA amendments did not limit the ability of interest groups to communicate with their members about elections or to endorse candidates. Nor did the amendments regulate "nonpartisan" voter mobilization efforts undertaken by nonprofit groups. Such efforts are under the regulatory eye of the Internal Revenue Service, which has the power to deny tax-exempt status to organizations whose activities are not genuinely nonpartisan. The new regulations did, however, impose a comprehensive framework on campaign financing—which was almost immediately altered by the Supreme Court.

Legal challenges to the FECA amendments were undertaken by an unusual coalition of liberal and conservative groups and activists, including the American Conservative Union and the New York chapter of the American Civil Liberties Union. The plaintiffs alleged that the law violated freedom of speech by limiting the amounts that individuals and groups could contribute and spend independently to advocate their ideas.

In January 1976, in *Buckley v. Valeo*, the Court ruled that campaign spending is protected by the First Amendment because it involves political speech but that Congress can regulate contributions in the interest of preventing corruption or the appearance of corruption. This ruling struck a delicate and tenuous balance between protection of free speech and prevention of corruption. It left intact all requirements that candidates, PACs, and party committees disclose the sources and use of their funds. The court also upheld limits on contributions from individuals, PACs, and party committees, as well as limits on spending by parties on behalf of candidates, holding that these limits helped government prevent corruption and the appearance of corruption.

However, *Buckley* eliminated all limits on spending by candidates and all limits on independent expenditures by individuals and PACs, holding that such limits would constitute an abridgment of free speech. The Court upheld the public financing of presidential elections and ruled that candidates who accepted public financing could be bound to spending limits in exchange for the public grant. Candidates who accept public funding therefore trade away their right to unlimited spending. In essence, the Court ruled that contributions could be limited because they might lead to corruption or the appearance of corruption, whereas spending could not be limited because it is protected free speech.

The distinction between contributing and spending seems arbitrary, and the logic does not withstand close inspection. For example, a PAC associated with a large group such as the National Rifle Association (NRA) can spend millions of dollars in independent expenditures to help elect a candidate but can give only $10,000 to that candidate for primary and general election campaigns. The rationale of the distinction is that a larger gift—of perhaps $50,000—might corrupt the candidate but that a huge independent expenditure would not. It seems likely, however, that an incumbent who has benefited from a massive independent spending campaign will be as grateful to the interests that financed that campaign as he or she would be to a group that gave the money directly to the campaign. Similarly, if the First Amendment protects the right of a group of citizens to spend unlimited amounts of money to argue that Sen. Barbara Boxer, D-Calif., deserves a another term in the U.S. Senate, why would it not also protect that group's right to give the money directly to Boxer so that she can make the case herself?

Although the distinction between spending and contributing may be arbitrary, the Court was attempting to balance two critical values that appeared to be in conflict. Political speech is clearly at the heart of the First Amendment, and election campaigns constitute a clear and central form of political speech. However, the government has a compelling interest in preventing corruption. Although it is easy to imagine other distinctions the Court might have drawn, any attempt to balance these two principles would perhaps be arbitrary.

In 1979 Congress passed additional amendments to the FECA that allowed individuals and interest groups to give gifts of unlimited size to political parties for "party building" and to help elect state and local candidates. When interest groups made these "soft money" contributions, they were not required to use money collected through PACs but could instead use treasury funds that came from business profits or membership dues. Technically, soft money could not be spent to advocate the election of specific candidates, nor could it be given to candidates for federal office. However, parties could use soft money for a variety of other purposes—for salaries and office facilities, for voter mobilization, to help local or state-level candidates, and to run advertisements for the party, for example.

In 1996 the Supreme Court allowed interest groups to spend money on "issue advocacy" campaigns as long as they did not expressly advocate the election or defeat of a particular candidate. Like funds for soft money contributions, funds for issue advocacy could be drawn from interest groups' treasuries. Thus an interest group could spend unlimited sums from its treasury on television advertisements criticizing an incumbent member of Congress—as long as the ads avoid a list of specified words and phrases such as "vote for" and "select." Although the advertisements themselves may be indistinguishable from those funded by independent expenditures, they differ in two important respects: they can be paid for with treasury funds, and the spending need not be disclosed to the FEC.

In the late 1990s, reformers were worried about two main elements of the current system. First, party leaders were spending increasing amounts of time raising large soft money contributions, primarily from corporations and business leaders but also from unions and citizen groups. These large contributions were seen as potentially corrupting. Second, issue advocacy became an important element in presidential races and in a handful of close House and Senate campaigns as well. This served to destabilize the system, since incumbents could raise and bank a large war chest of campaign contributions, only to face an unlimited outside campaign by a group that was essentially unknown.

In 2002 Congress passed the Bipartisan Campaign Reform Act (BCRA), which banned most soft money and limited issue advertising on television and radio during the final days of primary and general election campaigns. BCRA survived a challenge before the Supreme Court and has been in effect for only one full election cycle, so it is still quite early to know its full impact. (For a thorough assessment of the impact of BCRA in 2004, see Malbin et al. 2005.)

During the 2004 elections, many former soft money donors gave to special 527 committees, which then aired issue ads in the presidential and often other elections. Yet it appears that many soft money donors did not contribute to 527 committees, and their money was simply not in the electoral process (Malbin et al. 2005).

For the purposes of this chapter, let us look at two important changes that BCRA made in the law. First, it doubled the amount that individuals can give to candidates from $1,000 to $2,000 and in fact raised the limit even further for Senate candidates running against self-financed opponents. Second, it did not raise the limit on PAC contributions to candidates. In this way, the law gave candidates the incentive to pursue relationships with individual donors instead of interest groups, and it gave interest groups an incentive to convince their members to give directly to candidates, instead of directly through PACs.

Goals and Resources

We suggested in Chapter 2 that most intraparty electoral activity is undertaken by interest groups pursuing electoral strategies, which are designed to change the personnel of government. Campaign contributions are made by interest groups pursuing electoral strategies, access strategies, or both. Contributions to candidates in close elections can help influence who wins, and using contributions to maintain friendly relations with powerful incumbents—often committee chairs and party leaders—can help lobbyists gain access to policy makers. Because committee chairs and party leaders rarely face opposition in party primaries and are unlikely to be involved in close elections, interest groups have little incentive to pursue an access strategy to seek involvement in intraparty politics or to mount issue advocacy campaigns. For interest groups pursuing an access strategy, contributions to campaigns and political parties are thus most likely to be the primary form of electoral involvement.

Of course, interest group involvement in campaign financing requires money. For an interest group to make direct contributions to candidates, its members not only must be sufficiently motivated to give to their PAC and to candidates that the group endorses but also must have the financial resources to do so. Having a large membership is helpful because individual contributions to PACs and to specific candidates are limited. Because contributions come directly from interest group treasuries, an interest group's overall financial well-being is also a factor.

Tactics for channeling money into campaigns vary widely. Interest groups can form PACs, raise money from their members through voluntary contributions, and give this money directly to candidates—but there are limits on the amount that a PAC can give to any particular candidate. PACs can purchase or produce goods and services for a campaign and give them to the candidate as an in-kind contribution, and although such contributions are subject to the normal limits, accounting tricks are sometimes used to maximize the value of these kinds of gifts. Members of interest groups can also write a check directly to the candidate, and lobbyists or PAC directors can collect those gifts into a bundle and pass them along to the candidate. Although each member is limited in the amount he or she can contribute, there is no limit to the amount that a group can collect. Interest group members and their families can purchase seats at tables at fund-raising dinners; the candidate will credit the aggregate contributions to the group, although each donation is assessed against individual limits.

Interest groups can also help found and support 527 committees. These committees can collect resources from individuals and groups and use that money in issue advocacy, voter mobilization, and other activities. In some cases, 527 committees act like formal interest group coalitions. In 2004 America Coming Together (ACT) was formed by former AFL-CIO activists and was funded in part by unions, but it also received support from other liberal groups and activists. ACT focused primarily on voter mobilization. In other cases, 527 committees can serve as a conduit for funds from corporations that do not want to be seen explicitly backing candidates. Groups like Citizens for Better Medicare were funded primarily by corporations that sought to conceal their economic self-interest behind a name that sounded like a citizens' group. The issue advocacy campaigns by 527 committees are discussed more fully in Chapter 4. BCRA puts limits on 527 committee spending from corporate funds, however.

Before BCRA, interest groups could use their treasury funds as well, donating soft money in unlimited amounts to party committees. Although by law soft money could be spent only on party building or to assist state or local candidates, in practice much of this money ended up aiding candidates for national elections.

PACS: AN OVERVIEW

After the passage of the FECA amendments in 1974, the Sun Oil Company formed a PAC and asked the FEC to comment on its legality. In 1975 the FEC issued the SUNPAC advisory opinion, which approved of the corporate PAC and allowed Sun Oil to pay indirect and overhead costs from the corporate treasury. Once the FEC gave the green light to the business community, the late 1970s and early 1980s saw an explosion in the number of corporate PACs. The apparent success of ideological PACs (such as the National Conservative Political Action Committee) in the 1980 presidential election spawned a surge in the formation of other ideological PACs in the early 1980s. By the mid-1980s, more than four thousand PACs were registered with the FEC. Since then, the number of PACs has remained relatively constant, with nearly 4,200 registered at the end of the 2004 election cycle. (See Table 3-1.)

The sheer number of PACs is misleading. Only 2,900 PACs both raised and contributed money in 1996; by 2004 that figure had grown to 3,132.[4] PACs that have ceased campaign activity linger on the roster for several reasons. They may simply have neglected to file the paperwork to terminate the PAC, they may owe money to vendors, or they may hope to become involved in campaign finance again soon. The FEC periodically

TABLE 3-1

Number of PACs by Type and Election Cycle, 1978–2004

Election cycle	Corporate	Labor	Trade, membership	Nonconnected	Total[a]
1978	785	217	453	162	1,653
1980	1,206	297	576	374	2,551
1982	1,469	380	649	723	3,371
1984	1,682	394	698	1,053	4,009
1986	1,744	384	745	1,077	4,157
1988	1,816	354	786	1,115	4,268
1990	1,795	346	774	1,062	4,172
1992	1,735	347	770	1,145	4,195
1994	1,660	333	792	980	3,954
1996	1,642	332	826	953	4,079
1998	1,567	321	821	935	3,798
2000	1,545	317	860	1,026	3,907
2002	1,528	320	975	1,055	4,027
2004	1,622	306	900	1,223	4,184

Source: Compiled from Federal Election Commission data.

a. Includes PACs associated with cooperatives and corporations without capital stock, not shown separately.

removes the names of inactive PACs from its database, but it allows them to remain for a time because the PACs may become active again.

Most PACs are segregated funds of interest groups; that is, they are discrete accounts containing money raised according to FECA regulations and kept separate from the operating funds of the sponsoring organizations. A PAC need not have a separate office or even a full-time director— merely a separate bank account. PACs vary widely in their size and organization. Some are large bureaucratic bodies with full-time staff, offices, and equipment, whereas others are administered by an interest group official whose primary duties lie elsewhere and who can devote only a few hours per week to the PAC.

Corporations sponsored more than 40 percent of the active PACs in 2004. When trade association PACs are included, the proportion of PACs representing corporate America swells to nearly two-thirds. In contrast, labor represents only 7 percent (204) of all active PACs. Although PACs sponsored by professional associations or membership groups made up a very small portion of the total, committees sponsored by groups such as the National Association of Realtors (NAR), the AMA, and the NRA were among the largest and most innovative committees (Bedlington 1994, 1999; Gusmano 1999).

Not all PACs are sponsored by a preexisting interest group. Any individual or group of individuals may form a PAC, collect voluntary contributions from citizens, and make contributions to candidates. Nearly one-quarter of active PACs in 2004 were nonconnected (that is, had no sponsoring or parent organization), and more than two-thirds of these were either quasi-party groups seeking to assist Republican or Democratic candidates or ideological groups seeking to elect candidates with specific views.

Figure 3-1 shows the percentages of different types of active PACs in 2004. As the figure demonstrates, corporations and trade associations dominate the world of PACs. Corporate executives argue, however, that their numerical advantage is misleading because labor PACs are larger on average than corporate committees and give more money to candidates. There

FIGURE 3-1
Active PACs by Type, 2004

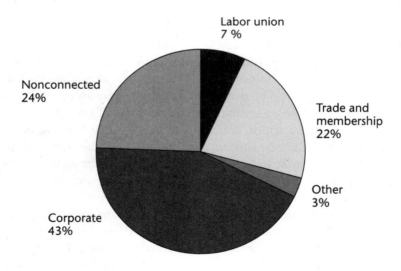

Source: FEC data provided by Robert Biersak.
Note: Values do not add to 100 percent due to rounding.

TABLE 3-2

PAC Contributions to Candidates for Federal Office by Type and Election Cycle, 1978–2004 (in millions of dollars)

Election cycle	Corporate	Labor	Trade, membership	Nonconnected	Total[a]
1978	9.8	10.3	11.3	2.8	35.2
1980	19.2	13.2	15.9	4.9	55.2
1982	27.5	20.3	21.9	10.7	83.6
1984	35.5	24.8	26.7	14.5	105.3
1986	49.4	31.0	34.4	19.4	139.4
1988	56.1	35.5	41.2	20.3	159.2
1990	58.1	34.7	44.8	15.1	159.1
1992	68.4	41.4	53.9	18.3	188.9
1994	69.6	41.9	52.9	18.2	189.6
1996	78.2	48.0	60.2	24.0	217.9
1998	78.0	44.6	62.3	28.2	219.9
2000	91.5	51.6	71.8	37.3	259.8
2002	99.6	53.9	75.1	46.4	282.0
2004	115.6	52.1	83.2	52.5	310.5

Source: Compiled from Federal Election Commission data.

a. Includes PACs associated with cooperatives and corporations without capital stock, not shown separately.

is some truth to this claim: in the 2004 elections, corporate and trade association PACs outnumbered labor committees by ten to one, but their net advantage in direct contributions to candidates was less than four to one.[5] Moreover, labor involvement in campaigns reaches far beyond campaign contributions. Table 3-2 shows the advantage that corporate PACs have in campaign contributions.

Who Forms PACs and Why

Interest groups can participate in elections without forming PACs. Most of the activities described in Chapter 2—recruiting and training candidates, sending delegates to party conventions, working to influence party platforms—can be undertaken without a PAC. Interest groups can select candidates to endorse and communicate those endorsements without ever forming a PAC. Interest group members can attend fund-raising dinners for candidates and parties without forming a PAC. An interest group must form a PAC, however, if its leaders want to gather contributions from members, aggregate those contributions, and—as official representatives of the interest group—give candidates money.

Although many PACs are active in American elections, a majority of corporations, trade associations, and membership organizations do not have PACs. PACs are more common among labor unions, but a number of unions have not formed PACs or have terminated PACs that were once active. Large companies, trade associations, and membership groups are more likely to form PACs than are their smaller counterparts—partly because larger organizations are able to raise more PAC revenue and are therefore better able to play the PAC game and partly because large firms, associations, and membership groups are more likely to be affected by legislation and regulations.

Among corporations, PACs are most common in regulated industries, in industries where companies frequently interact with government, and in industries that compete for government contracts. In many organizations the decision to form a PAC begins with an organizational entrepreneur who promotes the idea and takes responsibility for running the PAC (Ferrara 1994). PAC formation also appears to be contagious. When a few PACs have formed in a given industry, other companies may follow suit, perhaps because corporate officials believe that they must keep pace with their competitors. Indeed, political scientist Larry Sabato quotes one PAC official from the U.S. Chamber of Commerce who suggested "only slightly facetiously" that some corporations formed PACs because the CEO found himself surrounded on the golf course by CEOs from companies with PACs (Sabato 1984, 31).

For many interest groups, forming a PAC makes little sense. To begin with, PACs are expensive: overhead costs to the parent organization run between 50 and 100 percent of total PAC revenues (Sorauf 1984). To raise money, PAC officials may have to make awkward solicitations of colleagues. And incumbents constantly ask PAC officials for campaign contributions, creating potentially awkward refusals. Most important, however, many PACs raise so little money that they can make only a handful of contributions, which may be of little benefit to lobbyists. More than one-third of active PACs in the 2004 election gave to seven candidates or fewer. Many gave to only a single candidate. Most small PACs probably accomplish very little for their parent organizations. Even larger PACs sometimes do not live up to the expectations of their founders. In the 2002 election cycle, Siebel Systems formed a PAC that raised more than $2 million, in part because the company was interested in gaining a larger market share in homeland security spending. Yet the PAC ended up spending less than $400,000 in the 2002 election cycle and raised only $12,000 in the 2004 elections.

Forming a PAC does have certain advantages, however. In some organizations the PAC serves as the focus for the organization's involvement in elections. For members, it provides an alternative, easy form of political participation; for the parent group, it provides more frequent opportunities to communicate with members. And for those organizations that can raise enough money, the PAC may help influence a close election or help lobbyists maintain good relations with an important committee chair.

PAC Resources

A number of factors determine the resources available to PACs: regulations affecting fund-raising, the PAC's relation to its parent organization, and the size and complexity of the PAC organization itself.

The money that PACs contribute to candidates or spend independently must be raised in voluntary contributions from the members of the organization, and each member is limited to a contribution of no more than $5,000. The regulations are quite specific about who can be solicited by various types of organizations: corporations may solicit executive and administrative personnel and their families and stockholders and their families at any time; regular employees may be solicited twice a year. Labor unions may solicit members and their families at any time, and twice yearly they may solicit nonmember employees of a company where union members are employed. Membership organizations may solicit their members and executive and administrative personnel and their families at any time.

Nonconnected PACs are not sponsored by organizations with members and are thus allowed to solicit the general public. Most do so by mailing solicitations to individuals who might be sympathetic to their issue agenda. Potential contributors are usually identified through a process known as prospecting: PACs rent membership lists from sympathetic organizations or subscription lists from publications that have special appeal to individuals who might contribute, and then they mail solicitations to the individuals on the lists. Rental agreements usually allow the PAC to use the list only once, but anyone who responds to the initial mailing can be placed on the PAC's own mailing list and be solicited again.[6]

Being able to solicit the general public may appear to give nonconnected PACs an advantage, but the advantage in fact lies with PACs sponsored by interest groups. Interest groups that sponsor PACs can pay overhead costs (for example, salaries, supplies, postage) from their treasuries and can therefore channel all the money they raise into contributions to candidates and expenditures on their behalf. Because nonconnected PACs must pay all their costs out of the contributions they receive, much of the money raised goes not to candidates but to overhead expenses. Overall, less than 18 percent of the funds raised by nonconnected PACs in 2004 were used for contributions or independent expenditures; the rest paid for running the PACs. Some ideological PACs run up large debts to the direct-mail companies that solicit contributions for them, and the lifespan of such organizations is often short. Only 46 percent of nonconnected PACs registered with the FEC in 2004 were active in the election cycle, and many of the others had outstanding debts.[7]

Sponsored PACs vary in the resources they receive from parent organizations. Some organizations pay for several full-time employees, for example, while others pay for a single part-time staff position. AT&T PAC, sponsored by the telecommunications giant, has an executive committee, separate committees to handle fund-raising and contributions at the national level, and state and regional committees—a structure that allows the PAC to carefully gather and evaluate information about each race.

The AFL–CIO's COPE can draw on the expertise of local, regional, and state committees as well as on the capacities of the local, state, and national unions that are members of the AFL–CIO (Francia, forthcoming; Gerber 1999; Wilcox 1994). COPE has a professional staff that gathers and disseminates information to other committees; COPE briefings are attended not only by other labor unions but also by a number of other PACs in the Democratic coalition.

PACs with large staffs can gather—from party committees or other interest groups—information about the election: the closeness of the race, the positions of the nonincumbent, or the level of voter commitment to a candidate. A PAC with a single part-time employee, in contrast, operates with much less information. Taken together, such disparities in resources greatly affect the ability of some PACs to be active in national campaigns.

Within each type of PAC, there are a few large and sophisticated committees, a larger number of medium-sized committees, and a large number of small PACs with few resources. Interest groups with large and dedicated memberships are able to raise substantial sums of money. In the 2004 election cycle, EMILY's List, a PAC that helps fund the campaigns of pro-choice Democratic women candidates, raised more than $25 million in member contributions, for example, and the NRA's PAC raised more than $12 million. Both PACs have experienced significant growth over the past several years. In 1996 EMILY's List had raised just over $12 million and the NRA just over $7 million in individual contributions. Other PACs are associated with organizations with fewer and less supportive members and therefore had far less money to contribute to candidates.

Although PACs contributed more than $310 million to federal candidates during the 2004 election cycle, most of this money was given by a few very large PACs, and most PACs gave smaller amounts. Forty-four percent of all contributions in the 2004 election cycle were given by the largest 133 committees, and a quarter of all PAC contributions were made by just 48 PACs, each of which gave more than $1 million. In contrast, the 2,180 smallest PACs combined gave 10 percent of all PAC contributions (FEC data).

In 2004 United Parcel Service (UPS) PAC contributed more than $2 million dollars to hundreds of federal candidates, and those employed by UPS gave another $600,000 to federal candidates. In contrast, the EPI Corporation PAC, representing a nursing home in Louisville, Kentucky, gave less than $2,000 total to three Kentucky candidates, and there are no recorded contributions by employees of the company.

In the same election cycle, AFL-CIO's COPE gave approximately $600,000 to House candidates and another $100,000 to Senate candidates, almost all of whom were Democrats. In contrast, the Amalgamated Lithographers Local 1 PAC made a single contribution of $1,000 (FEC data). Among ideological PACs, the National Pro-Life Alliance gave more than $700,000 to candidates for federal office in 2004, while the Right to Life of Michigan PAC made a single contribution of $500 (FEC data). Although both of these committees were anti-abortion PACs, their organizational characteristics and capacities had little in common.

Table 3-3 shows the concentration of PAC contributions in 1990, 1996, 2002, and 2004. In each election cycle, many PACs made no contributions and most others gave small amounts to federal candidates. A quarter of all active PACs gave less than $5,000 in 2004, and two-thirds gave $50,000 or less. The largest and smallest PACs face very different decisions about how much to give and to whom. The data in this table make clear that those who are concerned that PACs may have disproportionate influence in American politics should concentrate on the few very large committees that dominate the PAC world.

TABLE 3-3

Concentration of PAC Contributions, 1990, 1996, 2002, and 2004

	Percentage of total contributions	Number of committees[a]	Percentage of committees
1990 contribution range			
$0	0	1,640	35
$1–$,5000	1	1,207	26
$5,001–$50,000	14	1,224	26
$50,001–$100,000	11	255	5
$100,001–$250,000	22	227	5
$250,001–$500,000	15	69	1
$500,001–$1,000,000	15	34	1
Over $1,000,000	21	21	0
1996 contribution range			
$0	0	1,517	34
$1–$5,000	1	910	20
$5,001–$50,000	12	1,307	29
$50,001–$100,000	11	353	8
$100,001–$250,000	19	261	6
$250,001–$500,000	15	93	2
$500,001–$1,000,000	17	54	1
Over $1,000,000	26	33	0
2002 contribution range			
$0	0	1,537	33
$1–$5,000	1	856	19
$5,001–$50,000	9	1,232	27
$50,001–$100,000	8	336	7
$100,001–$250,000	20	375	8
$250,001–$500,000	17	139	3
$500,001–$1,000,000	17	71	2
Over $1,000,000	28	48	1
2004 contribution range			
$0	0	1,648	34
$1–$5,000	1	810	17
$5,001–$50,000	9	1,370	28
$50,001–$100,000	8	369	8
$100,001–$250,000	19	382	8
$250,001–$500,000	18	163	3
$500,001–$1,000,000	19	85	2
Over $1,000,000	25	48	1

Source: Compiled from Federal Election Commission data.

a. The number of committees whose contributions fell within each range.

PAC Contribution Strategies

PACs routinely receive more invitations to fund-raising events than they could ever afford to attend, and they are solicited by more candidates than they could ever afford to support. In determining how best to use their resources, PACs generally make two kinds of decisions: first, what types of candidates to support, and second, which specific candidates to support.

Although many PACs lack any explicit statement of policy on what types of candidates to support, PACs making contributions to congressional candidates generally pursue a mixture of access and electoral strategies. PACs pursuing an access or legislative strategy give money as part of their lobbying effort, to gain the ear of incumbents who can influence legislation of interest to the parent organization. This usually means giving to party leaders, committee and subcommittee chairs, and other important actors in the policy network who can influence the content of a bill and its chances of passage, regardless of their ideology or whether they are involved in a close election. In the 2004 election cycle, 879 PACs gave only to incumbents. The National Structured Settlements Trade Association PAC, for example, gave over $100,000 to incumbents of both parties but did not contribute to a single nonincumbent candidate. A large majority of these incumbent-oriented PACs, which constituted approximately one-quarter of all active committees, were sponsored by small to mid-size corporate and trade associations.

Incumbents who hold powerful positions in Congress are generally able to solicit contributions from access-oriented PACs. The campaign staff of an influential incumbent may call a PAC director and ask for a contribution or offer an invitation to a campaign fund-raiser—an offer that the PAC director may feel reluctant to refuse. PACs whose sponsoring organizations hope to have continued access to party leaders or committee chairs give money to ensure that they are seen as friends of those in power. It is no accident that party leaders in the House routinely receive far more PAC money than do other members. For example, House majority leader Tom DeLay received more than $1.4 million in PAC contributions in the 2004 election cycle, mostly from business PACs, although he did not face serious competition in his House race (FEC data provided to authors by Robert Biersack, FEC statistician). He received an almost identical amount in individual contributions, mostly from business executives. He received other contributions to his leadership PAC, and to his legal defense fund, discussed later in this chapter.

Important committee chairs also receive disproportionate amounts of PAC money. In 2004 Rep. Bill Thomas, R-Calif., chair of the House Ways and Means Committee (which writes tax law) received more than $1.2 million in PAC contributions, 98 percent of which was from business PACs. He received more than $400,000 in individual contributions, most of which came from business executives (Center for Responsive Politics 2005a). Because businesses can gain windfalls from minor changes in tax law, access to Thomas was important for many companies. But contributions to Thomas were not aimed to help him win reelection; he ran unopposed in 2004. In contrast, Frank Wolf, a Republican incumbent representing northern Virginia who does not chair a powerful committee or hold a party leadership position, received only $400,000 from PACs in 2004.

An electoral strategy, in contrast, aims to ensure that Congress has the largest possible number of members who favor the policy positions of the interest group. Nonconnected and ideological PACs generally pursue electoral strategies, as do labor committees and a few corporate committees.

PACs that follow an electoral strategy often give substantial amounts of money to nonincumbent candidates who share their views. In 2004 one in five active committees gave at least 50 percent to nonincumbent congressional candidates. For example, Campaign for Working Families (a PAC representing conservative Christian interests) gave a total of $244,000 to congressional candidates, and 65 percent of that money went to challengers and candidates for open seats.

Since their goal is to elect as many sympathetic members of Congress as possible, PACs pursuing an electoral strategy give not only to nonincumbents, but also to incumbents in close races who share the parent group's policy goals. As the fortunes of the parties ebb and flow, electorally oriented PACs redirect their contributions from incumbents to challengers, targeting contributions where the money might influence the outcome of the election. If, for example, a PAC prefers policies that are more likely to be supported by liberal Democrats, then that PAC will support endangered Democratic incumbents in electoral cycles where Republicans are likely to gain seats, as in 1994. When Democrats are expected to gain seats, the same PACs will support Democratic challengers and candidates for open seats, as in 1996. Electorally oriented PACs that prefer the policies of conservative Republicans would follow the opposite course. The practice of supporting incumbents or challengers, depending on the prevailing electoral winds, is often called strategic contributing.[8]

The way that contributions are solicited makes it difficult for PACs to give solely to incumbents or nonincumbents. Party leaders routinely ask PACs to give to the most promising nonincumbent candidates, and committee chairs often echo the request, leading even the most access-oriented PACs to contribute to at least a few nonincumbent candidates in order to keep important policy makers happy. At the same time, many electorally oriented PACs find it difficult to refuse solicitations from powerful incumbents who have a strong record of supporting a particular ideological position. Such "friendly" incumbents may repeatedly ask an ideological PAC for a gift, and if polling data suggest that the incumbent could potentially face a close election, it is difficult for an ideological PAC to refuse.

Indeed, PAC directors often complain that when the most powerful members of Congress ask them to give, they have no choice but to comply. When the chair of the committee that writes the laws affecting your industry invites you to eat eggs and grits and talk taxes, it is hard to refuse. Party leaders also pressure PACs to give, and their staff scrutinize the contribution records of PACs to identify those that give "too much" to the other party.

Data on the patterns of PAC contributions help us take a closer look at which types of candidates receive PAC support. Table 3-4 shows both the amount and the proportion of money that PACs contributed to different types of candidates. In 1980, 63 percent of PAC contributions went to incumbents; in 1992, 73 percent; in 1996, 68 percent; and in 2004, 80 percent—indicating that most PAC contributions are given as part of lobbying efforts and reflect access strategies. Indeed, many of these contributions went to incumbents who faced no real prospect of defeat. In 2004 a majority of PAC contributions went to incumbents who were assured of victory. For example, corporate PACs directed 53 percent of their contributions to candidates for the House who received greater than 60 percent of the general election vote (FEC data, provided to authors by Robert Biersack, FEC statistician).

Contributions to nonincumbents are usually channeled to candidates for open seats, although this pattern may not be evident from the data in Table 3-4. Because challengers significantly outnumber candidates for open seats, especially in the House of Representatives, even when all challengers receive slightly more money than all candidates for open seats, open-seat candidates receive far more PAC money per candidate than do challengers. In the 2004 House general election, major-party open-seat candidates averaged $280,000 in PAC money, whereas challengers averaged just under

TABLE 3–4

PAC Contributions to Major Party Federal Candidates: 1980, 1992, 1996, and 2004

Type of candidate	1980		1992		1996		2004	
	Contribution	Percentage of total contributions	Contribution	Percentage of total contributions	Contribution	Percentage of total contributions	Contribution	Percentage of total contributions
House Democrats								
Incumbent	$16,934,165	29	$67,106,187	36	$51,712,687	24	$82,593,421	27
Challenger	2,342,807	4	7,866,490	4	16,737,142	8	8,670,117	3
Open seat	2,071,601	4	13,407,388	7	10,932,119	5	9,197,797	3
House Republicans								
Incumbent	$9,054,494	16	$31,978,807	17	$65,698,926	30	$110,166,758	36
Challenger	5,784,253	10	4,564,352	2	4,856,130	2	7,262,065	2
Open seat	3,004,611	5	7,394,537	4	9,135,646	4	13,307,241	4
Senate Democrats								
Incumbent	$7,459,436	13	$20,027,952	11	$7,511,408	4	$23,840,343	8
Challenger	1,011,366	2	6,455,164	3	2,843,745	1	2,126,581	1
Open seat	816,199	1	5,695,317	3	9,061,322	4	7,270,672	2
Senate Republicans								
Incumbent	$2,862,646	5	$16,598,062	9	$21,213,241	10	$27,741,962	9
Challenger	5,690,944	10	3,176,774	2	4,570,582	2	3,523,185	1
Open seat	1,319,888	2	4,272,660	2	10,273,264	5	11,573,322	4
All incumbents	36,310,741	63	135,711,008	73	146,136,262	68	244,342,484	80
All challengers	14,829,370	26	22,062,780	11	29,007,599	13	21,581,948	7
All open seats	7,212,299	12	30,769,902	16	39,402,351	18	41,349,032	13
Total	$58,352,410		$188,543,690		$214,546,212		$307,273,464	

Source: Compiled from Federal Election Commission data.

Note: Columns may not add up to 100 percent due to rounding.

$40,000. In contrast, incumbents averaged over $460,000 in total PAC receipts.

The data in Table 3-4 show some changes in contribution strategies following the GOP takeover of Congress in 1994. When the Republicans first took over Congress, Democratic-leaning PACs (especially those associated with labor unions) were eager to fund Democratic challengers who might unseat these new Republican incumbents. In 1996 Democratic House challengers received 8 percent of all PAC contributions. But over time these GOP incumbents became secure in their districts, and by 2004 Democratic House challengers received only 3 percent of all PAC contributions.

A comparison of the figures for 1992 and 1996 shows that many access-oriented PACs switched their contributions to Republicans when that party took control of Congress in 1994. Republican incumbents received 17 percent of all PAC contributions in 1992 and 30 percent in 1996. By 2004 the figure had grown to 36 percent. Meanwhile, Democratic incumbents' share of PAC contributions fell from 36 percent in 1992 to 24 percent in 1996; in 2004 contributions were back up to 27 percent. Of course, there were more Republican incumbents and fewer Democratic incumbents after the 1994 elections, but on average the GOP received far more PAC money when it had control of the congressional agenda. The average House Republican incumbent received slightly over $200,000 in PAC money in 1992, nearly $300,000 in 1996, and over $500,000 by 2004.

Many PACs switched their patterns of party giving after 1994. In 1992 the General Electric PAC contributions favored Democrats by a margin of three to two, but in 1996 Republicans were favored by a margin of almost two to one. In 2004 GE PAC continued to support Republicans by this margin, giving the party 64 percent of its total contributions. The Federal Express PAC gave 62 percent of its donations to Democrats in 1992 and 70 percent to Republicans in 1996. FedEx PAC continued this pattern and by 2004 was still giving 70 percent of its contributions to Republicans. AMPAC, the AMA's PAC, gave 51 percent of its contributions to the GOP in 1992, 81 percent in 1996, and then maintained at that level with 80 percent to the GOP in 2004. Overall, corporate, trade, and nonconnected PACs substantially increased their contributions to GOP candidates. (See Table 3-5.)

After taking over Congress, the GOP began pressuring pro-business groups to drop their bipartisan strategies and to increase contributions to Republican candidates (Stone 1997). Democrats tried to delay this change by arguing that they could well regain control of Congress and would

TABLE 3-5

Changes in PAC Allocation by Type: 1992, 1994, 1996, 2002, and 2004[a]

	1992		1994	
Type of candidate	Contribution	Percentage of total con- tributions	Contribution	Percentage of total con- tributions
Corporate				
Republicans	$31,976,016	50	$32,872,432	51
Democrats	32,308,294	50	31,430,922	49
Labor				
Republicans	1,914,644	5	1,598,642	4
Democrats	37,577,358	95	38,987,257	96
Trade, membership, and health				
Republicans	21,436,982	42	23,249,504	46
Democrats	29,899,090	58	27,015,672	54
Nonconnected				
Republicans	6,472,913	37	7,012,460	40
Democrats	11,010,957	63	10,471,935	60

remember those PACs that stood by them. By 2004, however, most corporate PAC executives were convinced that Republicans would hold control of Congress for many years to come, and many had switched their contribution strategy accordingly.

Influences on Strategy Selection

How do PACs decide what mix of access and electoral strategies to pursue? The most important factors are the policy agenda of the sponsoring organization, the type of sponsoring organization (for example, corporate, labor, or ideological), and the level of available resources.

POLICY AGENDA. Some interest groups seek narrow, particularistic policies that will benefit only their organization. Corporations and trade associations, which may seek a specific exemption from regulation or a narrowly targeted

TABLE 3-5
Continued

1996		2002		2004	
Contribution	Percent of total con- tributions	Contribution	Percent of total con- tributions	Contribution	Percent of total con- tributions
$52,057,218	73	$65,195,797	65	$77,171,806	68
19,096,942	27	34,358,151	35	36,820,297	32
3,023,413	7	5,238,808	10	6,603,456	13
43,379,845	93	48,569,737	90	45,176,253	87
36,539,188	65	45,322,870	60	52,458,878	63
19,758,192	35	29,800,754	40	30,255,852	37
13,413,910	60	25,585,834	55	33,399,591	65
8,947,346	40	20,749,925	45	18,349,772	35

Source: Compiled from Federal Election Commission data.
a. Without contributions to the president.

tax break, are especially likely to pursue particularistic policies. Other groups pursue broader policy goals. Labor unions, for example, support policies that stimulate employment and offer protection against the hardships of economic downturns; and business groups such as the National Federation of Independent Businesses (NFIB) support policies that will keep interest rates and labor costs low and reduce government regulation in general.

Interest groups that seek narrow benefits may find that they can be obtained from incumbents of either party; the PACs of these groups may therefore contribute funds to the campaigns of powerful committee chairs and leaders of the majority party. If a few or even one committee in the House or the Senate is able to distribute the benefits an interest group seeks, its PAC may focus contributions on members of those committees, perhaps members from both political parties. PACs that seek particular benefits from government seldom give to challengers or to candidates for open seats because such candidates are unlikely to be in a position to deliver special policy benefits in the near future.

Interest groups that seek broad economic policies such as cuts in business taxes or protection for striking workers are more likely to support candidates of a single party and to try to increase that party's strength in Congress. Interest groups with broad economic-policy goals pursue electoral strategies, targeting PAC aid to races where it will do the most good. Labor union officials generally believe that broad policies that help unionized workers are more likely to win support when the Democrats control government and thus seek to maximize the number of Democratic seats in Congress. The NFIB is closely linked to the Republican Party for similar reasons (Shaiko and Wallace 1999). Yet BIPAC has occasionally supported Democratic candidates, arguing that its goal is to create a "business-friendly" Congress, not merely a Republican one (Nelson 1994; Nelson and Biersack 1999).

Ideological groups that hold particular views on controversial issues such as abortion and gay rights sometimes create strong links with a single party. Some ideological groups, however, support candidates of both parties when it is in their interest to do so. For example, the National Abortion and Reproductive Rights Action League (NARAL) contributes mostly to Democratic candidates but also supports pro-choice Republicans (Thomas 1999).

Like other interest groups, ideological organizations use a mix of access and electoral strategies, and groups with the same objectives sometimes pursue competing strategies. For example, the NRA favors GOP candidates most of the time but backs Democratic candidates who favor gun rights. The more extreme Gun Owners of America (GOA) is less likely to consider a bipartisan strategy. In 1997 the two groups were at odds over endorsements in a state legislative race in Virginia, where the NRA backed the pro–gun rights incumbent Democrat over an even more conservative Republican challenger backed by the GOA. The NRA candidate won by just several hundred votes, giving the Democrats a bare legislative majority in the chamber.

The disagreement in this case mirrors a larger debate among leaders of ideological PACs. The NRA decision to back a pro–gun rights Democratic incumbent reflects the organization's desire to retain lobbying access to Democratic legislators. If the NRA tried to persuade Democratic lawmakers to support their bills but always backed Republican candidates—no matter how strongly the opposing Democrats hewed to the NRA line—their lobbyists would soon find the doors of many Democrats closed. The GOA's decision to back an even stronger pro-gun Republican reflects the view that the best way to protect gun owners' rights and roll back gun control is to create a legislature that has a strong GOP majority composed of members who favor gun rights.

RELATIONSHIP WITH THE SPONSORING ORGANIZATION. Corporations and trade associations have generally pursued access-oriented strategies, directing more than 80 percent of their total contributions to incumbents of both parties. Business groups generally prefer Republicans to Democrats, but they readily gave to Democratic incumbents when that party controlled Congress. When they did give to nonincumbents, however, they showed their partisan preference; in 1992 more than two-thirds of all contributions that corporate PACs made to nonincumbent candidates went to Republicans. Until 1994, partisan preferences and an interest in supporting incumbents pulled corporate PACs in opposite directions, but GOP control of Congress has eliminated most of this conflict and created a strong tendency to support Republican incumbents. In 2004 more than three-fourths of all contributions that corporate PACs made to nonincumbent candidates running for the House or the Senate went to Republicans.

Labor unions have long and deep ties to the Democratic Party and in most election cycles give 90 percent of their money to Democratic candidates. Many labor PACs practice strategic contributing, giving money to protect incumbent Democrats in years in which Republican gains are expected and shifting to nonincumbent Democrats in years in which gains are expected for that party. Figure 3-2 shows the percentage of all labor PAC contributions going to incumbents from 1994 through 2004. In years when Democrats have a chance to gain seats, unions invest more of their money in promising challengers and open-seat candidates. In years when Republicans are likely to defeat Democratic incumbents, unions channel more of their funds to protect sympathetic incumbents. Note for example the difference in the percentages of union contributions to incumbents in 1994, as the Republicans challenged (and defeated) many Democratic incumbents, compared with 1996, when labor invested in Democratic challengers seeking to defeat these new, and presumably somewhat vulnerable, Republican incumbents.

Although most labor PACs pursue electoral strategies, corporate committees showed significant diversity in the 1980s and 1990s. Some consistently threw their resources behind GOP challengers for the House and the Senate, despite the risk of irritating powerful Democratic committee chairs. In some cases these PACs are influenced by an entrepreneur—

FIGURE 3-2

Percentage of Labor PAC Contributions Going to Incumbents, 1994–2004

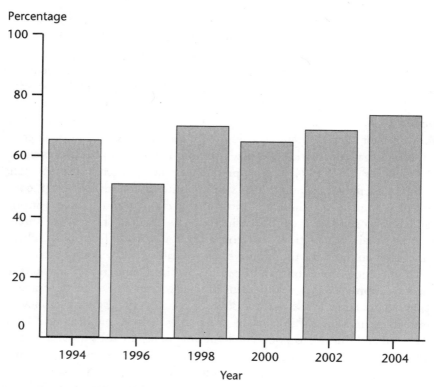

Source: Compiled from Federal Election Commission data.

perhaps the firm's founder, perhaps someone within the organization who pushed to form the PAC. The Eaton Corporation's Public Policy Association, for example, was formed in 1977 by former Eaton chairman John Hushen, who had served as deputy press secretary to President Gerald Ford. Hushen chaired the PAC and directed its contributions to Republicans, including many challengers and candidates for open seats. Most corporate PACs split their money, however, supporting key Democratic and Republican incumbents but investing some money in promising Republican open-seat candidates. After the GOP took control of Congress, corporate PAC contributions became more partisan since both access and electoral strategies implied greater GOP giving.

AVAILABLE RESOURCES. Sometimes the precise mix of access and electoral strategies is a function of the PAC's overall level of resources. Consider, first, the more than eight hundred PACs that gave $5,000 or less during the 2004 election cycle, most of which made a small number of small contributions to candidates. Smaller PACs generally have little discretion in their contribution decisions. They generally give to the chairs and perhaps other members of committees with jurisdiction over their issues and to incumbents from districts where they have facilities; there is little or no money left for other contributions. Small labor PACs give to Democrats on key committees and to Democrats from the districts in which the largest concentrations of their members live. Small ideological PACs may give to one or more incumbents who show particular support for important policies.

Larger committees, however, can give to the most important incumbents in their legislative area—party leaders, powerful committee personnel, incumbents who represent important geographic areas (such as districts with company plants), and their strongest legislative allies—and still have money left over to "invest" in nonincumbent candidates (Eismeier and Pollock 1984; Wilcox 1989). In some cases they may give to open-seat candidates who have proven friendly in state legislatures, or they may even give to challengers who appear to share their policy preferences. Sometimes this "venture capital" may go to a nonincumbent who is supported by a powerful incumbent patron or to a challenger to an antagonistic incumbent.

Influences on PAC Decision Making

Few committees have the resources to give in every race. Labor PACs are solicited by nearly every Democratic hopeful (including some who are running against each other in party primaries), and access-oriented corporate committees are often solicited by nearly every incumbent member of Congress. Whatever mix of access and electoral strategies a PAC ultimately chooses, it must make decisions about whom to support and must develop rules about how to make those decisions. Party leaders, committee chairs, and important policy advocates, for example, are more likely to be supported, a strategy that is sometimes officially articulated in PAC contribution guidelines (Bedlington 1999). Sometimes a PAC gives almost exclusively to party leaders and to members of a few crucial committees because these legislators are in a position to help the group achieve its policy goals.

Contribution decisions are shaped primarily by two factors: first, the structures and processes that operate within the PAC and within the sponsoring organization, and second, the amount and type of information on candidates that the PAC is able to obtain.

Although PACs vary widely in how they make their contribution decisions, most have one thing in common: they are not democratic institutions. PACs generally do not solicit advice from contributors, and donors are often technically powerless to influence PAC decisions. Nevertheless, donors who are unhappy with a PAC's contribution decisions can vote with their feet and simply refuse to contribute to the PAC in the future. Although few individual donors can exert much leverage with the threat of this sanction, few PACs can tolerate a significant decline in member giving. At least some PACs will therefore make small contributions to the favorite candidates of blocs of contributors, especially when these donors are local activists (Sorauf 1988). Few contributors make a big effort to influence PAC contributions, however. Instead, most appear to treat PAC contributions as investments in a political "mutual fund" that diversifies their contributions among important policy makers and oversees the management of their political interests (Eismeier and Pollock 1985).

INTERNAL STRUCTURES AND PROCESSES. PAC decision-making structures can change dramatically with new leadership, but significant differences exist in the decision-making structures and processes in large and smaller PACs. Smaller PACs may grant their director or an official of the sponsoring interest group complete discretion over contributions. One study of the American Association of Publishers PAC found that the committee was run by one woman who was both PAC director and lobbyist and had a virtually free hand to direct contributions to whichever candidates she chose (Stronks 1994). Small nonconnected committees often allow their founders complete control over the allocation of funds. For example, Morris Amitay, of the Washington PAC (a pro-Israel committee), ran the entire operation and had complete discretion over contribution decisions in the 1990s (Levick-Segnatelli 1994). Small corporate committees may be influenced by the founder of the company, who often pressures for a more electoral-oriented strategy, or the lobbyists, who generally push for a more access-oriented approach.

Larger PACs generally have formal rules that include explicit criteria for contributions; they may also have boards of directors whose members advise the PAC director and sometimes make final decisions about contributions. The board may be composed of individuals from all sectors of a conglomerate corporation, of individuals from state or local chapters of a union or other federated organization, or of individuals who have made large donations to a nonconnected PAC. Sometimes several committees participate in decision making. The NAR, for example, used to rely on one committee to determine contributions and another to determine independent expenditures. The committee that directed contributions had substantial representation from state and local realtors, whereas the committee that directed independent expenditures reflected the strategies of the NAR national leadership (Bedlington 1994). Although large institutionalized PACs often develop bureaucratic approaches to decisions, they have proven willing to change their decision-making approaches (Bedlington 1994, 1999; Gerber 1999; Mutch 1994, 1999; Wilcox 1994).

PACs whose sponsoring organizations have strong state and local chapters often rely on suggestions from those chapters. For example, local chapters of labor unions recommend candidates, as do local chapters of the Sierra Club (Cantor 1999). Although national PAC officials can and sometimes do override the recommendations of local units, they show restraint in doing so. Alienating local activists may deprive the organization of the ability to rally volunteers for voter mobilization and other efforts. The NAR has gone so far as to create programs that allow local organizations to make small contributions without the approval of the national office (Bedlington 1999). Through their In-State Reception Program, instituted in 1994, local NAR officials may attend in-district fund-raising events and contribute up to $1,000 to an incumbent without the approval of the national board. Similar guidelines apply to fund-raising events for nonincumbents.

INFORMATION ACCESS. PACs with electoral strategies value information on just how close a given race is likely to be so that they can target their money where it will have the greatest impact. Some PAC officials commission polls; others read poll results on the Web. Some attend Washington briefings given by the AFL–CIO, BIPAC, or party committees; others subscribe to special publications that provide detailed looks at various elections across the country. Many PACs require evidence—such as polling data or fund-raising prowess—of the viability of nonincumbent candidates. Some PACs are associated with federated interest groups that have state and local chapters, and these PACs are often able to tap the expertise of local political actors for information on the electoral viability of candidates.

Many PACs consider the legislative record of incumbents. The NAR, for example, refuses to give to incumbents who have not supported its policies on crucial issues, and the Sierra Club will not contribute to candidates with poor environmental records. The NRA rates all incumbents at the national, state, and local levels on their past record of support for gun rights, and it rates nonincumbents by their statements. More recently, even AT&T PAC—which had traditionally given to most incumbents to ensure access—has begun to consider incumbents' voting records in its contribution decisions.

Although it is relatively simple to determine the voting records of incumbent members of Congress, PACs that give to nonincumbents face a more difficult task. In some cases, local units or activists may provide information about a nonincumbent candidate's record in a local council or state legislature. Some ideological PACs mail surveys to candidates and use the responses to help determine whom to support. Some PACs serve as information conduits, providing cues to PACs in a particular community. COPE, BIPAC, and other groups provide information on candidates' views and their prospects for election. When BIPAC tells corporations that it supports a candidate, it essentially guarantees the candidate's pro-business credentials. A BIPAC endorsement helps candidates raise money from corporate PACs because smaller committees that lack the ability to gather their own information often rely on such cues (Nelson and Biersack 1999).

Since the mid-1990s, as fewer congressional races have been in play, separate networks of liberal and conservative groups have shared information about races, and polling results have been quickly distributed to interested PACs.

GIVING BEYOND THE LIMIT

Any single PAC can give only $5,000 to any national candidate in any single election. The effective limit is therefore usually $10,000, because all candidates are presumed to run in primary elections even if unopposed. (The occasional runoff elections allow PACs to give as much as $15,000 to a single candidate.) In fact, few PACs make contributions of this size (Wright 1996). But some PAC officials want to exceed the legal limits.

PACs seek to provide additional assistance to candidates for a variety of reasons. Electorally oriented PACs may identify a few close races that take on special symbolic significance (the election or defeat, for example, of an ideological candidate such as Sen. Rick Santorum, R-Pa.), or they may identify a few very close races that might tip the balance of the Senate or the House or increase the number of members who share their policy views. Access-oriented PACs may want to establish a particularly cozy relationship with party leaders, committee chairs, or other important policy makers. To do so, they may want to give beyond the limit—or the incumbent may ask them to.

How can PACs channel more money to a candidate than the legal limits allow? One method, discussed in Chapter 4, is through independent expenditures—money spent on behalf of a candidate in an effort to obtain voters' support. But contributions that exceed legal limits can also be channeled directly to candidates—principally through practices called bundling and coordinated contributing and through donations to affiliated organizations.

Bundling and Coordinated Contributing

The total limit on PAC contributions does not apply to members of a PAC, each of whom can give up to $1,000 to a candidate in a given election or $2,000 for the entire election cycle; family members of PAC members can also make individual contributions. Because the PAC and its individual members and their families can give money, this creates the possibility for a single interest group to contribute a much larger amount of money to one candidate than one might otherwise suppose.

Moreover, the law allows PACs to bundle contributions from members; that is, the PAC can collect contributions that either are made out to the candidate or are earmarked to the candidate through the PAC, and then distribute those contributions to the candidate. Thus the director of a corporate PAC might give $10,000 to an incumbent (the total permitted on behalf of the PAC) but also present an additional $30,000 in individual contributions from the corporation's executives and their families.

Bundling has become a controversial form of interest group electoral involvement, primarily because of the highly visible and successful efforts of EMILY's List, which bundled millions of dollars to pro-choice Democratic women candidates in recent election cycles. In 2004 EMILY's List claimed to have contributed—through the bundled contributions of its members—$10.8 million to candidates it supported. This figure is impossible to verify, however, because the FEC does not require PACs to disclose bundled contributions of less than $200 (EMILY's List encourages its members to make contributions of at least $100). EMILY's List has become the model for other ideological PACs—including WISH List (Women in the Senate and House) and the Gay and Lesbian Victory Fund—that want to channel individual contributions to candidates (Rimmerman 1994; Rozell 1999).

Bundling is not the only way that interest groups can channel money from their members into the campaign coffers of candidates. PACs and interest groups can coordinate the giving of their members, even when they do not assemble their funds into a bundle. One such method is to sponsor tables at fund-raising events for candidates, a practice especially common in presidential and senatorial campaigns. This approach can be implemented through a PAC or by an organization without a PAC. Major events often have tables sponsored by several large companies and interest groups.

Coordinated giving also occurs when campaigns recruit fund-raisers from within an organization, who then ask their colleagues for contributions. For example, when Michael Dukakis ran for president in 1988, the Dukakis for President campaign recruited the principal owner and chairman of Fidelity Investments, who successfully solicited fifty additional corporate executives and their spouses (Brown, Powell, and Wilcox 1995). The presidential campaigns of most mainstream candidates are financed by networks of contributors, many of whom are linked to interest groups. George W. Bush has refined this strategy to create an unprecedented fundraising machine. In 2004 Bush had 327 "Pioneers" who each raised at least $100,000, and 221 "Rangers" who each raised $200,000 or more, enabling him to collect over $76 million through this strategy, according to Public Citizen (www.whitehouseforsale.org). The finance industry led all others in bundled contributions, giving over $24 million in 2004. The thirty biggest utility companies produced ten Rangers and Pioneers. Bush has rewarded these super-contributors handily. Utility companies along with their lobbyists and trade association met with Vice President Dick Cheney's energy task force at least seventeen times to help formulate the country's energy and pollution policies. Many of these energy companies have been sued by the Environmental Protection Agency for violating pollution standards, but cases against them have been dropped by the Bush administration (Public Citizen 2004a).

Each of these techniques allows interest groups—in some cases through their PACs and in some cases without them—to channel far more money to candidates than the FECA would allow through direct PAC contributions. Indeed, because historically some candidates have refused to accept PAC contributions, some interest groups have resorted entirely to coordinated individual giving. For example, Sen. David Boren, D-Okla., consistently returned any unsolicited PAC contributions, but the individuals who gave to his campaigns included many oil company executives, wildcatters, and their families. Collectively, coordinated giving from the oil industry provided Boren with significant resources, although none of it came through PACs.

Some interest groups sponsor fund-raising events and invite their own members. This tactic is especially popular with federated organizations because the candidate attends the event and therefore has multiple opportunities to interact with group members. In some cases such events are sponsored jointly by several interest groups, or the sponsoring interest group may invite representatives from or members of another group to the event.

However, not all contributions from company executives are coordinated through company or PAC officials. In fact, little research has examined the level of coordinated giving by corporations, but employees of companies do not always give in coordination with their company PACs, and in some cases they may support different candidates. Interest groups do bundle contributions and coordinate the giving of their members, but not all giving by interest group members is bundled or coordinated.

Finally, interest groups can rent out their mailing lists to candidates, who can then solicit group members directly for contributions. If the solicitation includes a personal endorsement by an interest group leader or activist, the mailing can raise significant sums for the candidate. In Virginia, the Family Foundation (a conservative pro-family group) rents its list to candidates, and the solicitation often includes a personal endorsement from the group's founder and former leader, Walter Barbee. According to Barbee, such mailings usually yield many individual contributions from group members. In the 2004 election cycle, James Dobson of Focus on the Family recorded personal endorsements of GOP Senate candidates, some of which were then mailed by the GOP to conservative Christian households (Larson 2005).

Giving to Affiliated Organizations

Thus far we have focused on direct contributions to candidates' principal campaign committees, but some powerful incumbents have other affiliated organizations as well. Many have formed or head their own national PACs, which raise money from individuals and other PACs and give that money to candidates. These "leadership PACs" serve a variety of functions. They can help a candidate launch a presidential bid by paying for travel costs and consultants (Corrado 1992), help a candidate in a bid for party leadership or the chairmanship of a committee, or help a candidate build legislative coalitions (Wilcox 1990).

For example, House minority leader Nancy Pelosi's PAC to the Future helps solidify her position as Democratic party leader in the House. Many corporate, labor, and ideological PACs have contributed to Pelosi's PAC. Pelosi's PAC as well as House majority leader Tom DeLay's PAC attract contributions from committees with electoral as well as access goals. Some PACs give to these leadership PACs because they can channel the money into those campaigns that need it most, thereby influencing the composition of Congress. Yet many others give simply as an additional way of ensuring that the group's lobbyists have access to influential party leaders.

DeLay's leadership PAC, Americans for a Republican Majority, raised over $3.6 million in 2004, including $1.3 million from other PACs. Some PACs gave DeLay's campaign committee the maximum contribution of $10,000 for the primary and general elections and then contributed to DeLay's PAC as well. Not all PACs that gave to DeLay's PAC did so to avoid contribution limits; indeed, most had not given the maximum to his campaign committee. A few even gave to DeLay's PAC instead of to his campaign committee, presumably because DeLay solicited contributions to his PAC to make it easier to centralize the distribution of this money to other candidates.

DeLay's aggressive fund-raising tactics and his use of Americans for a Republican Majority have created significant controversy. Three of DeLay's allies, including Jim Ellis, director of Americans for a Republican Majority, have been indicted by a Texas grand jury for possibly criminally laundering corporate money into Texas state elections (Copelin 2004). The House Ethics Committee, the official watchdog of the House of Representatives, has admonished DeLay several times for violating House norms. One of the admonishments was directly related to the fund-raising tactics for his leadership PAC—a Kansas energy company gave $25,000 to DeLay's political committees and claimed they received legislative help in return (Public Citizen 2004b). Democratic leaders, including Representative Pelosi, have called for DeLay to resign, but he has denied wrongdoing (Babington and Eilperin 2004). In November 2004, House Republicans had voted to change their party rules to allow DeLay to continue to serve as their leader even if he were indicted for criminal charges, but then the party reversed its decision two months later (Allen 2005). DeLay continues to serve as House majority leader. He has set up a legal defense fund to which certain groups such as the American Trucking Association have made contributions.

In addition to PACs, some candidates sponsor foundations that can collect contributions from PACs and even from interest group treasuries. Although these foundations are not supposed to engage in explicitly political activity, some skirt the law, helping candidates from one party or those who share an ideological view or helping a candidate launch a presidential bid. Some foundations wish to influence the ideological direction of a party, others to spread democracy abroad, still others to raise and distribute charitable contributions. In each case, however, when an interest group contributes to the foundation, the candidate is aware of the donation, and the interest group generally hopes that the contribution will help its lobbying efforts.

CONTRIBUTIONS TO PARTIES

In addition to contributing directly to candidates, PACs and interest groups can donate to party committees. Unlike the activities described in Chapter 2, contributions to parties are generally not meant to influence the ideological positions of the parties but to gain access to party leaders or to help the party's candidates win election. In 2004, 39 percent of active corporate PACs gave to at least one party committee, as did one-quarter of active committees associated with trade associations and membership groups, one-third of active PACs associated with labor unions, and one-quarter of nonconnected PACs. Some of the largest PACs gave to several national and state party committees. (See Table 3-6.)

Although PACs can give to party committees, these gifts are limited by law to $15,000 to any one party committee in any one year. Prior to BCRA, interest groups could also give more in the form of soft money, and these contributions did not need to come from PAC receipts. As long as the parties kept the funds in a separate account for specific activities, they could receive unlimited contributions directly from interest group treasuries. Soft money could be given only to political parties, but contributions were often earmarked to help particular candidates, especially presidential candidates.

Soft money gave interest groups the opportunity to contribute millions of dollars, and some corporations and unions did just that. Both political

TABLE 3-6

United Parcel Service PAC Contributions to Party Committees, 2004

	Number of gifts	Total
Democrats		
Arizona State Democratic Central Executive Committee	1	5,000
Democratic Congressional Campaign Committee	2	30,000
Democratic Party of Illinois	3	15,000
Democratic Party of Oregon	1	5,000
Democratic Senatorial Campaign Committee	2	30,000
Democratic National Committee	2	30,000
Iowa Democratic Party	1	5,000
Kansas Democratic Party	2	5,000
Nevada State Democratic Party	1	5,000
Pennsylvania Democratic Party	1	5,000
South Dakota Democratic Party	2	10,000
Texas Democratic Party	1	5,000
Republicans		
Arizona Republican Party	1	4,725
Colorado Republican Federal Campaign Committee	1	5,000
Michigan Republican Party	1	5,000
Mississippi Republican Party	1	4,900
Missouri Republican State Committee-Federal	1	5,000
National Republican Congressional Committee	2	30,000
National Republican Senatorial Committee	2	30,000
Republican Campaign Committee of New Mexico	1	5,000
Republican Federal Committee of Pennsylvania	1	5,000
Republican National Committee	4	30,000
Republican Party of Kentucky	4	10,000
Republican Party of Texas	2	10,000
Republican State Central Committee	1	1,500

Source: Compiled from Federal Election Commission data.

parties crossed ethical boundaries in soliciting soft money contributions, and corporations in particular frequently felt that they had little option but to give when asked, often to both parties. Such soft money contributions are now banned.

As discussed in Chapter 2, interest groups also help finance party conventions. In addition, they give to institutions affiliated with parties, though not directly involved with elections, that may ultimately help the party's electoral fortunes. For example, the GOP National Policy Forum helps identify and develop issues that Republican candidates can use in their campaigns. The forum is financed largely by interest groups, which contribute in order to gain access to important policy makers. The forum holds conferences at which interest group representatives share their views with prominent members of Congress, including committee chairs. In some cases these conferences are held on the very day of major Senate or House committee hearings. Corporations that attend the conferences are usually asked to donate $25,000 (Marcus 1997a).

Contributions of Goods and Services

Although most PAC contributions are simple cash transactions, PACs also contribute services, staff, and products—rather than money—to campaigns. Under FEC guidelines, in-kind contributions are subject to the same limit of $5,000 per candidate per campaign that applies to direct financial support. The worth of an in-kind contribution is estimated at fair-market value—that is, the price at which the candidate would have purchased the goods or services. If, for example, an interest group donates services worth $5,000 during a primary, it can give only $5,000 in cash or services during the general election. Approximately one in six active PACs in 1996 made in-kind contributions; nonconnected PACs and those associated with trade associations and membership organizations were the most likely to do so.

PACs make in-kind contributions for several reasons. First, such contributions enable a PAC to control how money is spent. PACs with electoral goals may be better able to help nonincumbents by providing a needed service than by giving them cash, which the campaign might spend on a less essential service. Second, a PAC may be able to produce some services below market cost, thus maximizing the use of its resources. For example, although a PAC may have only $20,000 in cash to give directly to candidates, it may be able to produce $35,000 in services to contribute instead. Third, because of the way that campaign law values certain in-kind contributions, they may be more valuable than cash.

One of the best bargains for a campaign is the donation of a poll. PACs that commission a number of polls can usually get them at a discount, and the value of the data turned over to the candidates varies with time. After fifteen days, a PAC can depreciate a poll by 50 percent; after sixty-one days, by 95 percent. Thus a poll that costs $20,000 can be donated to a candidate for a value of only $1,000 after two months. In the final weeks of a campaign, such old news would be worthless—but early in a campaign, data even two months old can prove quite useful. In March of an election year, polls can warn incumbents of potential weaknesses or indicate the strength of a challenger's name recognition. In addition, polls can identify issues that are salient to voters in a particular district or state and help campaign committees determine how best to approach those issues.

Although few corporate PACs provide surveys to candidates, BIPAC has recommended that corporate committees donate polls early in the election cycle, when they can help candidates develop campaign themes and positions on issues (BIPAC 1996, 12). Focus groups, another popular in-kind contribution in recent years, can also help candidates hone their message.

In addition to funding polls, interest groups make in-kind contributions by training and providing campaign staff. Membership organizations with ideological agendas—like the Sierra Club, the League of Conservation Voters (LCV), and the Human Rights Campaign (HRC)—are especially likely to provide volunteer support. According to Kim Mills, spokesperson for the HRC, that organization sponsors campaign training seminars for volunteers aged eighteen to twenty-five and then lends the trainees to key candidates. The group will even lend some of its full-time staffers to priority campaigns. In 2004 the LCV announced a plan to recruit some 25,000 volunteers to work in campaigns and make personal contacts in key battleground states. Both HRC and NARAL set up centers to help train volunteers in effective political action.

Interest groups increasingly employ the services of political consultants and pollsters to test and develop messages and issue emphases. Such services can be shared with political campaigns and may influence how the candidates themselves choose and address policy issues. Perhaps most prominently, a number of conservative groups, including the Christian Coalition and the NFIB, financed research and polling in 1994 that led to the development of the Contract with America, the GOP's ten-point plan for policy change. The efforts of these groups helped to develop a national GOP message (including the Contract with America) and an agenda for the midterm congressional campaign. The groups benefited from having their principal issues articulated in the elections and can be given partial credit for the Republican takeover of Congress.

Interest groups can also provide candidates with targeting information to help them reach sympathetic voters (Herrnson 1994), training for candidates and campaign officials, and transportation for candidates. The variety of in-kind assistance that PACs can provide is vast, but since in-kind contributions require PACs to make a special effort to purchase or produce the goods or services and provide them to campaigns, by far the majority of active PACs do not engage in in-kind contributions.

Summary

Although campaign contributions have occurred throughout history, contributions have varied in form because of changing fund-raising styles, changing technology, and—most important—changing laws. How funds from interest groups enter elections is currently determined by federal campaign finance laws passed in 1974, 1979, and 2002, and by a series of U.S. Supreme Court rulings that have overturned, modified, and clarified portions of these laws. This legal framework creates the opportunity structure for interest group involvement in campaign financing.

Interest groups make direct contributions as a means of communicating with candidates and party leaders. Indeed, most PAC and soft money contributions are made at fund-raising events where interest group lobbyists have an opportunity to meet the candidate or party leader directly. Incumbents meet with PAC officials at breakfasts, cocktail parties, and dinners, and nonincumbents meet PAC officials when they can, often at events sponsored by party leaders or other patrons of the candidate. Some interest groups not only attend fund-raising events but also host them. A few set up events for nonincumbent candidates and invite officials from other PACs to attend.

Interest groups vary not so much in the way they make contributions as in the candidates to whom they choose to give: access-oriented groups are likely to give to committee chairs and party leaders regardless of whether they are in close elections, whereas electorally oriented groups give to candidates in close elections and try to channel their resources where they can make the largest impact.

Overall, however, interest group money for campaigns is mostly access money. The fact that most PAC money goes to incumbents makes elections less competitive. Challengers face long odds in any event, and these odds are made longer still by the fact that incumbents can raise money quickly by issuing invitations to fund-raising events that many PAC directors feel powerless to refuse.

For groups that hope to influence the outcome of an election, the limits on the amount of direct contributions to candidates pose a barrier to efficient allocation of available funds. A PAC with $300,000 to contribute cannot give all that money to candidates in two close races but is required by federal law to distribute it to at least thirty candidates.

In Chapter 4 we focus on spending to influence voters—through issue advocacy, independent expenditures, and voter mobilization efforts—spending that occurs, in most cases, without any limits on the amount that can be directed to a particular race.

NOTES

1. Occasionally candidates in southern states are involved in runoff elections; in such cases, individuals can give an extra $1,000.
2. A party or candidate that receives 5 percent of the popular vote in a presidential election is eligible to receive public funds in the next election. The public grant is equal to the percentage of the winning candidate's popular vote received by the candidate from the minor party. Thus, if the minor party candidate received 10 percent of the popular vote and the winning candidate received 50 percent, then the minor party candidate would be eligible to receive a public grant in the next election equal to 20 percent of the grant awarded to the major parties.
3. Campaign finance information from the FEC is available at the commission's web site (www.fec.gov). Other groups begin with FEC data, add their own research, and repackage the data for public consumption. For example, the Center for Responsive Politics allows access to records from interest groups and their members at their web site (www.crp.org/index.html-ssi).
4. In this chapter and Chapter 4, "active" PACs are defined as those that both raised and contributed money in the election cycle.
5. Estimates provided to the authors by Robert Biersack of the FEC.
6. To ensure that names on a rented list are solicited only once, many groups "salt" their lists with a few fictional individuals. A group or candidate that sends more than one mailing to the fictional group member has clearly violated the rental agreement.
7. An additional 12 percent received contributions but did not make contributions or independent expenditures.
8. PACs pursuing an electoral strategy sometimes become involved in primary elections. In the GOP, for example, interest groups on both sides of the abortion issue have mobilized behind their preferred candidates in intraparty contests. Other electorally oriented committees are active only in general elections, hoping to help their preferred party obtain the highest possible number of seats (Herrnson 1994).

CHAPTER 4

Interest Groups and Voters

Interest groups that pursue electoral strategies often try to persuade their members and other voters to support or oppose candidates. They may communicate endorsements to their members in newsletters or e-mails, or rate candidates on scorecards that their members might use to make vote decisions. They may distribute voters' guides in churches or outside welfare offices or mail them to their members with a letter urging them to distribute the guides in their neighborhoods. They can produce advertisements on television, radio, or the Internet, often targeted at voters who are not group members. Such efforts are far more complicated than simply giving money to a candidate or party: a political action committee (PAC) contribution rarely involves more than writing a check and attending a cocktail party or a fund-raising dinner, but communicating with interest group members and other voters requires research, planning, and production. Many groups also research the effectiveness of their campaign involvement, to help improve their success in the next election.

In the 2004 elections, interest groups mounted unprecedented campaigns to help elect or defeat various presidential and congressional candidates, often spending more money than the candidates themselves. Such efforts allow interest groups to define the issues of a campaign and to frame the debate, a change that threatens to transform American elections from races centered on individual candidates to races centered on coalitions of interest groups.

One of the most striking examples of an interest group's ability to define the debate is the case of the Swift Boat Veterans for Truth during the 2004 election. Beginning on August 5 with a relatively small ad buy in just three states—West Virginia, Ohio, and Wisconsin—attacking Senator John Kerry's war record, Swift Boat Veterans for Truth was able to dominate the news for almost an entire month. The ads were simple and repetitive, claiming that Kerry had lied about his record during the Vietnam War. The media, especially talk shows and cable news programs, repeated the group's charges, providing an echo chamber for the ads' message. Though the group's allegations contained substantial inaccuracies, within just a few weeks of the original ad purchase, over 50 percent of the public had heard the charges (Jurkowitz 2004). The group was able to aggressively attack Kerry in a way that Bush could not, and although Bush pointedly did not renounce its attacks, he did not suffer from the negative feelings that the group's negative advertising aroused.

In this chapter we examine how interest groups get the word out to their members and to the electorate at large. We begin by looking at the strategic context of interest group activity: the laws and common practices that create opportunity structures and the goals and resources that determine interest groups' strategies and tactics. We then describe specific tactics in more detail.

THE STRATEGIC CONTEXT: REGULATIONS, GOALS, AND RESOURCES

Communication among interest groups and their members, and with other voters, is regulated by tax law, by the Federal Election Campaign Act (FECA; discussed in Chapter 3), and by recent Supreme Court rulings. The law in this area continues to evolve, as interest groups probe the limits of both the legal regulations and the willingness of regulators to enforce those regulations.

Tax law limits the ways in which certain groups may engage in electoral activity, including the endorsement of candidates. Section 501(c) of the Internal Revenue Code permits organizations that promote the social welfare of the country to qualify for tax-exempt status. Groups that qualify for 501(c)(3) status can thus receive tax-exempt contributions, which is an enormous benefit because it allows wealthy benefactors to write off donations on their taxes. The 501(c)(3) groups cannot lobby Congress or engage in partisan political activity, but they are permitted to educate voters on issues and to encourage citizen participation in elections. Many groups with this tax status do engage in campaigns, however, including distributing voters' guides, running advertisements that educate the public on the candidates' stances on particular issues, and developing lists of potential voters that other organizations can contact.

Other groups are organized under section 501(c)(4), which means that although they are not required to pay taxes on their revenues, contributions they receive are not tax deductible. Organizations classified as 501(c)(4) can engage in partisan politics, endorse candidates, and even sponsor a PAC, as long as electoral activity is not their primary purpose. The Internal Revenue Service has issued guidelines to help determine when the principal purpose of a group is electoral activity. In the 1990s it ruled that the Christian Coalition was primarily involved in electoral politics and stripped the organization of its tax-exempt status, although the case brought protests from conservatives and is still being litigated.

To protect their 501(c)(3) or 501(c)(4) status, many citizens' groups do not issue formal endorsements; they nevertheless distribute information to their members (and to other voters) that makes it clear which candidate they support. For example, in 2004, Focus on the Family, a conservative religious group organized as a 501(c)(3), distributed talking points and model sermons to pastoral members that sought to focus voting decisions on issues that benefited Republicans. The organization's director, James Dobson, expressed his own preference for George W. Bush for president but made it clear that he was speaking as a private citizen and not making an endorsement on behalf of his organization. Nonetheless, when group leaders make partisan statements, they may run the risk of endangering their groups' tax-exempt status. In 2004 the Justice Department announced an investigation into the tax status of the National Association for the Advancement of Colored People (NAACP), based on public statements by the group's leaders during the campaign. The investigation by the Republican-led Justice Department has been criticized by Democrats as an effort in political intimidation.

Other committees are organized under section 527 of the tax code, which regulates political committees instead of charities. Such committees can raise money through contributions that are not limited in size, and they can spend that money in issue advocacy campaigns. A single wealthy individual can form a 527 committee and give it millions of dollars, which it can then spend in thinly veiled campaign ads. These 527 committees can also be supported by other organizations. In the 2004 campaign, liberal groups formed 527 committees that acted as formal coalitions to raise and spend funds for various purposes, from running advertisements to register- ing voters.

Some large interest groups have separate entities organized under differ- ent sections of the tax code. The Sierra Club, for example, has a 501(c)3 committee called the Sierra Club Foundation that educates citizens on environmental issues and helps to mount nonpartisan voter mobilization efforts. The core of the Sierra Club is organized as a 501(c)(4) membership association that engages in a range of activities including lobbying and electioneering. The organization also has an associated 527 committee and a PAC.

The FECA allows groups to spend unlimited amounts of treasury funds to communicate with their members. The American Federation of Labor–Congress of Industrial Organizations (AFL-CIO), the National Rifle Association (NRA), and other groups focus on mobilizing their own members first, and these communications are largely unregulated. Federal election campaign law comes into play when groups try to broaden their communications to persuade voters who are not group members.

When interest groups try to persuade voters to support or oppose par- ticular candidates, they generally undertake either independent expendi- tures or issue advocacy. Both independent expenditures and issue advoca- cy were allowed by the Supreme Court's 1974 *Buckley v. Valeo* decision. PACs began to engage in independent expenditures soon after that deci- sion, but case law on issue advocacy was not clarified until 1995. Issue advocacy campaigns exploded soon thereafter, in the 1996 elections. By 2004, issue advocacy by 527 groups dominated the airwaves and often set the terms of the political debate.

Independent expenditures are defined as spending by a PAC or by an individual to advocate the election or defeat of a specific candidate. Such efforts must be genuinely independent and cannot be coordinated with the candidate or with a party committee. Independent expenditure campaigns are usually conducted through PACs, which fund these campaigns through member contributions that are limited to $5,000 per member. Independent expenditures made by individuals or PACs must be disclosed to the FEC. The expenditures themselves are not subject to FECA contribution limits—there is no limit on the amount that a group or individual can spend in any single campaign or in all campaigns combined.

Issue advocacy is spending that advocates particular positions on issues but not the election or defeat of particular candidates. Advertisements may mention candidates by name as long as they do not use specific words such as *vote for* or *defeat*. As is the case with independent expenditures, there are no limits on spending by interest groups or individuals in issue advocacy campaigns. In contrast to funds for independent expenditures, however, money for issue advocacy may come from interest group treasuries—funded by company profits, union or organization dues, or large contributions from group members. Issue advocacy by 527 committees must be disclosed but not as often or as clearly as other campaign activity. Issue advocacy by groups organized under other sections of the tax code is less transparent.

Although it might appear initially that independent expenditures are a more effective tool for interest groups because they can feature explicit language urging voters to elect or defeat specific candidates, the vast majority of issue advocacy ads in 2004 mentioned a candidate by name and included the candidate's picture. The ban on explicit endorsements is thus a minor hindrance. The advertisement by Swift Boat Veterans for Truth did not advocate the defeat of John Kerry, but its intention was transparent to all who saw the ad. Ultimately, issue advocacy campaigns are less restricted because they allow interest groups to use funds not only from PACs but also from their treasuries and from member and nonmember donations.

Why do interest groups go to such effort to communicate directly with voters? For groups that have broad policy goals and are seeking to influence the outcome of elections, direct communication with voters has several advantages over a simple campaign contribution. First, there are generally no limits on the amounts that interest groups can spend to communicate with voters, although procedural rules affect how the money is spent. If an interest group especially wants to influence the outcome of a single or a dozen House races, it can concentrate most or even all of its financial resources in those districts. A PAC that only makes contributions would have to spread $100,000 across at least ten congressional districts (with maximum size contributions), but it could spend all of that money in independent expenditures in a single race.

Second, when interest groups communicate directly with voters, they control the content of the message, which enables them to more effectively mobilize their members and to highlight important issues among the larger electorate—and possibly to persuade some voters to support their position on those issues or to support candidates that they favor. In 2004, for example, the Chamber of Commerce ran advertisements linking Democratic vice presidential nominee John Edwards to his prior career as a trial lawyer. The ads were intended not only to build business opposition to Edwards but also to increase voter support for limits on product liability lawsuits. Finally, direct communication with voters enables interest groups to put the candidate on the record in favor of their positions, which may make the candidate more likely to continue to support those positions in the future.

Consider, for example, television ads run by an environmental group urging support for a candidate who favors increased spending to clean up toxic waste sites. Members of the environmental group and other supporters of environmental causes are likely to respond well to this message, and many will be more likely to vote for the candidate. If the advertising is successful, district voters who are not members of the group may become increasingly concerned about toxic wastes; some may tell pollsters that more money should be spent on cleanup, and a few may even join the environmental group. If exit polls show that the candidate carried the environmental vote, then the interest group's lobbyists may find it easier to gain access to the candidate if he or she is elected. Finally, by publicizing the candidate's promise to support increased spending on cleanup, the environmental group makes it more likely that the candidate will follow through on this promise.

Interest groups use a variety of resources to communicate with voters. Groups with money buy television ads; groups with a large and active membership distribute voters' guides; and groups with prestige endorse candidates and allow the candidates, the parties, and other interest groups to disseminate the endorsement. Thus even cash-poor groups can use non-cash resources to attempt to sway voting decisions.

Interest groups can choose among many tactics in their efforts to persuade voters to support or oppose a particular candidate. They can publicize the candidate's record or positions to the group's members, perhaps along with an endorsement. They can identify incumbents with—in their view—particularly undesirable voting records and publicize this information among group members, urging them to vote against these candidates. They can publicize voting records among the larger electorate by distributing voters' guides and by sending information to group members to distribute in their communities. Finally, they can fund advertising through the mail, radio, television, or the Internet, urging voters to support or defeat a candidate, although some forms of advertising must take a more subtle approach.

Endorsements

Many organizations formally endorse candidates to signal to their members which candidate best represents their viewpoint. Endorsements are first and foremost an attempt to persuade the membership to vote for the candidate, so they are inevitably distributed to group members, often by various means. The Sierra Club issues its endorsements for important national offices in its monthly magazine, and local chapter newsletters include these endorsements along with endorsements for state and local offices. Contributors to the club's PAC receive special communications on the group's endorsements. Other organizations distribute endorsements on the Internet, through chains of members who receive and send faxed copies of endorsement lists, at local meetings, and through other channels.

Although endorsements may seem to be the most basic of all forms of interest group participation in elections, in fact, most organizations do not issue endorsements. Many corporations and trade associations make contributions to candidates without endorsing them, and some citizens' groups devote considerable resources to electing candidates without issuing formal endorsements.

Why would a group give money and resources to a candidate but withhold a formal endorsement? Citizens' groups often refrain from giving endorsements because doing so might cost them their tax-exempt status. Some organizations, such as the Sierra Club, have separate 501(c)(3) organizations that do not endorse, allowing the main body of the organization to issue endorsements. But endorsements can be tricky for all kinds of tax-exempt groups.

Even among corporations, trade associations, and business groups that do not qualify as tax exempt, endorsements are not common. Endorsements can create controversy within an organization. Corporations and trade associations, for example, refrain from issuing endorsements partly to avoid long and contentious stockholders' meetings or consumer boycotts of their products. An endorsement implies a high level of support from an organization, whereas a contribution from a PAC merely implies an ongoing relationship with a candidate. Moreover, an endorsement of a candidate might become an embarrassment if the candidate is later involved in a scandal.

The Endorsement Decision

Most organizations have a formal process for deciding whom to endorse, and the decision criteria are generally similar to those used for making contributions (see Chapter 3). For incumbents, interest groups consider voting records; for nonincumbents, they consider any voting record in state or local government, answers to the group's questionnaires, and information provided by local activists. Many groups also assess candidates' viability and withhold their endorsement from those who have no chance of winning. To determine viability, larger and more complex organizations rely on committees and boards; smaller ideological groups often delegate the task to their director.

For example, WISH List—a PAC that works to identify, train, support, and elect more pro-choice Republican women—has a Candidate Review Committee that reviews its prospective endorsees. Candidates who are seeking WISH List support fill out a questionnaire and in some cases schedule interviews with the group's leadership. On the basis of the questionnaire responses and the interview, the Candidate Review Committee assesses two factors: whether the candidate shares the PAC's policy positions, and whether the candidate has a realistic chance of winning. A candidate who is "right" on the issues but lacks political viability may not be endorsed.

Groups such as WISH List—and EMILY's List, its larger, Democratic counterpart—use their endorsements to signal members not only to vote for the candidate but also to contribute to her campaign. Because their members trust WISH List to endorse only viable candidates, they feel confident making contributions on the basis of the organization's endorsement. Pro-choice GOP women are thus especially eager to obtain a WISH List endorsement. They are aware that it will make fund-raising easier and attract grassroots support. WISH List also sends its members a mailing containing profiles of endorsed candidates. This visibility is sought by candidates, who recognize the value of publicity that reaches like-minded contributors and activists.

The NRA makes its political endorsements based on a variety of information, especially on the candidate's voting record in public office. Other information used to evaluate candidates and their positions on issues includes questionnaire responses, public statements, virtually anything that can be documented. However, actions do speak louder than words, and voting records carry much more weight than does any other information. NRA officials believe that past behavior is the best predictor of future behavior. Consequently the NRA is most likely to support friendly incumbents (who are tested and proven), even when they are being challenged by candidates who are in nearly perfect agreement with NRA positions on issues.

The national AFL–CIO has a general executive board made up of leaders from its more than fifty affiliated unions. According to Bill Samuel, legislative director of the AFL–CIO, the board's endorsement in presidential campaigns is based primarily on candidate questionnaires and in some cases on appearances before the board, although not every declared candidate actually fills out a questionnaire or visits the board. For House and Senate races, decisions on endorsements begin at the local level and must be ratified by regional and then by state AFL–CIO councils. In all cases a two-thirds vote is required for endorsement.

One side benefit of the endorsement process is the opportunity it provides for an interest group to force candidates to commit publicly to supporting the group's goals. Interest groups can make it clear that endorsements depend on public statements of support for or opposition to particular policies; groups may then create a record of a candidate's commitment, which can be used later by lobbyists when a measure is under consideration by legislators.

Contested Endorsements

Although endorsement decisions are often easy and straightforward, they sometimes provoke significant controversy within an organization. In the 2004 Democratic presidential primary, candidates eagerly sought the endorsement of the AFL–CIO, one of the most important groups in Democratic Party politics. John Kerry, Richard Gephardt, John Edwards, Howard Dean, and the other primary candidates were supportive of labor's agenda and were strongly favored over George W. Bush. By selecting one of these candidates, the AFL–CIO could potentially determine the ultimate winner of the Democratic primary, and who would face President Bush.

Richard Gephardt, the former Democratic leader in the House, was one of labor's staunchest allies, with a proven track record of support for the AFL–CIO's issues. However, Gephardt was not doing well in the polls or in fund-raising and was likely to lose even with the AFL-CIO's strong support. The AFL-CIO faced a tough choice: to reward a strong supporter and hope to provide a needed boost to his campaign, or to support a candidate with a greater chance of success. Many of the unions that make up the AFL-CIO chose to endorse Gephardt, but others could not decide who to support or favored other candidates. As a result, no candidate received support from two-thirds of the AFL-CIO's unions, and the AFL-CIO did not issue an early endorsement (Greenhouse and Swarns 2003). Only after Gephardt withdrew from the race, and John Kerry had won several state primary elections and emerged as the clear favorite to win the Democratic Party nomination, did the AFL-CIO endorse his candidacy.

Similarly, in the 2002 Alaska governor's race, labor unions were torn between Republican senator Frank Murkowski and Lieutenant Governor Fran Ulmer, a Democrat. Senator Murkowski had a better record on labor issues than most other Republicans, but Ulmer was a stronger friend of labor. After much disagreement, the AFL-CIO endorsed Ulmer, but some unions supported Murkowski instead (Associated Press 2002).

The dilemma faced by the AFL-CIO—to support a strong GOP ally or to endorse an even more loyal Democrat—is common to groups that attempt to maintain a bipartisan strategy. Many groups have faced this dilemma more frequently in recent years, when close divisions in Congress have made supporting a candidate of the "other" party less attractive. For example, in 2002, liberal groups faced a difficult choice in the contest between moderate Republican Connie Morella, R-Md., and her Democratic challenger. Morella had long been one of the most moderate Republicans in the House and had enjoyed the support of feminist, environmental, and gun control groups. But these liberal groups were eager for the Democrats to gain seats and possibly take control of the chamber, and they believed that every seat mattered. Ultimately some groups endorsed Morella, some abandoned her and endorsed her Democratic challenger, and a few issued rare "dual endorsements" of both candidates.

Some groups have resolved contested endorsement decisions by leaning toward incumbents, whereas others have sought to balance the partisanship of their endorsements so as to maintain a bipartisan stance. The bipartisan stance might aid in gaining access to leaders of both parties in Congress, and it helps to maintain support among members of both parties. For example, the Sierra Club has frequently operated under guidelines that are a sort of "affirmative action" for Republicans—endorsing GOP incumbents with acceptable environmental records even when they are challenged by much "greener" Democrats. In recent years, the Sierra Club has begun to endorse Democratic challengers thought to have a good chance of winning while continuing to support GOP incumbents who seem likely to be reelected.

Public versus Private Endorsements

Endorsements are generally intended to swing the votes of interest group members, but some organizations seek to influence nonmembers as well. Whether an interest group chooses to communicate its endorsements primarily to members or to publicize them further depends critically on how the group is perceived by the electorate at large. Popular organizations may seek to influence nonmembers by publicizing their endorsements, whereas more controversial groups may even attempt to keep their endorsements from the public eye.

Environmental organizations generally publicize their endorsements. Sierra Club political director Dan Weiss noted that "the Sierra Club is unique in that the endorsement is meaningful because the name means something. There is a noneconomic benefit to a Sierra Club endorsement. In effect, we offer the environmental version of the Good Housekeeping Seal of Approval" (Cantor 1999). Similarly, the League of Conservation Voters (LCV) issues an "Earth List" of legislators with the strongest environmental records, which is widely believed to influence environmentally minded voters who are not league members. In 2004 the LCV had eighty names on its list, including sixty-five Democratic candidates and fifteen Republicans.

Organizations held in mixed regard may be forced to exercise caution with their endorsements. In the early 1980s, several pro-choice candidates asked the National Abortion and Reproductive Rights Action League (NARAL) to withhold endorsements because they feared mobilization by anti-abortion activists (Thomas 1999). Christian conservative groups have used endorsements from gay and lesbian rights groups to mobilize their members to help defeat candidates. Similarly, endorsements from Christian conservative groups often lead moderate and liberal voters to mobilize against endorsed candidates (Rozell and Wilcox 1996). This has led some candidates to try to avoid endorsements by Christian Right groups. For example, in 2004 John Thune, a GOP Senate candidate in South Dakota, did not fill out a candidate survey for Concerned Women for America, probably because he preferred not to have an endorsement from the group.

For a time, some Christian conservative organizations even recommended that candidates deliberately hide endorsements and wage "stealth candidacies." The practice of concealing endorsements occurred most often at the local level, where some school board candidates allowed endorsements to be disseminated in local churches but withheld them from the media.[1]

Sometimes, organizations with opposing views may use the same endorsements simultaneously to mobilize their members. NRA endorsements, for example, are used to mobilize citizens who are for or against gun control. The net impact of an NRA endorsement appears to vary widely: in many states it is almost always an advantage; in some cities it may be a liability.

Endorsements and Voting Decisions

Do endorsements influence the voting decisions of interest group members? Generally endorsements matter most among interest groups when membership is voluntary, when members share common positions on particular issues and consider those issues central to their politics, and when members trust the organizational leadership to evaluate candidates. Ideological interest groups—such as the National Right to Life Committee, NARAL, the NRA, the Sierra Club, and the NAACP—are the most likely to fit this profile. Endorsements probably matter most in the House and in state and local races, where interest group members may have less information about the records and policy positions of the candidates than they do for national elections.

Although there has been little research on the value of endorsements, mounting evidence indicates that they influence the votes of at least some members of interest groups. When endorsements are combined with voter mobilization efforts (discussed later in this chapter), they can help swing close elections. For example, with the NRA at 3.8 million members, many of whom are willing to base their votes on gun rights issues, an NRA endorsement can be an enormous asset to candidates in some regions. According to Chris Cox, executive director of the NRA Institute for Legislative Action, in 2004, thirteen of the fourteen Senate candidates profiled in the November NRA magazine won their races. Of the 251 U.S. House candidates endorsed by the NRA Political Victory Fund (the organization's PAC), 241 won. The NRA argues that its efforts were instrumental in helping defeat Senate minority leader Tom Daschle, D-S.D. In Daschle's race, the NRA ran 300 ads in 150 South Dakota newspapers, aired 1,200 radio spots and 750 television spots, put up 30 billboards, and made 150,000 combined mailings and phone calls (National Rifle Association Political Victory Fund 2004). Scholars have confirmed in previous elections that NRA endorsements influence election outcomes (McBurnett, Kenny, and Bordua 1996).

One of the most important reasons that endorsements might fail to influence votes was articulated many years ago by David Truman in *The Governmental Process* (1951). According to Truman, membership in more than one group or interaction with members of other groups may subject voters to conflicting cues. Conservative gun owners, for example, may also belong to the Sierra Club and to a labor union, or they may talk politics with Sierra Club activists at NRA meetings, with union activists at the factory, and with liberal activists at PTA meetings. In the 2000 presidential race the NRA mailed packets to coal miners in West Virginia who also had hunting licenses, attempting to overcome union endorsements of Al Gore.

Ironically, although labor unions are more likely than any other type of interest group to issue endorsements, they do not fit the profile of organizations whose endorsements are most likely to carry weight. To begin with, labor union membership is not necessarily voluntary: in many states, certain places of employment are closed shops, meaning that anyone who works there must join the union regardless of their political views. Although union members may share a common belief that management gives itself too many bonuses while underpaying the workers who make profits possible, they do not necessarily agree on abortion, affirmative action, welfare reform, or foreign aid. And in times of economic prosperity, union issues may seem less salient to workers than do social, racial, and other issues. All of this suggests that union endorsements may not be especially effective in influencing workers' voting decisions.

In 1984, for example, the AFL–CIO endorsed Walter Mondale early in the Democratic primaries and worked hard to defeat President Ronald Reagan, who had dissolved the Air Traffic Controller's Union and allowed corporations to replace striking workers. But Reagan used a variety of issues to target union voters: he sought the votes of inner-city ethnic whites by opposing affirmative action and taking a strong anticommunist stance, wooed workers by opposing welfare for those who would not work, and appealed to Catholic workers by opposing abortion and posturing on moral issues. Ultimately, 48 percent of members of labor union families voted to reelect Reagan in 1984 (Gallup Organization 1984). Clearly, union endorsements failed to deliver a sweep of the labor vote to Mondale.

In 2004, however, labor endorsements may have been somewhat more important. Union members voted for John Kerry by 65 percent compared to 33 percent for President Bush. In contrast, non–union members voted for Bush over Kerry by 54 percent to 45 percent. Union households also comprised a higher portion of the electorate than they had in many previous elections. The AFL-CIO attributes Kerry's strong support by union members to its aggressive efforts to contact members. According to a poll conducted for the AFL-CIO, 92 percent of union members heard from their unions during this election cycle, and 81 percent heard from unions at least three times (AFL-CIO 2004).

Hit Lists

In addition to endorsing some candidates, interest groups may single out others for defeat. The "hit list" is generally thought to have originated with Environmental Action, which in the early 1970s created the "Dirty Dozen"—a list of legislators with the worst environmental records. The familiar and catchy phrase drew more negative attention to candidates than would any straightforward listing of those with environmentally unfriendly voting records. In the course of five election cycles, Environmental Action included fifty-two different incumbents on its list, and twenty-four were defeated in the years they were listed (Schlozman and Tierney 1986).

More recently the Dirty Dozen list has been issued by the LCV, which uses the hit list to target electoral efforts. In the final two weeks of the 1996 election, the LCV spent heavily, using independent expenditures to run 472 television and 382 radio advertisements in efforts to defeat targeted candidates (Gugliotta 1996). In 2004 the LCV for the first time included the president of the United States on its Dirty Dozen list. Other groups target incumbents for defeat without explicitly calling them hit lists. In 1996 the AFL-CIO targeted 104 members of Congress for defeat, 45 of whom—including 11 GOP House freshmen—lost their elections (Herrnson 1997).

Just as endorsements can sometimes backfire against a candidate, so can being placed on a hit list. In 1996 the Human Rights Campaign (HRC) conducted its first-ever independent spending campaign against a candidate, openly targeting North Carolina Republican senator Jesse Helms for defeat. The HRC spent about $250,000 against Helms, assisted with phone banks and literature drops, and contributed the services of several staff members to assist Democratic challenger Harvey Gantt's campaign. Given his long-standing hostility toward gay rights and his sometimes vitriolic statements about homosexuality, Helms was a logical first target for this organization. But North Carolina is a culturally conservative state, and Helms carried opposition from the gay community as a badge of honor and believed that he gained more than he lost from the organized opposition.

For a variety of reasons, hit lists are far less common than endorsements. First, the leaders of many interest groups believe that if their organizations concentrate on hit lists, they will be perceived by the media and the political community as excessively negative. Second, hit lists greatly antagonize incumbents, most of whom are likely to win reelection and become even more energetic in opposing the interest group's agenda. For groups pursuing either legislative or electoral strategies, hit lists run the risk of decreasing access to important policy makers. Finally, some groups that have tried to target incumbents with negative campaigns have received strong feedback from group members who disapproved of the tactics and threatened to withhold support in future elections.

RATINGS, SCORECARDS, AND VOTERS' GUIDES

Like endorsements, ratings, scorecards, and voters' guides enable interest groups to provide convenient voting cues to members and the public alike. Ratings and scorecards evaluate incumbent legislators' support for an interest group's agenda, usually by listing votes on important bills and amendments and summarizing that information as a numerical score that ranges from 0 to 100 percent support. Ratings, which generally provide longer and more complex evaluations of incumbent votes, are aimed primarily at activists, lobbyists, and journalists. Scorecards, usually shorter and simpler, are aimed primarily at interest group members. Voters' guides present incumbent and nonincumbent candidates' positions on issues of concern to interest groups and their members.

For interest groups that claim or seek 501(c)(3) tax status, ratings, scorecards, and voters' guides allow the group to influence the voting decisions of their members and the broader electorate without specifically endorsing candidates. By avoiding an explicit endorsement, the group can claim to have merely provided nonpartisan information to assist voting decisions. In 2004, for example, many churches had sermons and other materials on the theme "How Would Jesus Vote?" Although these materials did not endorse a candidate per se, they made it clear that the pastor at least believed that Jesus would vote for Bush.

Interest groups (such as the AFL–CIO and the Sierra Club) that endorse candidates may also issue ratings, scorecards, and voters' guides. Ratings and scorecards provide more nuanced information than a simple endorsement. Although an organization may endorse two candidates for separate seats in the House, for example, one may have a 100-percent score and the other a 60-percent score. Ratings and scorecards thus clarify for interest group members the precise extent to which each candidate has supported the group's policies. Such a signal can sometimes influence fund-raising by the candidate among interest group members and sympathetic PACs. Moreover, ratings can help interest groups' lobbyists: informing a member of Congress that an upcoming vote is going to be a part of the next scorecard may provide an extra incentive to support the group on the issue in question.

The National Farmers Union was the first group to use the legislative scorecard, in 1919 (Hrebenar 1997, 187). The oldest continuous congressional voting record has been maintained by Americans for Democratic Action (ADA), which first issued a scorecard in 1947. The scorecards of the ADA and the American Conservative Union (ACU) include a wide variety of issues designed to assess candidates' general ideology, and the ADA and ACU ratings are often used by political scientists to measure the liberalism and conservatism of members of Congress. For many years, in order to attract greater publicity and influence voting decisions, the ADA and ACU released their scorecards in a joint press conference after Labor Day each election year.

Some interest groups evaluate candidates' positions on a range of issues in a single domain. The Family Foundation of Virginia, for example, rates state legislators' "family-friendly" votes on issues that range from sex education to abortion to tax rates. In 2004 the Family Research Council, another conservative Christian group, issued a scorecard rating members of Congress on twenty-one votes. The scorecard gives legislators a plus or a minus for their votes on issues such as abortion, gay marriage, and even the estate tax (Family Research Council 2004). Scorecards generally address votes and not behavior, which can lead to occasional problems. In the 1980s, the Christian Voice issued the "Morality Scorecard," which attracted widespread attention and derision when it was revealed that the group had given some ordained religious leaders scores of 0 and awarded scores of 100 to some House members who had been convicted in the Abscam corruption probe or censured for sexual affairs with teenage pages (Wilcox 1992).

Most interest groups rate candidates on a narrow set of issues of special interest to the group's membership. The LCV describes its National Environmental Scorecard as "an annual report card on how Congress votes on the environment" (Mundo 1999). The National Federation of Independent Businesses rates legislators according to roll call votes on bills affecting small business.

The HRC scorecard for the 108th Congress rates "where members of Congress stand on equality issues" for gay and lesbian voters (Human Rights Campaign 2004). The votes in the scorecard may have been taken on final passage of legislation, on amendments, or on procedure. HRC devised a rating scale based on representatives' records on crucial votes, such as the Federal Marriage Amendment. The scorecard included a brief explanation of each of the eight issues that the House voted on and then identified the organization's formal position (in favor or opposed). For each vote, the group gave each member of the House either a blue-filled circle (for voting right) or an empty circle (for voting wrong). A representative who voted "right" seven times out of eight, for example, received an 88-percent positive rating from the group.

Scorecard ratings depend critically on which votes are selected for counting. For example, if ten or fewer votes are counted, then the selection of two roll calls can change an incumbent's score by 20 percent or more. In some cases interest groups deliberately—sometimes quite transparently—manipulate the ratings to inflate or deflate candidates' scores. In early 1996 the Christian Coalition released a congressional scorecard that gave incumbent GOP senator John Warner, of Virginia, a 100-percent rating. Yet several months later, challenged in a GOP primary by the more conservative James Miller, Warner suddenly found himself with only a 23-percent favorable rating from the Christian Coalition's voters' guide. After Warner won renomination and was challenged by a pro-choice Democrat, the coalition issued a new voters' guide that focused on different issues and gave Warner an 86-percent positive rating (Rozell and Wilcox 1997).

Like endorsements, legislative scorecards do not always have the positive impact hoped for by the organization that issues them. Candidates sometimes use positive ratings from particular groups to mobilize voters against their opponents. Southern Democrats, for example, often find it difficult to defend a high ADA score. Nevertheless, scorecards do signal to interest group members and others sympathetic to the group's goals precisely which incumbents are the most supportive, enabling the group to target its resources to those candidates.

Ratings and scorecards generally rate all incumbent members of the House and Senate on selected roll call votes on bills, amendments, and motions of concern to the organization. Voters' guides differ in several ways. First, they provide information on the policy preferences of incumbents and nonincumbents alike. Second, they are generally tailored to particular electoral constituencies. Wyoming voters, for example, would receive a guide rating presidential, Senate, and House candidates in that state; voters in Montgomery County, Maryland, would receive similar information about presidential candidates, but the information about Senate and House candidates would apply only to their jurisdiction. Finally, voters' guides are usually distributed a few days before an election and are designed to be taken into the ballot box to guide voting directly.

Voters' guides sometimes provoke controversy because they can contain misleading information. In the 1994 Virginia Senate campaign, despite Democratic incumbent Charles Robb's support for the "Helms amendment" to cut federal funding for "offensive art," a Christian Coalition voters' guide characterized Robb as favoring funding for "obscene art." Robb had voted for a federal budget package that included funding for the National Endowment for the Arts, and included in that package was funding for art that many social conservatives considered offensive. Of course, many conservative senators also voted for the federal budget, and in states where the coalition supported conservative candidates who had voted for the budget, it did not characterize them as supporting "obscene art." The Christian Coalition distributed some 1.7 million voters' guides in the Virginia Senate race alone (Rozell and Wilcox 1996).

Sometimes the same voters' guide would have different impact if distributed in different places. Consider a guide distributed by the Palmetto Family Council, a conservative Christian group in South Carolina affiliated with the Family Research Council. The guide focuses on three issues: abortion, gay marriage, and education (Palmetto Family Council 2004). The education section expresses the Palmetto Council's concern with gay teachers in schools. The education headline reads, "On who could teach our children." Above the headline are photographs of the two South Carolina Senate candidates separated by a blue line. Below the headline is a quote from Republican Jim DeMint: "Openly gay teachers should not be teaching in public schools. We need the folks that are teaching in schools to represent our values." DeMint's quote is paired with one from Democrat Inez Tenenbaum: "A person who is a homosexual and who wants to teach in our public schools has to be allowed to." When distributed in conservative churches, the Palmetto Family Council guide would doubtlessly help DeMint, but if distributed instead in liberal churches, it might well have helped Tenenbaum.

Voters' guides are produced for all kinds of elections. The Mississippi Center for Public Policy, also affiliated with the Family Research Council, issues voters' guides for state Supreme Court justices. In 2004 the group issued a voters' guide listing judicial candidates' answers to four questions (Mississippi Center for Public Policy 2004). One of the questions asked the candidates to list any group of which they had been a member in the past ten years. Another asked, "Which one of the current Justices of the U.S. Supreme Court most reflects your judicial philosophy?"

VOTER MOBILIZATION

An interest group's impact on an election is a function of its size, its voting cohesion, and its participation rate. Even small groups can influence elections if their members vote in large numbers and vote for the same candidates, whereas even large groups can have little influence if their members stay at home on Election Day or divide their votes among the candidates. Thus, when interest groups communicate with their members, supporters, and the general public, they are seeking not only to influence voting decisions but also to increase turnout at the polls.

Groups that can effectively deliver their members to the polls are sought after by parties and candidates trying to assemble electoral coalitions. Moreover, such groups can often use the cohesiveness of their membership as a lobbying asset. For example, when NRA leaders first approach a new member of Congress, they may tell her the number of NRA members in her district. The intent is to convey that many NRA members base their voting decisions primarily on gun rights issues and NRA endorsements. A simple membership count would thus indicate to a new House member that the NRA can help deliver those votes to her—or to her opponent—in the next election and that her degree of support for NRA issues could swing many votes.

Like endorsements and ratings, voter mobilization efforts sometimes have unanticipated consequences. The coordinated efforts in the 1960s to mobilize black voters in the South succeeded impressively, but white turnout increased at a similar rate (Rosenstone and Hansen 1993). In many states, voter mobilization efforts by the Christian Right have caused countermobilizations by moderate suburbanites, helping Democratic candidates to win elections (Rozell and Wilcox 1995). Nevertheless, such countermobilizations are often less enduring than the effects of sustained efforts by interest groups to politicize their members.

Steven Rosenstone and John Mark Hansen (1993) argued that voter mobilization efforts by social movement organizations succeed because they lower the costs of participation and increase the benefits. Many citizens find elections confusing and may not even be sure how and where to register to vote. Phone calls and other contact by interest groups can help citizens register to vote, and groups sometimes even transport voters to the polls, greatly reducing the cost of the voting act. Voters' guides and endorsements reduce the information costs of the voting decision. By creating a network of social expectations, voter mobilization efforts increase the benefits of voting as well.

In the past several elections, voter mobilization has become more central to group efforts. With the public closely divided between the two parties, and party control in Congress hinging on a few votes, groups have sought to mobilize their members and even citizens who are not members or supporters of their groups. In the 1998 Senate election in Wisconsin, for example, environmental groups targeted black voters concerned with lead-based paint, rather than environmentalist citizens (Wilcox 2000).

In addition to undertaking voter mobilization, many groups attempt to recruit activists to participate more broadly in elections—to volunteer their time and money on behalf of candidates, to work within their social networks and communities to persuade friends and acquaintances to support candidates, and to perform many other tasks that benefit candidates and parties. The usefulness of this tactic depends not on how many members an interest group has but on the size and devotion of its activist core.

Tactics

Many groups communicate directly with their members to urge them to vote. A week before the elections, the NRA distributes a bright orange 3 x 5 endorsement card as a reminder to its members—a tactic that the group's executive director for legislative affairs calls one of its most effective communication tools. (See Figure 4-1.)

FIGURE 4-1

NRA-PVF Endorsement Card

NC-state

VOTE FREEDOM FIRST -- VOTE FOR *RICHARD BURR FOR U.S. SENATE* ON NOVEMBER 2

Dear North Carolina NRA Member: October 25, 2004

The Second Amendment needs your help -- today. **The NRA Political Victory Fund (www.NRAPVF.org) has endorsed Richard Burr for U.S. Senate to protect your gun rights and hunting heritage, and he needs your vote to win!**

Your vote on Election Day -- Tuesday, November 2 -- will determine the future of the Second Amendment. If we win at the polls, we can move forward to strengthen our Right to Keep and Bear Arms. But if we lose, it will only be a matter of time before Congress moves to restrict your rights, register your guns and regulate your freedoms.

During his tenure in Congress, Richard Burr has always stood with the NRA in our fight to protect the constitutional rights of law-abiding Americans, and he has earned his "A" rating from the NRA-PVF. In contrast, his opponent -- Erskine Bowles -- served as Chief of Staff for the most anti-gun President in history and he supports banning guns. The choice is clear!

That's why it's critically important for you and every freedom-loving voter in North Carolina to vote for Richard Burr for U.S. Senate. The NRA Political Victory Fund has endorsed Richard Burr for Senate because he is a tested and proven friend of gun owners and sportsmen who deserves your vote.

Vote for Richard Burr for Senate on November 2, and encourage all of your family, friends, and fellow hunters and shooters to do the same! The future of your Second Amendment rights depends on it!

NATIONAL RIFLE ASSOCIATION INSTITUTE FOR LEGISLATIVE ACTION

P.S. Please vote for George Bush for President

Source: Used with the permission of the National Rifle Association of America Institute for Legislative Action.

A highly innovative approach to communicating with interest group members and supporters was the 1996 Interfaith Alliance "voter's pledge." Modeled after the candidate pledges (for example, not to raise taxes) of other organizations, the Interfaith Alliance pledge asked voters to commit to taking the elections seriously by studying the issues, learning the candidates' positions, and actually voting. The goal of the pledge was not merely to provide a public service by asking people to focus on the elections, but more directly to help turn out voters who shared the organization's faith-based moderate and progressive views.

Most often, interest groups reach voters by telephone. Labor unions generally organize phone banks in districts and states with close elections, calling union members and their families and encouraging them to participate. In 2000, labor unions were credited with making some eight million phone calls. Many other interest groups call selected members before an election and urge them to vote. In closely contested races, voters may get many phone calls from different groups urging them to vote. In one state legislative race in Virginia in 2003, Democratic voters received calls from NARAL, the National Organization for Women, the Sierra Club, and several other groups during the last week of the campaign. Many were prerecorded messages designed to be left on answering machines (calling machines are frequently programmed to disconnect if they reach a live voter). Most observers believe that a personal phone call is far more effective than a recorded one. Some groups mail glossy reminders and sample ballots to members in carefully targeted districts, and a few are beginning to experiment with Internet (e-mail) reminders to vote.

In some cases, groups send their members door-to-door to personally talk with group members and encourage them to vote. Research suggests that these personal contacts are the most effective in increasing voter turnout (Gerber and Green 2000). Such personal contacts are quite expensive, but in very close elections they may make the difference. In 2000 the NAACP created two new advocacy organizations and sought to register new minority voters in thirteen states. More than eight thousand volunteers went door-to-door in minority neighborhoods, explaining the importance of the election and urging citizens to register and vote. The group also created a registry of some 3.8 million African Americans in major cities in forty congressional districts. The group made more than seven phone calls to each of more than one million minority households. The group also mailed mobilization messages to select households (Biersack and Viray 2004). The mail and phone efforts do not appear to have had a major effect on turnout (Green 2004), but there has been no systematic study of the impact of face-to-face mobilization by volunteers.

Interest groups can also try to mobilize potential voters who are not group members. Often interest groups target potentially sympathetic voters and help them register to vote. In 2000 the AFL-CIO was credited with helping to register some 2.3 million people (Biersack and Viray 2004). In 2004, interest groups worked in coalitions to register voters in battleground states.

Observers have estimated that interest groups spent more than $350 million in get-out-the-vote drives in the 2004 elections. In Florida, unions and civil rights groups coordinated their efforts to reach targeted precincts. The Chamber of Commerce and other business groups sought to reach employees of companies that had benefited under the Bush administration through e-mails, fliers, and even messages included in envelopes with paychecks. Some groups sought to mobilize absentee voting among the military and among contractors in the Persian Gulf. Many groups sent volunteers door-to-door, urging voters to cast early absentee votes in states where this was easy to do. Much of this effort was conducted by new groups, such as Floridians for All, Americans Coming Together, National Voice, and the Prosperity Project. Although most of these new groups were 501(c)(3) organizations and therefore were not required to disclose their donors, many clearly were funded by existing interest groups or by the wealthy members of those groups (Moss and Fessenden 2004).

Interest groups that have strong attachments to particular parties often try to mobilize not only their own members but also other potentially sympathetic voters. Thus Democratic-leaning groups have sought to mobilize minority voters, regardless of whether they support the group's agenda, and Republican-leaning groups have sought to mobilize conservative Christians, even if the groups were not individually concerned with social issues.

Churches provide a special forum for voter mobilization efforts because they are full of active individuals who share common beliefs and always have a meeting two days before an election. Both Christian conservative groups and liberal civil rights groups make a special effort to recruit ministers, who can be instrumental in mobilizing voters. In the black community, churches often mount voter registration drives, and on the Sunday before Election Day, pastors inevitably exhort their members to vote, often for particular Democratic candidates. In recent years, white evangelical churches have become the locus of voter mobilization efforts as well. In the early 1980s, the Moral Majority mounted voter registration drives in fundamentalist churches; and in 1988 many Pentecostal pastors encouraged their members to participate in the GOP primaries and caucuses in support of Pat Robertson. As mentioned in Chapter 1, in 2004 Let Freedom Ring produced a video that highlighted George W. Bush's personal faith and distributed this video to pastors in Ohio and Pennsylvania to show in their churches prior to the election. The video was accompanied by a flier offering free legal help if this action endangered the church's tax-exempt status.

Because churches are tax-exempt charities, they cannot endorse candidates, although to date only one church has lost its tax-exempt status, for buying an advertisement that claimed that "A vote for Bill Clinton is a vote against God." Republicans have pushed for a "Houses of Worship Freedom of Speech Act" that would allow churches to endorse candidates and maintain their tax-exempt status. But many conservative pastors who personally support Republican candidates do not support the act, for fear that there will be internal dissention in their church and strong pressure to endorse particular candidates.

Financing

Voter mobilization efforts often involve creative financing, with money transferred freely between interest groups, political parties, and special voter mobilization projects. Special ad-hoc, "nonpartisan" voter mobilization projects can receive tax-exempt contributions from individuals and organizations as long as they do not advocate the election of specific candidates. An example of a truly nonpartisan voters' drive is Rock the Vote, a group formed in 1992 with the goal of mobilizing young voters, who are notoriously apathetic. In that election year, the group relied primarily on concerts, mass rallies, and targeted television advertising on youth-oriented programs to deliver its message. In 2004 Rock the Vote used similar high-visibility tactics such as targeting the electronic music scene by using as its spokesperson DJ Paul Van Dyk, voted America's favorite DJ in *BPM Magazine*. However, the group also uses more subtle approaches, such as helping young people to register to vote on its Web site, answering frequently asked questions, and providing downloadable forms. A wide range of other nonpartisan organizations made significant efforts to encourage young people to vote in 2004, including the New Voters Project, Hip-Hop Summit Action Network, World Wrestling Entertainment Smackdown Your Vote!, and P Diddy's Citizen Change.

Because most voter mobilization efforts are officially nonpartisan, they are not permitted to focus on just one party or candidate. In practice, such efforts often subtly (or not so subtly) help one party or candidate more than another—for example, by targeting precincts where most voters are likely to support candidates of one party. In 2004 labor gave millions of dollars and lent staff assistance and expertise to nonpartisan voter registration projects working primarily in districts targeted by the AFL-CIO. During the election the AFL-CIO paid for more than 5,500 full-time staff or union members to do such work, up from 1,500 in 2000. Democratic voter mobilization efforts might be centered in poor inner-city areas with substantial minority populations, and GOP projects might be focused in rural white areas of the South.

Interest groups can contribute money or services to other interest groups that are mounting voter mobilization campaigns or can coordinate with those groups and provide them with goods and services. The National Committee for an Effective Congress (NCEC) specializes in producing studies that help candidates and interest groups target their resources to maximum benefit. The NCEC shares its information with Democratic Party officials, with special voter mobilization projects, and with the AFL-CIO and other liberal groups to enable them to more successfully reach likely Democratic voters.

At times, political parties have contributed money to interest groups to help them mobilize their members. The Republican National Committee (RNC) steered millions of dollars in contributions from its major donors to sympathetic organizations, including the National Right to Life Committee and Americans for Tax Reform. The largest contribution went to the American Defense Institute, which runs voter mobilization campaigns for military personnel (Marcus 1997b). Toward the end of the 1996 election cycle, the RNC gave large donations to these three groups—including more than $4 million to Americans for Tax Reform—to help mount get-out-the-vote drives. The Bipartisan Campaign Reform Act of 2002 makes such aide by parties problematic, and some conservative activists noted that the National Right to Life Committee was far less active in the 2004 campaign when it could not rely on Republican funding for its efforts. In 2003–2004 the Democratic National Committee gave money to consulting firms that helped organize 527 committees such as America Coming Together, which sought to mobilize voters in the 2004 election. America Coming Together was also backed by the AFL-CIO, the Sierra Club, and other groups that sought the defeat of President Bush.

Coalitions

Just as individuals become more effective political actors by forming groups, groups become more effective by forming coalitions. If a single interest group mobilizing its base of supporters is a formidable force in electoral politics, then a collection of groups is that much more so. Some coalitions are formal, featuring their own letterheads with a list of member groups.

But an informal coalition of groups can be every bit as influential, perhaps even more so. During the late 1990s, Grover Norquist assembled the "Leave Us Alone" coalition, which played an important role in bringing together conservative groups with disparate interests. The coalition included leaders and members of groups such as the U.S. Chamber of

Commerce, the Christian Coalition, the Eagle Forum, the Heritage Foundation, the National Right to Life Committee, Republicans for Choice, the Small Business Survival Committee, property rights groups, and home-schooling groups.

Although the members of the coalition had clear differences on certain issues, they agreed to put aside these differences when working together to help elect conservative candidates. As Norquist explained to reporter Elizabeth Drew:

> If everyone in the room can agree—the gun owners agree not to throw condoms at the Christian kids, and the Christian groups agree not to steal anybody else's guns, and the small business groups agree not to raise anybody else's taxes, and the tax groups agree not to take other people's property—as long as everybody agrees not to screw with anybody else—everyone's happy. And everybody can leave and spend the rest of the day crushing the left. It's a low-maintenance coalition. (Drew 1997, 6)

The coalition met regularly in the 1996 campaign to discuss strategy. In one meeting, the day after the New Hampshire primary, representatives from about seventy groups discussed strategy for the rest of the campaign. Dismayed by the victory of conservative commentator Patrick Buchanan, who many feared would cost the GOP its control of Congress, coalition members agreed to cooperate throughout the campaign to prop up GOP House members and challengers in competitive races. The coalition continued to exist in 2004, although less is known about its more recent activities.

In 2004, liberal groups formed many formal and informal coalitions to coordinate their efforts to defeat President Bush. Labor, civil rights, feminist, and environmental group leaders spoke often about strategy and formed a variety of 527 committees designed to help coordinate their actions. They shared polling information and voter contact lists, and they frequently divided key states precinct by precinct so that there was less duplication of effort in voter mobilization.

In election years, interest groups often work together to push politically charged issues onto the legislative agenda. This strategy increases the likelihood that particular policies that the groups support will become law. Alternatively, if the proposals do not pass, coalition members are better able to use the issues to mobilize their own groups in the election. In 2004, Christian conservatives pushed George W. Bush hard to endorse an amendment to the U.S. Constitution that would define marriage as between a man and a woman, thereby stopping gay marriage in Massachusetts. Republicans agreed to schedule a vote on the measure, even though there was no chance that it would pass the Senate, just to put Democratic candidates John Kerry and John Edwards on record as opposing the amendment.

In other cases the bills pass, which helps advance the group's policy agenda but deprives it of an issue on which to mobilize. In 1996, labor groups pushed hard for enactment of an increase in the minimum wage—legislation unlikely to emerge from a GOP Congress. But the proposal was enormously popular, and under the implicit threat that unions would be able to mobilize their membership and appeal to the larger electorate over this issue, many Republicans voted for the bill, which passed and was signed by the president. Similarly, in 1996, social conservative groups—betting that President Clinton would issue a veto—pushed for enactment of the Defense of Marriage Act. Their strategy was to inject the issue of gay rights into the campaign and provoke a massive mobilization of social conservatives at the polls. Despite reservations, the president signed the bill—a decision few believe he would have taken in a nonelection year.

INDEPENDENT EXPENDITURES AND ISSUE ADVOCACY

Under the tax laws, activities classified as voter mobilization must be nonpartisan efforts to encourage citizens to participate in elections and are not permitted to show or recommend support for specific candidates and issues. To persuade their members and other citizens to elect or defeat a particular candidate, interest groups must use other means—principally, independent expenditures and issue advocacy.

Independent Expenditures

PACs have made independent expenditures in support of candidates since 1976, when a Supreme Court ruling allowed them to do so. Ideological groups discovered the efficacy of the technique in 1980 and began using it effectively. In the 1980 New Hampshire presidential primary, Republican candidate Ronald Reagan benefited from more than $250,000 in independent expenditures undertaken by the Fund for a Conservative Majority—

spending that some observers credited with helping Reagan prevail in that "must win" election. In the 1980 general election, the National Conservative Political Action Committee (NCPAC) targeted for defeat a number of Democratic House incumbents and six Democratic senators who had voted in 1978 for the Panama Canal Treaty. NCPAC spent more than $1 million in advertising in those races, airing commercials that attacked the incumbents on issues such as government spending, defense spending, and abortion. One advertisement against Idaho's Frank Church aired throughout the state 150 times daily for five weeks (Schlozman and Tierney 1986, 216). Four of the senators lost, although it is unclear how much NCPAC's ads contributed to their defeat. NCPAC's director, Terry Dolan, bragged that NCPAC "could elect Mickey Mouse to the House and Senate" and said that his group could issue false statements in its advertising without tainting the candidate—because the candidate would have had nothing to do with the ad. The PAC's ads severely distorted the records of the candidates they targeted for defeat (Sabato 1984; Schlozman and Tierney 1986).

The NRA and the American Medical Association (AMA) spent more money on independent expenditures than did any other group from 1989 to 2004, according to the Center for Responsive Politics (Center for Responsive Politics 2005c). The NRA spent over $14 million during this time period, and the AMA spent over $7 million. More than 80 percent of these groups' independent expenditures supported Republican candidates.

Independent expenditure campaigns are sometimes launched in the primary elections as well. One such effort occurred in the 2004 Pennsylvania Senate primary for the Republican Party. Incumbent Arlen Specter, a moderate Republican, was challenged by conservative representative Patrick Toomey. The Club for Growth, a conservative anti-tax group, spent over $400,000 to help Toomey (Wayne 2004). The Club for Growth ran television ads attacking Specter, saying his voting record was as liberal as that of Senator John Kerry. In response, the Specter campaign filed a complaint with the FEC, asserting that the organization illegally coordinated campaign expenditures with the Toomey campaign, an accusation the club denies. Specter won the primary and the general election and was endorsed by President Bush.

In 2004, PACs spent nearly $100 million to advocate the election or defeat of candidates for federal office. The vast majority of this spending was by nonconnected, trade, and membership PACs. Most independent expenditures were targeted to the presidential election and to congressional candidates in close primary or general election contests. This is in

TABLE 4-1

Group Involvement in 2004 U.S. Senate Race in South Dakota

For Daschle	Against Daschle	For Thune	Against Thune
American Chiropractic Association	Campaign for Working Families	American Watercraft Association	League of Conservation Voters
International Association of Firefighters	Capital Hill Prayer Alert Committee Election Fund	Associated Builders and Contractors	Planned Parenthood Action Fund, Inc.
	National Right to Life Committee	Ave Maria List PAC	
	South Dakota Pro-Life Committee	Club for Growth	
	You're Fired	Focus on the Family Action	
		National Federation of Independent Businesses	
		Free Enterprise Trust	
		National Right to Life Committee	
		National Right to Work Committee	

Source: Compiled by authors.

sharp contrast to PAC contributions, described in Chapter 3, which often go to candidates who face little or no competition. Independent expenditures are made to influence elections, not to gain access to incumbents.

As illustrated in Table 4-1, a number of groups made independent expenditures in the 2004 South Dakota Senate race, where Democratic Party leader Tom Daschle was defeated by John Thune. The table shows the groups that ran ads for and against the two candidates. One ad, aired by the Ave Maria List PAC, a pro-life Catholic group, charged

> What's happened to Tom Daschle? When Tom Daschle ran for Congress, he sent a letter to South Dakota voters. He called abortion an abhorrent practice. Strong words. Tom Daschle sent another letter; not many South Dakota voters got this one. In this letter he urged people to support and send money to the largest pro-abortion group, NARAL. Tom Daschle even sent $10,000 in campaign funds to another pro-abortion group. Still, Tom Daschle tries to claim he's pro-life even though his voting record and actions in Washington prove he's not. Tom Daschle has changed and it's time for South Dakota voters to make a change of their own. (Lopez 2004)

Issue Advocacy

Although issue advocacy was allowed by the Supreme Court in 1976, not until the 1990s were its legal limits articulated by circuit courts. In 1996 the Supreme Court distinguished between speech that is "express advocacy," which includes exhortations to vote for a particular candidate, and speech that merely advocates particular positions on issues. In 1991 the First Circuit Court allowed the Maine Right to Life Committee (MRLC) to distribute voters' guides that included (1) candidate and party positions on abortion, (2) information on whether a particular vote was consistent with the position of the National Right to Life Committee, and (3) a statement claiming that the publication did not represent an endorsement of any candidates. In addition to allowing the distribution of the guides, the circuit court allowed the MRLC to use corporate revenues to finance publication of the voters' guides.

In 1995 the Fourth Circuit Court upheld a lower court ruling that a 1992 advertisement funded by the Christian Action Network did not expressly advocate the defeat of Bill Clinton.[2] The ad opened with a full-color picture of Bill Clinton's face

> superimposed upon an American flag, which is blowing in the wind. Clinton is shown smiling. As the narrator begins to describe Clinton's alleged support of "radical" homosexual causes, Clinton's image dissolves into a black and white photographic negative. The negative . . . gives Clinton a

sinister and threatening appearance . . . . The commercial then presents a series of pictures depicting advocates of homosexual rights . . . demonstrating at a political march . . . . As the scenes from the march continue, the narrator asks in a rhetorical fashion, "Is this your vision for a better America?" . . . The narrator then states, "for more information on traditional family values, contact the Christian Action Network." (advertisement cited in Potter 1997, 234–235)

This court decision and others like it opened the way for interest groups to spend millions of dollars on advertising and other efforts that were clearly designed to support or attack specific candidates but that avoided using the "magic words" that constitute express advocacy. Early in the 1996 election cycle, the AFL-CIO announced plans to spend $35 million on issue advocacy in carefully selected House districts where newly elected GOP representatives might be vulnerable to defeat. The organization initially targeted 75 House Republicans, eventually expanding that number to more than 100 (Herrnson 1997). In an advocacy campaign that was coordinated with voter mobilization efforts by labor and with the grassroots activities of many other organizations (Gerber 1999; Herrnson 1997), the AFL-CIO spent $25 million to air 27,000 television commercials in forty-four House districts and distributed more than 11 million voters' guides comparing Democratic and Republican stances without explicitly endorsing candidates.

Issue advocacy campaigns have increased sharply since that time. Most interest groups prefer issue advocacy to independent expenditures because its funding is more flexible. Independent expenditures are funded through PACs, with limits on the amounts that a single individual can give. As mentioned earlier in this chapter, issue advocacy campaigns can be funded from treasuries: from corporate profits, labor union dues, and large contributions from individuals. In the 2000 presidential races, Planned Parenthood launched a television issue advocacy campaign against GOP candidate George Bush, spending $7 million dollars that was apparently raised from a single donor (Malbin, Wilcox, Rozell, and Skinner 2002).

A few issue advocacy campaigns are humorous. In 2000 an ad that ran in the New York Senate race showed a host of babies of different races and ages, wearing different styles of clothing. The voiceover asked, "What do all of these babies have in common? They have all lived in New York longer than Hillary Rodham Clinton." Other ad campaigns take a generally positive tone: Let Freedom Ring featured a contest with a cash prize for the best advertisements to run on its Web site, and these ads were required to be positive in tone because the most generous patron of the group and its president both agreed that campaigns had become too negative.

In the 2004 presidential campaign, the NRA sought to portray Democratic nominee John Kerry as a supporter of gun control. The Kerry campaign created photo-ops of the candidate hunting ducks, showing him comfortably handling rifles. The NRA ad featured a French poodle wearing a Kerry sweater, with the caption "That dog don't hunt." (See ad, following page.) The ad was featured (with sound) on the NRA's Web site and was included in mailings to NRA members. The organization also created T-shirts, caps, and other novelty items. "It became the centerpiece image in a "No quiero John Kerry" campaign that included more than six million postcards and letters, nearly as many fliers and bumper stickers, and an expensive media campaign made up of 28,000 television commercials, 20,000 radio spots, 1,700 newspaper ads, and more than 500 billboard messages" (Miller 2005).[3]

But most issue advocacy campaigns are very negative in tone, pushing charges that candidates themselves would never make for fear of alienating voters. One Swift Boat Veterans for Truth ad showed John Kerry testifying before the Senate Committee on Foreign Relations in 1971 arguing against the U.S. role in Vietnam. The advertisement concluded that Kerry "dishonored his country, but more importantly, the people he served with. He just sold them out" (Center for Responsive Politics n.d.). Other ads by the same group showed many individuals charging that Kerry had lied about his war record. The ads brought a sharp rebuke from Republican senator John McCain, himself a decorated war hero.

In 2004 MoveOn.org made defeating George W. Bush a priority. The group ran many issue ads attacking the president, some of them produced by famous movie directors. One of the group's ads entitled "Platter" aired in the battleground states of Ohio, Missouri, Oregon, Nevada, as well as in Washington, D.C. The ad focused on claims that Halliburton (a defense contracting firm that Vice President Dick Cheney formerly headed) drastically overcharged the government after receiving no-bid contracts for Iraq. The ad charged President Bush with "A failure of leadership" (Center for Responsive Politics n.d.).

One of the nastiest issue advocacy campaigns was conducted in a race for the West Virginia Supreme Court. An interest group, And For the Sake of the Kids, ran issue advocacy ads highly critical of the incumbent

That dog don't hunt.

John Kerry says he supports sportsmen's rights. But his record says something else.

John Kerry voted for Ted Kennedy's amendment to outlaw most ammunition used by deer hunters.[1]

John Kerry supports higher taxes on firearms and ammunition.[2]

John Kerry voted in favor of banning semi-automatic firearms, including many firearms favored by sportsmen.[3]

John Kerry voted to allow big city politicians to sue the American firearms industry and hold legitimate firearms manufacturers and dealers responsible for the acts of criminals.[4]

John Kerry voted to close off hundreds of thousands of acres to hunters.[5]

John Kerry voted to commend Rosie O'Donnell's Million Mom March, an organization calling for gun owner licensing, gun registration, and other radical restrictions on law-abiding gun owners.[6]

With a 20-year record of voting against sportsmen's rights, it's no wonder John Kerry has been called a "hero" by the Humane Society of the United States, an extremist group that wants to outlaw hunting in America.[7]

If John Kerry wins, you lose.

NRA-POLITICAL VICTORY FUND
11250 Waples Mill Road · Fairfax, Virginia 22030 · www.NRAPVF.org · Chris W. Cox, Chairman

VOTE FREEDOM FIRST

[1] Voted for Kennedy Amendment to S.1805 (3/2/2004). [2] On CNN "Late Edition" (11/7/1993) Kerry said "I think you ought to tax all ammunition more, personally. I think you ought to tax guns." [3] Nine separate votes for gun ban legislation. Most recently, Kerry voted to amend S.1805 to include the Feinstein amendment to reauthorize the Clinton gun ban for ten years (3/2/2004). [4] Voted to amend S.1805 to include gun ban legislation, effectively killing lawsuit reform legislation. [5] Voted against Wallop Amendment to S.21 (8/25/1994). [6] Voted for Daschle Amendment to S.2521 (5/17/2000). [7] Humane Society of the United States (not the American Humane Society), which wants to ban all sport hunting in America, called Kerry a "hero" for his anti-hunting record (see www.HSUS.org).

Democratic justice for extending the probation of a convicted sex offender. The sharp ads helped the Republican challenger, who won the state Supreme Court seat in a close election. The name of the group implied that it was a citizens' group formed to protect children against sex offenders, but in fact the group was funded primarily by a single donor, Don Blankenship, chief executive of Massey Energy Co., a coal company. According to the *Washington Post*, "The coal company is one of the largest employers in the state, and it is expected to have several cases on appeal before the state Supreme Court" (Morello 2004). In this case the coal company expected to do better before the Court with a Republican judge, and its president formed an "organization" to attack the Democratic incumbent.

As the preceding example illustrates, the organizations that mount issue advocacy campaigns are sometimes not groups at all, but rather are fronts for one or a few individuals. The names chosen for these pseudogroups are often misleading. In John McCain's 2000 primary election contest against George W. Bush in New York, a group called Republicans for Clean Air ran the following television advertisement:

> Last year, John McCain voted against solar and renewable energy. That means more use of coal-burning plants that pollute our air. Ohio Republicans care about clean air. So does Governor Bush. He led one of the first states in America to clamp down on old coal-burning electric power plants. Bush's clean air laws will reduce air pollution more than a quarter million tons a year. That's like taking 5 million cars off the road. Governor Bush, leading, for each day dawns brighter.

At the time, the law did not require the group to publicly disclose the names of its funders. Voters may have assumed the ad was financed by an environmental group, but later the news media revealed that the ad was paid for by Charles and Sam Wyly, two Texas billionaires and long-time friends and contributors to Bush (Public Citizen 2005). In fact, environmental groups were quite positive in their assessment of John McCain, who was named among the environmental heroes by the LCV in 2004. As mentioned earlier, the league named Bush as one of its Dirty Dozen in 2004, the first time a sitting president has made the list. So the advertisement by Citizens for Clean Air created a totally false image that environmentalists supported Bush over McCain.

Similarly the United Seniors Association spent more than $2 million in a 2002 Pennsylvania House race that featured two redistricted incumbents from different parties, and more than $7 million overall during the campaign. The ads in Pennsylvania praised the Republican candidate for helping pass a prescription drug bill that aided seniors. The bill was strongly backed by the pharmaceutical industry, which helped to organize and principally fund the United Seniors Association. Voters might understandably think that the group was a citizens' organization of senior citizens, rather than a political arm of drug companies.

The 2004 campaign was the first conducted under the new Bipartisan Campaign Reform Act, and the FEC declined to regulate issue advertising by 527 committees and other groups, although the law gives the commission the authority to declare certain types of advertisements as campaign spending and require that they be paid for through a PAC. Senators McCain and Feingold have gone to court to try to force the FEC to implement regulations on this advertising consistent with the new law.

Issue advertising campaigns are controversial for several reasons. First, as we have noted, they are often conducted by entities with names that convey the notion of citizens concerned with a particular set of issues, when in fact they are funded by one or two wealthy individuals or companies with a very different agenda. Second, their charges are frequently misleading. Third, with few exceptions their tone is overwhelmingly negative, and the ads are frequently aimed at demobilizing supporters of the other candidate. In other words, many issue-advertising campaigns are designed to sow doubts among supporters of a candidate and, therefore, to discourage them from voting. There is considerable debate among political scientists as to whether the ads actually succeed in reducing turnout, but clearly campaign professionals believe they do, and intend them to do so.

Many candidates resent these ads, even when they seem to benefit their campaigns. In Pennsylvania's twenty-first district in 1996, for example, interest groups and party committees together spent more than $1.4 million on issue advocacy campaigns promoting the election or defeat of one candidate or the other, whereas Republican incumbent Phil English spent $1.2 million and Democratic challenger Ron DiNicola only $468,000. Both candidates complained that they were sometimes blindsided by advertising promoting their candidacies in ways that they did not approve (Gugliotta and Chinoy 1997). In Chapter 5 we return to the concerns raised by issue advocacy campaigns.

REFERENDA, INITIATIVES, AND RECALLS

Many citizens are increasingly put off by traditional political parties and their candidates, but interest groups have discovered that they can mobilize voters by creating opportunities for them to vote directly on issues of concern. A direct popular vote—through a referendum, an initiative, or a recall—is an increasingly common, albeit controversial, way for interest groups to mobilize their members and other voters.

Although interest groups place referenda on the ballot for many reasons, the most important is the opportunity to bypass state legislatures and governors and write the group's policy preferences directly into law—to expand or contract civil rights protections for gays and lesbians, to protect or restrict abortion rights, to favor one type of automotive insurance over another. Referenda serve other purposes, however, and interest groups sometimes place them on the ballot even when they are sure to lose. Referenda can (1) mobilize group members to become more politically active, (2) help groups recruit new members, (3) provide a forum to help persuade the public on an issue, and (4) increase voter turnout in other races that are also on the ballot.

In the 2004 elections, 163 initiatives and referenda appeared in the thirty-four states that permit the procedure. California voters approved a measure that earmarked $3 billion for embryonic stem cell research, after President Bush ordered a freeze on certain types of funding from the federal government. Colorado voters defeated a measure to change the state's winner-take-all electoral vote system to proportional allocation. But perhaps the most significant initiatives were the anti-gay-marriage proposals on the ballots in eleven states.

Several of the states with anti-gay-marriage initiatives, such as Ohio, Oregon, and Michigan, were battleground states in the presidential election, leading some observers to argue that the initiatives were part of presidential advisor Karl Rove's strategy to increase turnout among evangelical Christians. Rove had long maintained that a key to the 2004 election would be to increase turnout of evangelicals by four million because evangelicals tend to vote strongly in favor of Bush (Jacoby 2004). In postelection interviews, Rove stated that opposition to gay marriage was one of the most powerful forces in American politics and fundamental to the president's victory (Nagourney 2004). However, Rove also noted that though the anti-gay-marriage initiatives won in all eleven states, Bush did not carry Michigan or Oregon. In addition, some evangelical leaders argued that the president was slow to support their anti-gay-marriage efforts (Cooperman and Edsall 2004). Although the exact role of presidential politics in placing these initiatives on the ballot is unclear, their presence may well have helped Bush.

In some states, such as California, ballots typically include a long—sometimes numbing—list of initiatives. In 1996, for example, the California State Board of Elections sent every voter a book over two hundred pages long explaining all the ballot initiatives. Because only the most highly motivated voter is likely to have the time and energy to become informed on so many issues, many voters fail to vote on any initiatives. Thus ballot issues are often decided by a relatively small percentage of those who actually voted—a circumstance that strengthens the ability of organized groups to influence policy development directly. Among those most likely to have sufficient interest and inclination to vote on ballot initiatives are members and supporters of interest groups that have a stake in the outcome.

For many groups, the major challenge in promoting an initiative is meeting all the requirements to get on the ballot. State laws allowing initiatives to be placed on the ballot vary dramatically. In many cases the number of signatures required is so large that interest groups have begun hiring firms that pay workers to collect signatures. In California in 1996, Common Cause and the League of Women Voters worked with other public interest organizations to collect the required 700,000 signatures for a campaign finance initiative, hiring firms that were ultimately responsible for collecting about half of the signatures. The state director of Common Cause said that to have been able to collect as many as half of the needed signatures through volunteers was an outstanding achievement, noting that interest groups in California typically paid for most of signature collection (Tollerson 1996).

Paying for signature collection is controversial because the principle behind the popular referendum is that an issue with substantial grassroots support—but perhaps lacking the clout that comes with big money—can have a chance at success through direct popular vote. A large base of volunteers, intense enough in their beliefs to invest time and effort in collecting the required number of signatures, is strong evidence of an issue's popularity and legitimacy. With paid signature collection, however, moneyed interests have a substantial advantage in using the initiative process to promote their agendas.

SUMMARY

Interest groups with large memberships or well-stocked treasuries frequently try to influence election outcomes by communicating with their members and other voters in efforts designed to help specific candidates. Although tax law forbids some interest groups from endorsing candidates, the law is sufficiently vague and enforcement lax enough to enable most groups to find ways to communicate their preferences to members and other voters. Moreover, spending on such activities is often unregulated, meaning that it can be financed by interest group treasuries and need not be reported to the FEC.

Issue advocacy—the latest form of direct communication with voters—is increasingly the major activity that interest groups use to mobilize and convince potential voters. Issue advocacy campaigns raise many important issues. They frequently involve very negative advertisements, often with misleading charges. And although there is some disclosure for 527 committees that run issue ads, 501 committees are not required to disclose their donors. This means that we are often unsure precisely who is behind a particular set of advertisements. We return to this issue in Chapter 5.

NOTES

1. The number and extent of stealth candidacies was always exaggerated in the media, and few groups now encourage such tactics.
2. *Federal Election Commission v. Christian Action Network,* 92 F.2d 1178 (4th Cir. 1996).
3. The NRA depiction of the dainty French poodle ad was humorous and doubtlessly effective, although in fact the poodle is used in Europe as a hunting dog.

CHAPTER 5

Evaluating the Role of Interest
Groups in Elections

Chapters 2, 3, and 4 described the myriad ways in which interest groups participate in elections—from grassroots mobilization to cash and in-kind contributions, from recruiting and training candidates to conducting independent expenditure and issue advocacy campaigns. This concluding chapter addresses two questions: First, what are the positive and negative elements of interest group involvement in elections? Second, what kind of changes might we make in laws, regulations, and practices to improve the ways in which interest groups are involved in elections, and thereby also improve the ways in which American elections are conducted?

POSITIVE AND NEGATIVE ASPECTS
OF INTEREST GROUP INVOLVEMENT

There is little agreement among political scientists, journalists, or even interest group activists about the role of interest groups in elections. At one extreme, interest groups can be viewed as pure democracy in action: aggregating the voices of individual Americans, articulating their concerns, drawing them into the electoral system, and raising money to finance candidates' campaigns. Most observers who offer an unqualified defense of interest group involvement in American politics argue that although short-term disturbances may temporarily favor one group or set of groups, competing forces will mobilize to redress imbalances, and the interest group universe will achieve balance over the long term. Others reject the notion that balance is a goal: in their view, the participation of interest groups in electoral processes embodies the basic principles of American democracy—freedom of speech and the right of assembly— and any regulations, including those already on the books, are infringements of individual liberty.

At the other extreme are those who believe that almost every aspect of interest group involvement in politics is damaging to the electoral process. According to this view, when interest groups seek nominations for their own members, they usurp the power of parties. When they create advertisements to sway the larger electorate, they usurp the role not only of parties but also of the candidates themselves. When they help finance elections, they buy or "rent" members of Congress, influencing the content of legislation in ways that may be harmful to the nation as a whole. When they endorse candidates, they create misleading and oversimplified messages and distort incumbents' records, often sponsoring "attack" advertising campaigns that increase public cynicism and decrease voter turnout. Finally, when interest groups place ideological purity above all else, they undermine the pragmatic compromise that is the bedrock of American democracy.

In sum, analysts and observers who are concerned about interest group participation in electoral politics see it as the embodiment of the factionalism that James Madison feared. Many view the interest group universe as highly unbalanced—dominated by corporate America or by corporations and unions, each out for its own financial gain. Critics note that although many Americans are not members of interest groups, their voices go unheard, drowned out amid the shouting of interest group activists.

Few people take such extreme positions, of course. We believe that there is some truth to what both defenders and critics of interest groups have to say. In our view, the current and evolving role of interest groups has positive and negative implications for the conduct of American elections and for democracy more broadly. To get a closer look at these implications, we reconsider the major activities covered in Chapters 2, 3, and 4: communication with parties, with candidates, and with voters.

Interest Groups and Parties

Although interest groups and social movements have long been active in American political parties, today this activity is more visible—and perhaps more vitriolic—than ever before. There is a substantial debate among scholars about the role of interest groups in American political parties, with some arguing that interest groups help democratize parties and others contending that they eviscerate them.

One positive consequence of interest group involvement in party affairs is that the recruitment process has become more inclusive, drawing into the candidate pool many Americans who might never before have sought office. For example, many talented women, African Americans, and conservative Christians have become candidates because of the recruitment efforts of interest groups, expanding the scope of demographic and issue representation.

Of course, in political systems where parties control nominations, it is possible to make even more rapid progress toward the inclusion of outgroups. In 1997 the British Labour Party decided to increase the proportion of women in its legislative delegation. The party increased the number of women Labour candidates from 138 to 159, boosting the number of Labour women members of Parliament from 37 to 102 and doubling the proportion of all women in Parliament to 18.2 percent—all in a single election (Lovenduski 1997). Many countries have lists of candidates, and some parties have chosen a "zippered list" of candidates that alternates between men and women and thus guarantees gender equality in the party's legislative cohort.

In the United States, however, parties are generally neutral in primary elections that choose candidates. This means that women's groups must work hard to increase the numbers of women in Congress, first recruiting and helping to train candidates, then helping them raise money and campaign to win the party nomination, and finally helping them win the general election. As a result, the percentage of women in Congress is far lower than in the legislatures of many other nations. But without interest group involvement, women would be even less common on Capitol Hill.

When interest groups contend for influence in parties and create more vigorous competition for party offices, the party leadership is less likely to be a static, "inbred" group that may have lost touch with the larger electorate (Baer and Bositis 1993). The ability to infuse new life into party elites is especially important because party leaders in the United States resisted the inclusion of blacks in the Democratic Party, women in both parties, and Christian conservatives in the GOP.

In addition, by mobilizing members of previously apolitical or disenfranchised groups—drawing them into political parties; encouraging them to seek nominations as delegates to local, state, or even national conventions; helping them to run for party office; enlisting them to work to influence party platforms—interest groups help develop the political skills of their members and increase their capacity for participation in democratic processes. Many union workers, African Americans, women, and Christian conservatives who are active in party politics today may have started without the socioeconomic background and resources that are generally associated with political activism, but their involvement in interest groups enabled them to develop the skills needed for politics.

Finally, by compelling debate on party platforms, interest groups sometimes force parties to confront important issues they might prefer to ignore. Promoting debate within parties is especially important in the American political system: in European multiparty systems, policy debates are often conducted among several political parties; because we have a two-party system, internal party debates and disagreements become all the more important. For example, when members of the civil rights movement began working within the Democratic Party, party officials and candidates had to confront racial inequality, an issue that both parties had been more comfortable ignoring. Similarly, the Christian Right incursion into the Republican Party sparked a heated debate about issues such as abortion and gay rights.

Despite these advantages, interest groups can also do significant damage to political parties. Chapter 2 discussed several instances in which social movement organizations worked to nominate unelectable candidates and saddled other candidates with platforms that brought intense and derisive media attention. At times, interest groups can fragment parties into contending factions. In Virginia and Minnesota in the 1990s, for example, survey data showed that the moderate and Christian Right factions were extremely antagonistic, rating each other's candidates and leaders below even those of the Democratic Party. Indeed, both moderates and conservative Christians surveyed in Virginia found that assigning a score of 0° on a "feeling thermometer" was not enough to signal their dislike of the other faction; some penciled in scores of −10,000°, along with some nasty comments in the margin (Rozell and Wilcox 1996). The internal GOP debate on abortion has frequently been more of a shouting match than a genuine policy debate (Wilcox and Larson 2005).

Political scientists have written extensively about the rule changes that opened up the presidential nomination process to active involvement by ideological groups. In the 1970s and early 1980s, many analysts felt that social movement organizations had hijacked the nomination process. Because the new procedures favored ideological groups and candidates at the expense of party regulars and moderates, the parties often nominated "outsider" candidates who were either unelectable or unable to govern effectively once elected. Critics held further that interest groups had usurped traditional party functions such as recruitment, nomination, and the development of party platforms, always to the detriment of the parties (Broder 1972; Ceaser 1979, 1982; Polsby 1983).

Although we agree that these arguments have some truth, we think they are overstated. Since the move toward more open nomination systems in the early 1970s, the Democratic Party has nominated one social movement candidate, George McGovern, who ran to the left and lost badly. It has nominated three establishment liberals—Walter Mondale in 1984, Michael Dukakis in 1988, and John Kerry in 2004—and it has nominated three moderate-centrist candidates in Jimmy Carter (1976, 1980), Bill Clinton (1992, 1996), and Al Gore (2000). The Republican Party has nominated two movement candidates who ran emphasizing their moderation and won (Ronald Reagan, 1980, 1984, and George W. Bush, 2000, 2004), and more centrist conservatives such as George H. W. Bush (1988, 1992) and Bob Dole (1996).

In the 1970s and early 1980s, critics of interest group politics argued that the Democratic Party had been taken over by feminists, environmentalists, and peace activists. More recently, many critics have suggested that the Christian Right has taken over the Republican Party. In the 1990s, Christian Right groups consciously sought to gain control of many local and state Republican Party organizations (Rozell and Wilcox 1997). In March 2005, former U.S. senator and ambassador to the United Nations John Danforth, a political conservative and an ordained minister, wrote an editorial in the *New York Times* that charged that the Republican Party "has gone so far in adopting a sectarian agenda that it has become the political extension of a religious movement" (Danforth 2005).

Danforth described efforts by Republicans in his home state of Missouri to criminalize all research into stem cells, and the extraordinary efforts of Republican (and some Democratic) legislators to keep alive Terri Schiavo, a woman who doctors in Florida had declared to be in a "persistent vegetative state" for the past 15 years. With pro-life groups mobilized and active, Republican lawmakers convened an extraordinary special session to pass a personal bill allowing Schiavo's parents to appeal in federal court a Florida court decision to allow her husband to remove her feeding tube, and they actually issued a subpoena for her to testify before Congress. Although surveys suggested that pro-life forces had helped Republicans in the 2004 elections, public reaction to these actions in the Schiavo case was universally negative, even among conservative white evangelicals.

Clearly, Christian conservatives are a powerful force within GOP politics, and many policies are aimed at winning their votes. Yet in 2005 the Christian Right is but one powerful faction within the Republican Party, and it must bargain with business interests and others to achieve its goals. Indeed, it could be argued that the Christian Right has gotten far less from the Republican Party in concrete policy payoffs than have other elements of the GOP coalition (Wilcox and Larson 2005). Business interests have gained considerably under GOP government, as have foreign policy hawks.

Overall, interest group involvement in the internal life of parties can lead to more vibrant and inclusive party organizations, but it can also divide parties into contentious, uncompromising factions. We join with many other political scientists in preferring a system with stronger parties than now exists in the United States, although we also value the role of interest groups in creating a more diverse and representative system and in raising important issues on the political agenda.

Political parties are private associations, and they can change their rules to limit or expand the role of interest groups in internal party politics. For example, although Republican moderates face an uphill battle against Christian conservatives, it would be possible to create a stronger national party organization and to give that organization more control over the selection of state and even local party chairs. Such changes are unlikely, however, in the American political culture, especially given the GOP's long-standing support for local autonomy.

Interest Groups and Candidates

The role of interest groups in financing American elections is a source of great controversy. Supporters of the current system argue that campaign contributors are merely good citizens, providing money to support candidates and parties that share their policy goals. Surveys show that many individuals who give to candidates indeed give out of a sense of civic responsibility (Brown, Powell, and Wilcox 1995; Francia, Green, Herrnson, Powell, and Wilcox 2004).

Critics of the current system routinely charge that interest groups have "bought" or "rented" politicians, parties, or even all of government. Consider the title of a book by a prominent advocate of reform: *The Best Congress Money Can Buy* (Stern 1988). Media stories frequently show a list of government policies that benefit interests that give to candidates and parties. The clear implication is that the policies are a reward for contributions. The same surveys that show that many individuals give for civic reasons show that many give for business reasons.

Interest group funding of candidates has important positive consequences for elections. For many nonincumbent candidates, interest group resources are essential to launching their campaigns. Running for office costs money, and many unknown candidates have a hard time attracting contributions. Nonincumbent candidates must often invest large amounts of their own money (Wilcox 1988), but interest groups can provide crucial resources at this stage, contributing the seed money that helps nonincumbents get their campaigns under way (Biersack, Herrnson, and Wilcox 1993). EMILY's List, WISH List, and the Gay and Lesbian Victory Fund all contribute and bundle money to nonincumbents early in the campaign, helping many promising candidates win election.

Moreover, interest group money enables candidates to get their message out. Although critics charge that Americans spend too much on elections, in fact we spend less on national, state, and local election campaigns than we do marketing consumer products such as beer and toilet paper. Ours is a complicated political system. Voters must sort out differences not only between parties but also among candidates within parties, a task that requires a great deal of information. By providing services to help candidates develop their messages and by providing funds to help them articulate and deliver their messages, interest groups play a valuable and important role in a privately funded political system.

Finally, by encouraging their members to give to political action committees (PACs) and to candidates that their group supports, interest groups provide members with an additional avenue for political participation. Although contributing is a specialized form of participation that does not automatically lead to greater political involvement, it is nonetheless a form of participation (Francia, Green, Herrnson, Powell, and Wilcox 2004; Verba,

Schlozman, and Brady 1995). Many women who would never have considered becoming politically active have joined EMILY's List or WISH List and now attend fund-raising dinners and meet candidates. Similarly, corporate and business PACs seek to engage the interest of executives who might otherwise tune out politics.

Nevertheless, the role of interest groups in financing elections is not all positive. Because PAC contributions go primarily to incumbents, they render American elections less competitive. Incumbents begin with a long list of advantages—name recognition, political contacts, and the perquisites of office, among others—but PACs have enabled them to enjoy a tremendous fund-raising advantage as well. In 2004 the average House incumbent raised $1.2 million dollars, while the average challenger raised less than $200,000. Even in contested races in which the challenger received 40 percent of the vote or more, incumbents raised more than twice as much as challengers: $1.6 million to $750,000 (Campaign Finance Institute 2004c).

Critics often charge that PAC contributions do more than help incumbents win reelection: they also buy incumbents' votes, or at least "rent" their policy-making power for a time. Sometimes this connection is implied. The Center for Responsive Politics lists on a Web page entitled "Tracking the Payback" a description of action by the U.S. Senate that will probably open the Arctic National Wildlife Refuge to drilling by oil companies. The site notes that "the oil and gas industry contributed $23.8 million in individual and PAC donations during the 2004 election cycle, 80 percent to Republicans. Environmental interests contributed $1.9 million, 88 percent to Democrats" (Center for Responsive Politics 2005b).

In other cases, critics explicitly charge that policy is made in exchange for contributions. In *Return on Investment: The Hidden Story of Soft Money, Corporate Welfare, and the 1997 Budget and Tax Deal*, Common Cause (1998) charged that soft money donations to both parties led to a series of specific provisions that appeared, after no debate, in budget and tax bills. The report charged that Amway Corporation, which helped fund the 1996 Republican National Convention and gave more than $1 million in soft money to the GOP in the first six months of 1997, benefited from a provision that changed the rules for determining whether assets in foreign subsidiaries are passive investments and therefore subject to taxation. Designed principally for Amway, the provision gave the company a huge tax break. Similarly, tobacco companies initially benefited from a budget provision holding that revenues from a tax hike on tobacco would be used to pay off any settlement the industry negotiated with some forty state governments over tobacco-related health costs. Public outcry eventually led Congress to repeal this provision, although without media efforts to stir up public outrage, it would have become law. The Common Cause report quoted Kenneth Kies, staff director of the Joint Committee on Taxation, as saying that "the industry wrote it and submitted it and we just used their language." The tobacco industry had previously made major hard and soft money contributions to both political parties.

Yet it is difficult to be certain when policies are made because of contributions, or when instead contributions are made because of policies. Numerous studies by political scientists have found that PAC contributions have only a small impact on roll call votes by members of Congress, which suggests that contributions have only a modest impact on legislative voting (for example, Chappell 1982; Grenzke 1989; Welch 1982; Wright 1985, 1996). Nevertheless, insider accounts of policy making often focus on the importance of money. Why does political science research indicate that PAC money has only a small influence on policy, while insider accounts portray money as having a large impact?

Political scientists and political activists have reached different conclusions for several reasons. First, critics who have observed a simple relationship between PAC contributions and votes have assumed that this pattern inevitably implies that money bought political support. But PACs give to members of Congress not only to try to gain access to influence policy but also to reward past support. Consider, for example, Louisiana Republican David Vitter, who in 2004 was elected to the U.S. Senate from Louisiana. In his campaign, Vitter received more than $25,000 from PACs associated with pro-life and Christian Right groups. Yet this does not mean that these PACs have bought Vitter's vote—or that if pro-choice PACs would simply give him more money he would switch his vote. These social conservative PACs contributed to Vitter because of his record supporting their issues in the Louisiana state legislature and, later, in the U.S. House of Representatives. This suggests that some of the statistical relationship between PAC contributions and roll call votes arises because PACs give money to members of Congress who already support them—even if those members would likely support them without a contribution.

Political scientists first try to determine how a member of Congress might have voted had he or she not received a PAC contribution—on the basis of influences such as personal convictions; constituents' views; arguments and pressure from colleagues, party leaders, and the president; and arguments and pressure from interest groups. In some cases when a PAC contribution matches a roll call vote, there are other explanations for the vote. Often an interest group is successful at lobbying members of Congress because it represents large numbers of voters in a state or district or because other important political players support the group's views. The tobacco industry, for example, could gain access to senators and representatives from North Carolina or Virginia even without contributing to their campaigns, simply because the industry employs many voters in those states and the income of those voters indirectly supports many other businesses. Thus the apparent relationship between PAC contributions and roll call votes is more complex than it may seem to political activists.

Moreover, many political scientists believe that because incumbents are able to raise large sums of money from many sources, even a coordinated effort by a major industry generally amounts to a small portion of donation receipts. Iowa Republican senator Chuck Grassley received more than $575,000 in PAC contributions from the finance industry for his 2004 reelection bid. Yet Grassley raised more than $2.8 million in PAC contributions in the election cycle and more than $3.9 million in individual contributions of more than $200. Altogether Grassley raised $7,638,488 for a reelection campaign in which he received 70 percent of the popular vote. Having contributed less than 10 percent of Grassley's campaign totals, finance industry PACs were scarcely in a position to demand that Grassley deliver any specific policy benefit. Any single PAC likely accounted for less than 1 percent of Grassley's total funds. In most relationships between PACs and incumbents, it is the incumbent who is more powerful.

In sum, one of the reasons for the discrepancy between the observations of political scientists and those of some critics who are concerned about PACs is that the critics do not take into account the complexity of the relationship between PACs and incumbents. At the same time, however, political scientists' findings may have been influenced by the fact that their studies investigated the relationship between PAC contributions and roll call votes, which may not be where political contributions have their greatest impact. Money may be more likely to influence the content of legislation than individual members' votes on bills. Since the late 1970s, Congress has increasingly voted on large bills that fold together spending on many areas. These votes frequently take place with little debate—in some cases before the bill has even been printed for members of Congress to read. Because their passage is often a foregone conclusion, what ends up in these bills is quite important. Interest groups therefore have a strong incentive to affect the content of such legislation.

Consider, for example, when GOP leaders in 2004 removed, from a Senate tax bill, a provision that would have enabled the U.S. Food and Drug Administration to regulate tobacco. The relationship between money and policy would not have shown up as PAC contributions affecting roll call votes because there was no roll call vote on the decision; instead the vote would have been on a broader tax bill. But the tobacco industry clearly benefited from the decision, and tobacco companies and their executives gave $2.7 million to Republicans in the 2004 election cycle.

Media reports have brought to light a number of cases in which specific favors for major donors were embedded in obscure language in legislation. It seems likely that the provisions were the direct result of political contributions. It is worth noting that in many cases, once the media have made an issue of these favors, Congress has repealed them. Political contributions are thus less influential than public outcry but are nonetheless probably important in influencing the content of some legislation.

Thus, it may well be that PAC money does not buy roll call votes but does have an important influence on the content of legislation. This was even more important in recent years because legislation is increasingly likely to be worked out by party leaders in closed-door sessions (Sinclair 1997). This pattern is particularly characteristic of the new Republican Congress, where party leaders have put considerable pressure on committees and even bypassed them on important occasions. Although this approach has enabled the House to move quickly to pass important legislation, it has also made it easier for party leaders to insert language into bills without having it subject to the committees' deliberative processes.

Regardless of whether money actually buys public policy, the public overwhelmingly believes that wealthy interests receive favors for their political contributions, and this belief exacerbates the growing cynicism about the American political system. Public opinion expert Robert Shapiro concluded after examining many public opinion polls over a span of years that

> the public has seen the need to reform the campaign finance system in order to limit the influence of money in the political process; the public has seen politics and politicians consumed and harmed by fundraising; the public has perceived corruption in politics connected to the influence of political donations and campaign contributions; the public has associated political contributions with the undue influence of "special interests"; . . . [and] the public was deeply troubled by the undesirable influence they

associated with political contributions in the Enron scandal. (Shapiro 2003)

Although political parties and incumbents have long used their power over the policy agenda to extract resources from interest groups, such activity appears to have increased in recent years. During the visibly frantic fund-raising undertaken during the 2004 campaign, both Republicans and Democrats were increasingly likely to design and schedule fund-raising events so that interest groups were being asked for contributions immediately before scheduled deliberations on legislation that would affect them. Interest group leaders were pressured to provide money to 527 committees that would help finance voter mobilization efforts, with the suggestion that access to policy makers might be contingent on such contributions.

Interest Groups and Voters

With the American electorate often poorly informed about the political positions of the members of the House and the Senate who represent them—and even about the positions of major presidential candidates—communication between interest groups and voters is often vital to the democratic process. Endorsements, hit lists, and voters' guides provide members of interest groups and other citizens with information they need to enable them to "vote their interests." Voters for whom abortion is a salient issue, for example, can easily find a voters' guide from a pro-choice or anti-abortion group to guide their choices at the ballot box. In an era of weak political parties and candidate-centered, media-driven campaigns, interest groups play a crucial role by assessing the candidates' records, not just their rhetoric.

Moreover, the extensive voter mobilization efforts by interest groups in the 2004 election helped produce a sizable increase in voter interest and voter turnout. Although political scientists debate how to best measure voter turnout, all methods suggest a sizable increase between 2000 and 2004. Increased participation is almost certainly a good thing, and although other factors help to explain the increase in 2004, it is clear that interest groups played a key role.

Finally, interest group involvement in elections can be a participatory process that involves activists in politics in new and important ways. The thousands of volunteers who were trained and then fanned out across

Florida, Ohio, Michigan, and many other states learned about retail politics in a way that no college class could convey. They acquired personal and political skills that will help them to engage in politics more effectively. Many groups such as MoveOn.org and Let Freedom Ring encouraged individuals to create advertisements, and the best of them were then produced professionally and either placed on the group's Web site or run on broadcast television or radio. Interest groups helped to inspire and coordinate "bloggers" who followed the campaign closely and wrote about it regularly.

But interest group communications with members and voters have negative aspects as well. Often voters' guides provide misleading and even false information. Moreover, they are increasingly likely to be published by tax-exempt organizations claiming to be nonpartisan; given the content of the guides, such claims make a mockery of tax and campaign finance laws. And when partisan actors set up these tax-exempt groups to conduct "nonpartisan" voter mobilization efforts, it is clear that everyone involved is doing their utmost to evade the law.

Issue advocacy campaigns are relatively new and were undertaken in 2004 in record numbers. It is difficult to say what their ultimate impact will be on American elections. On the one hand, organized and coordinated efforts to inform the voters of candidates' positions and records can serve a valuable educational function. Moreover, to seek to persuade voters to adopt a particular position on the issues of the day is a clear exercise of the constitutional right to freedom of speech.

Nevertheless, issue advocacy campaigns seem to raise some thorny problems. First, they have the effect of shifting policy debate from candidates to loose coalitions of interest groups. Although political scientists disagree strongly about whether policy messages should be shaped by the parties or by candidates, few would argue that interest groups should dominate the dialogue. When interest groups frame the issues, attack the character of candidates, and otherwise run shadow campaigns, accountability suffers. Candidates are not responsible for the claims and attacks in the advertisements, and it is more difficult to hold candidates to campaign promises when those promises are made by interest groups and not by the candidates themselves. This was evident in the 2004 Swift Boat Veterans for Truth campaign, which was able to mount effective but misleading attacks on John Kerry, with no ill effects on President Bush's credibility.

Second, as mentioned in Chapter 4, many of the "groups" that mount issue advocacy campaigns are not groups at all but rather are conduits for the money of a handful of wealthy individuals or even just one individual. Sometimes they are funded by corporations or industries that wish to hide their obvious self-interest in an issue or candidate behind a name that sounds like a citizens' group. To fully evaluate campaign communications, voters need to consider the source. When candidates attack one another, voters discount the attacks because they expect candidates to be aggressive in their charges. When citizens have no information about the source of an advertisement, they may look to the name of the group as a clue. For example, Republicans for Clean Air sounds like an environmental group, and the advertisement they aired against Arizona senator John McCain during his 2000 Republican primary campaign seemed like the kind of ad that an environmental group would broadcast. If the public had known that the ad was paid for by two very wealthy Texans who were longtime backers of George W. Bush, they would have discounted the charges. Believing that it was aired by an environmental group, some voters proba-bly failed to discount the information properly.

Current disclosure rules do not require some types of groups to disclose their financial patrons, and others must disclose this information partially to the Internal Revenue Service, which is not obliged to try to publicize the information. Thus voters are faced with a barrage of advertising from a group they have not heard of, with little or no information to help them determine the credibility of the charges. A number of organizations like Public Citizen, the Center for Responsive Politics, and the Annenberg Center's FactCheck.org are available to voters willing to spend consider-able time researching particular advertisements, but that is a tiny portion of the electorate.

Third, issue advocacy campaigns are often a way to skirt campaign finance laws. Technically, the purpose of these campaigns is to advocate issues, not the election of candidates, but that technicality is entirely ignored by almost all campaign actors. Such disregard for the law breeds cynicism and makes it difficult to craft a rational system of campaign finance rules. Moreover, by allowing wealthy individuals go give millions of dollars to finance such campaigns, the utility of contribution limits is eroded further.

Fourth, and perhaps most important, because issue advocacy campaigns are mounted with only minimal disclosure, they undermine the trans-parency of the system, the most successful aspect of the current campaign finance regime (Wilcox 2004). To determine whether a candidate appears to have been unduly influenced by special interests, it is vital for the media, the parties, citizens, and interest groups to be able to discover where contributions have come from and how extensive they are. When interest groups can spend unlimited amounts of undisclosed and untraceable funds, the disclosure system is perhaps fatally damaged—which is likely to further increase public cynicism about the political system.

REFORMING THE SYSTEM

The rules and regulations that channel interest group activity in American elections are not fixed. Other countries deal with elections very differently from the United States. Most have stronger political parties that choose candidates and therefore have the resources to impose discipline on members who stray from the party line. Many countries have far shorter election cycles and rules about spending money outside of the election period. Some have spending limits, and many have public funding. Moreover, in the United States, the rules governing interest group activities in statewide elections vary widely from state to state.

In this section we explore some of the reforms proposed for improving the conduct of American elections, including the role of interest groups in those elections. Many reforms have been proposed by scholars, activists, and concerned citizens, and many contradict one another. Often the differences among them relate to balancing key values, such as equality, freedom, and transparency, and to different visions of what an ideal electoral system would look like.

We are not offering our own comprehensive plan of reform in this section. Nonetheless, we evaluate many of the reform proposals with our own values in mind. We believe that campaigns should allow for a vigorous debate of the key issues, between candidates who have the resources to reach the voters with their messages. We value citizen involvement in elections, including contributions to candidates and parties from a wide spectrum of citizens, but we also believe that equality of political voice is important, and that curbs on the size of contributions and activity can help to achieve that equality.

We focus here on reforms that would directly influence interest group activities, but it is important to note that some reforms that do not directly influence interest groups would nonetheless influence their roles in elections. For example, currently, incumbent politicians draw the boundaries of House districts in ways that maximize the seats to a single party or that maximize the number of incumbents who are safe from challenge. As a result, most House districts do not experience a vigorous debate of issues, because the incumbent politician is judged sufficiently safe that quality candidates do not challenge her, and interest groups do not marshal their resources in the campaigns. It is possible to craft legislative districts that instead maximize electoral competition, and this would greatly affect the way that interest groups recruit candidates, target their resources, and contribute to candidates.

Interest Groups and Parties

The role that interest groups play in the nomination process is central to their relationship with political parties. Scholars have proposed a variety of reforms for the nomination process, the most common of which would give party leaders greater control—in some cases complete control—over nominations. Such proposals are not new. In the 1970s and early 1980s, for example, many political scientists argued that the system for nominating presidential candidates should return more control to party elites. In the Democratic Party, the creation of "superdelegates," who are primarily elected officials, was in part a response to such suggestions. The decision to compress the schedule of primaries and caucuses was also intended to provide greater influence for party moderates and to give an advantage to well-known "insider" candidates. Similarly, the GOP has retained its winner-take-all system of selecting delegates, in part to prevent ideological candidates with limited appeal from sending large delegations to the national convention. Although party nomination rules clearly affect who wins (Lengle and Shafer 1976), whether such rules consistently help or hurt different types of candidates is unclear, largely because campaign professionals are constantly looking for new ways to help their candidates win under different sets of rules.

Another proposed reform would create a single national primary election or four regional primary elections. The goal would be to weaken the impact of Iowa and New Hampshire on the nomination process; both are states in which interest groups are strongly represented. The current system forces candidates to run for several weeks in many states, appealing to groups that are perhaps disproportionately important in each state. In 2000, for example, George W. Bush ran a compassionate conservative campaign until the South Carolina primary, where he was forced to move sharply to the right and embrace the Christian Right in order to win the state's primary. In 1988 Democratic candidate Michael Dukakis announced his support for the American Civil Liberties Union (ACLU), in part to appeal to party activists and members of liberal interest groups in Iowa. The move came back to haunt him in the general election, when George H. W. Bush attacked the ACLU for defending some unpopular causes. Proponents of national or regional primaries argue that they will lead to the election of more centrist candidates who are established national politicians and that they will help candidates resist making promises to interest groups that are especially influential in states that are crucial to the election calendar.

How a national primary, or four regional primaries, might affect interest group activity is not immediately clear. With much at stake on a single day, wealthy groups would be asked to marshal their money behind particular candidates—in PAC contributions, contributions from their members, and independent spending and issue advocacy. Candidates with significant name recognition would certainly be advantaged, but it might be that campaigns would simply start earlier, and that ideological groups would have time to help introduce candidates to voters. Indeed, interest groups with motivated members who could volunteer and work for a candidate would be in hot demand, as would those with strong communication channels to their members, like the National Rifle Association, National Organization for Women, and National Right to Life Committee.

Depending on the rules for allocating delegates, candidates might choose to campaign in particular areas, appealing to narrow constituency groups. In 1988, southern Democratic Party leaders created a Super Tuesday primary in order to help moderate and southern Democrats win more votes. But the two big winners were liberals Michael Dukakis and Jesse Jackson, who targeted particular constituencies and ran in only certain parts of key states (Norrander 1992).

Although there has been less discussion of changes in the nomination process for congressional candidates, allowing party leaders to choose the nominees for these races would have a profound impact on the relationship between parties and interest groups. In most countries, party leaders choose candidates for the legislature. Because legislators could be replaced on their party's list in the next election, they almost always vote with the party leaders. Allowing party leaders to choose nominees for congressional office would increase party discipline and greatly simplify the tasks facing voters. If all members supported and opposed the same policies, voters would merely have to determine what each party—rather than each candidate—stood for. It would be much easier for them to blame the incumbent party for bad policies and to understand the promises of the other party.

Such a change would not mean, of course, that interest groups would cease to play any role in party nominations. Instead, interest groups would bargain with party leaders to help choose the composition of the party slate. Groups with significant resources—including ardent followers who contribute money to campaigns, vote loyally for party candidates, and volunteer to distribute voters' guides—might be in an even better position than now to insist that candidates share their policy preferences and probably also that some candidates come from the activist ranks of the group itself. But party leaders would bargain with interest groups centrally and could determine, to a certain extent, the ideological composition of their congressional delegation.

If American parties became disciplined, unified organizations like European parties, then interest groups would have even more at stake in battles over party platforms. In most European democracies, party programs are the promises that the parties make to voters, and these unified parties usually try to implement these promises. As the pro-life and Christian Right movements came to dominate the Republican platform committees, moderates simply ignored the platforms. If platforms bound all members, they would take on more importance. It is possible that parties would fragment, for the United States is a large and diverse society, and two rigidly ideological parties might not have sufficient diversity to represent America. The Republican Party might not be able to contain both George W. Bush and Arnold Schwarzenegger if they were bound by a single party platform.

Of course, parties are free to tinker with the rules that affect nominations, delegate selection, and the writing of platforms. If the Democratic Party chose to, it could adopt a winner-take-all system of delegate selection, although many important party constituencies would react with outrage. It could include many more superdelegates at the convention, or it could allow all delegates to be free agents regardless of the outcome of primary elections in their states. The GOP could change the way its delegates are selected, requiring that delegates come from the lists provided by the candidates; it could also change the way the party platform is drafted to give the nominee much more say in the language. Such changes would affect the balance of power between contending interests in the parties for a time, although the long-term consequences are unpredictable.

Interest Groups, Candidates, and Voters

Controversy over the relationship between interest groups and candidates and interest groups and voters is almost exclusively focused on campaign finance. During the 1990s, the campaign finance system crafted by Congress in response to the Watergate scandals finally unraveled. Spending limits were overturned by the Supreme Court. Contribution limits were undermined by soft money. Disclosure was limited to issue advocacy campaigns by 527 and 501 committees. And the public funding system was weakened as inflation eroded the value of matching funds, leading George W. Bush, John Kerry, and Howard Dean to refuse matching funds in 2004 and avoid spending limits.

For many years, Congress debated campaign finance reform, and different measures routinely passed the Republican-controlled House in the late 1990s, only to die of a filibuster in the Senate. The 2000 election brought new supporters of reform to the Senate, and in 2002 Congress passed the Bipartisan Campaign Reform Act (BCRA). BCRA was designed to fix two of the biggest problems with the system: soft money and issue advocacy. It was not designed as a systematic reform package but rather as a fix for the most pressing problems.

BCRA is enforced by the Federal Election Commission (FEC), which is run by six commissioners divided evenly among the two major parties. Not surprisingly, the commission is not an aggressive regulator. Soon after BCRA passed, the FEC began creating rules to implement the legislation. The rules frequently weakened or even eviscerated provisions of the legislation. For example, BCRA prohibits federal officials from soliciting money for nonprofit groups that help to mobilize voters and air issue ads. The purpose of this provision was to prevent party leaders who once pressured interest groups for soft money contributions from merely redirecting those contributions to new nonprofit groups that performed quasi-party functions. But the FEC implemented regulations allowing elected officials to appear at fund-raisers for the nonprofit, to make the keynote address, and to do everything except explicitly ask for a contribution.

Some observers point to the complexities of campaign finance regulations, and the slow collapse of the Federal Election Campaign Act framework, as evidence that money in politics cannot, and perhaps should not, be regulated. They argue that spending is speech and that government efforts to regulate interest group activity are futile. Proponents of deregulation often offer a hydraulic metaphor, saying that money is like water, and if you build a dam the stream will eventually find a way around it, over it, or under it.

We believe the hydraulic metaphor is a good one, for somewhat different reasons. Dams do not seek to totally block streams but rather to channel their energy. Dams do not inevitably fail at this, but they do need to be repaired and reinforced from time to time, and they need close monitoring to help determine any problems they may be causing. Park service officials have implemented controlled flooding of the Grand Canyon to help clear water channels and to restore the ecosystem that would occur in an unregulated stream.

Campaign finance rules have not been updated and monitored regularly. The FEC lacks the authority, the resources, and the political will to monitor campaign finance practice and to develop new rules and regulations to keep the system stable. The commission has too few attorneys, which leads to an enormous backlog of enforcement actions. It lacks the power to implement random audits or to respond to anonymous complaints (Mann 2005). The same is not true in other countries. Elections Canada is headed by a single, nonpartisan bureaucrat with the resources and authority to prosecute those who violate the law and the ability to issue new guidelines and regulations to deal with changing campaign finance practices. For this reason, reforming the FEC must be a central part of any other package of reforms (Wilcox 2004).

Reforms can have unexpected consequences and should be carefully considered before being implemented. Over the years, many critics of interest group involvement have advocated eliminating all PACs. Yet PACs provide contributions that are institutional and transparent. Individuals who work for a company or who belong to an interest group are more difficult to trace. It is easy to track PAC contributions from the National Association of Realtors, for example, but if the PAC was abolished and the group instead encouraged its members to give more, it would be virtually impossible to trace all of the contributions. Thus banning PACs would not by itself remove interest group money from elections, and it might in the process make existing money less transparent. Moreover, a ban on PACs without changes in the regulations on issue advocacy campaigns would lead many interest groups to channel their funds into issue advocacy.

Sometimes the impact of a potential reform is fully understood by politicians, who attempt to sell the reform with a very different logic. Some proposed reforms seem less attractive to us. For example, GOP politicians frequently extol the benefits of a "payroll protection act" that would ban unions from using member dues for politics without the members' explicit approval. In its most onerous form, the proposal would require that unions get separate permission from their members each time they spend money on campaigns. Debated in isolation, it seems only fair to let union members, many of whom are forced by state law to join unions in the first place, determine where their dues are spent.

Yet unions are the major counterweight to corporations in American politics, and, not surprisingly, the GOP is not proposing a "dividends protection act" that would require companies to get permission from their shareholders for separate acts of political campaigning. Owning stocks is sometimes involuntary as well, when companies direct pension deposits into stock accounts or mutual funds that hold a basket of stocks. Limiting unions without similarly limiting corporations would create a serious imbalance in the political power of these two groups.

Let us first consider two substantial changes in the regulatory regime: deregulation and public funding of campaigns. Then we explore some more modest reform proposals that we believe can help improve the role of interest groups in American campaigns.

DEREGULATION. Many libertarians, and some Republicans, have proposed that we abolish all contribution limits. Most of these proposals include expanded disclosure. One of the most eloquent cases for deregulation is made by FEC commissioner Bradley Smith in his book *Unfree Speech*. Smith argues that campaign contributions have never been proven to cause corruption and that committed contributors generally find ways around restrictions. He argues primarily that contributing money is speech, and that campaign finance regulations are contrary to the First Amendment. Moreover, Smith suggests that disclosure is enough to deter corruption, although he also hints that perhaps disclosure has its own problems (Smith 2003).

Surveys of political donors show that nearly all Democrats oppose deregulation, as do a sizable majority of Republicans (Francia, Green, Herrnson, Powell, and Wilcox 2004). Donors presumably fear that deregulation will make it impossible for them to fend off aggressive fund-raising by incumbents, because they will no longer be able to say that they have already given the maximum. Most Democrats fear that eliminating all regulations would allow corporations to dominate elections with their deep treasury coffers.

Although most scholars believe that disclosure plays a vital role in controlling corruption, few agree that disclosure by itself would deter abuse. For disclosure to fully control corruption, incumbent politicians would have to fear that the public would turn them out of office if people believed these officeholders had supported policies in exchange for campaign contributions. But most incumbents do not face serious challenge, and most voters cannot name a single interest group that has contributed to their incumbent. Thus it seems likely that few voters would seek out information on contributions, compare them to the actions that incumbents have taken on behalf of interests, and cast ballots based on that information. This would not mean that voters do not care about campaign contributions or believe them to be corrupting, but it would mean that disclosure alone would not deter abuse.

PUBLIC FINANCING. At the other extreme are proposals that would eliminate private money from elections altogether, substituting public funds. Many Western European democracies currently have systems in which the government provides money to the parties to spend on behalf of their candidates, and many states also provide public funding for candidates. Proponents of public financing argue that it would actually save money, first, by eliminating the need for legislators to provide interest groups with particularistic economic benefits such as tax cuts and corporate welfare and, second, by eliminating not only most corruption but the appearance of it as well. Candidates who accepted public funding would agree to refuse private money and to limit their spending to the public grant, a policy that the Supreme Court has already upheld.

Although public funding has worked well in other democracies, it is difficult to know how it might work in the United States at the national level. Independent expenditures and issue advocacy would still be permitted, although there may be ways to make them less attractive to interest groups. Critics charge that public funding would create yet another entitlement program, this time for politicians. Moreover, they argue that the system would be costly and would give public money to candidates who might espouse unpalatable and even offensive views. A more limited form of public funding—perhaps providing a small amount to all general election or even primary election candidates to help them launch their campaigns— would be less expensive and would foster electoral competition. Moreover, if candidates accepted these funds they could be bound to abide by other limits in the law.

Many reform proposals include voluntary spending limits for candidates, which the Supreme Court has ruled enforceable only for those who accept some form of public subsidy. Under such proposals, candidates would agree to spend only a certain amount, perhaps $500,000 in House races, with a variable amount—depending on the size of the state—for the Senate. The case for spending limits is that by preventing incumbents from simply drowning out their opponents' messages with a constant barrage of advertisements, they create a more level playing field and foster genuine competition. The case against such limits is that limits set too low would protect incumbents (because challengers must spend large sums to achieve the name recognition necessary to compete), and limits set too high would serve little purpose at all. Moreover, spending by candidates is clearly political speech in its most pure form, and any limits on it must be approached with caution.

Some proposals would ban or severely limit PACs. Proponents argue that such restrictions would reduce the power of special interests in financing elections. Yet a ban or sharp limits on PACs would likely produce exactly the opposite effect: with access to PACs restricted or denied, interest groups would channel their money into issue advocacy, and individual members would contribute directly to candidates instead of to the PAC. Both tactics would render it much more difficult to assess the total amount contributed or spent by an interest group. Although it is easy to determine, for example, that a PAC is sponsored by a particular corporation, it is much harder to discover which individuals are associated with that corporation.

DIRECTIONS FOR CAMPAIGN FINANCE REFORM

Although we support different political parties and disagree on a number of political issues, we do agree on a set of general principles that should guide reformers and on many specific reforms as well. Some of the reforms that we supported in the first edition of this text were incorporated into BCRA, but there is more work to be done in campaign finance reform.

Underlying Assumptions

Our sense of where campaign finance reform needs to be directed is based on a number of assumptions. First, we wish to protect interest group activities that help group members develop political abilities and that educate and inform voters about issues and candidates' positions. By training their members and educating them in the workings of the political process, interest groups help democratize the political system, ensuring that political expertise is not confined solely to the wealthiest and best-educated citizens. Because we also value the diversity of voices in the political system and the inclusion of previously disenfranchised groups, we favor reforms that promote grassroots activity and that encourage individual members of interest groups to participate in elections by volunteering time and money.

Second, we greatly value the freedoms of speech and association that interest groups claim as the basis for many of their activities. Nevertheless, we do not equate limits on spending with limits on speech. Unlimited campaign spending drives up the costs of advertising, which puts less-wealthy groups and less well-funded candidates at a disadvantage in getting their message out. Because voters have a limited attention span when it comes to politics, they tend to focus on the most frequent and familiar themes. Although there will always be disparities among interest groups in their ability to compete in and influence elections, we favor reforms that help level the playing field, enabling diverse interest groups to make their positions public. When the wealthiest interest groups can spend unlimited amounts to advocate their positions, political debate and deliberation are perhaps least inclusive, and many important voices are likely to go unheard.

Third, we value electoral competition and therefore generally support activities that allow nonincumbent candidates to achieve the name recognition and media attention needed to communicate their views. Our views on this issue are not based on the assumption that incumbents win elections only by outspending their opponents: most incumbents are experienced candidates who have survived many elections because they have strong political skills and are a good fit in their state or district. Instead, we believe that challengers deserve the right to state their case in an election, and to do so they must be able to raise and spend sufficient sums.

Fourth, we value a fully transparent system of disclosure of campaign activities. Although too comprehensive and rigid a disclosure system could have a chilling effect on small and local interest groups, it is also true that operating in secret creates opportunities for corruption. Perhaps more important, voters are much more likely to perceive the system as corrupt when they cannot discover precisely how interest groups have aided political candidates. We therefore believe that political activities conducted without disclosure of the amounts spent and the sources of the revenue are potentially damaging to democracy.

Finally, we prefer that interest groups' campaign activities strengthen the candidates' and parties' accountability to citizens. Thus we support proposals that would encourage interest groups to channel money to candidates and parties and that would discourage them from engaging in issue advocacy and independent expenditures. Stronger political parties and campaigns in which the candidates articulate the issues are preferable to campaigns driven by interest groups.

Goals of Reform

Generally, we support reforms that would channel money through candidates, parties, and PACs; that would limit the size of contributions; and that would push more financial activity into the disclosure system. Moreover, we support proposals that would increase the competitiveness of campaigns, fostering a flow of resources to nonincumbents in the crucial early stages of their campaigns. Many contending proposals claim to achieve these goals, but continued dialogue and study will be needed to uncover the implications of these plans. In addition, whatever individual reforms are adopted must be part of an ongoing process that modifies the rules as fundraising technologies and practices change.

To create more competitive campaigns, some analysts have proposed partial public funding for general election candidates (as now exists in the presidential nomination process). Others prefer free or subsidized media time for candidates, and still others have proposed increasing the limit on the initial amount of money raised by candidates so that they can more expeditiously launch their campaigns. Such proposals could be expanded to include candidates in primary elections as well. We are especially drawn to the idea of free or subsidized media. The Brookings Institution Working Group, for example, calls for a "broadcast bank" of minutes of television and radio time to be distributed to major party candidates and to major and minor political parties.

A system of partial matching funds—perhaps matching three to one the first $10,000 in individual contributions of $100 or less raised by a candidate—would also enable candidates to more effectively launch their campaigns, thereby helping to make elections more competitive. Such a system would have the additional benefit of creating an incentive to raise small contributions. Tax credits for small individual contributions are worth exploring, although we are not certain that they would provide a strong incentive to give.

We would eliminate the limits on coordinated spending by political parties, allowing them to channel their resources into competitive races without the artifice of creating separate independent expenditure campaigns. Some analysts have proposed increasing the limits that PACs can give to candidates from $5,000 to perhaps $7,500, and this might be worth exploring as another mechanism for interest groups to channel money to candidates in close races without allowing any individual group excessive influence.

Although BCRA dealt with issue advocacy by 527 committees, the explosion of issue ads by 501 committees in 2004, and the lack of effective regulation of 527 issue campaigns, point to the need for further reform. We favor requirements that would channel such activity through PACs, which would mean that treasury money and large contributions from wealthy individuals could no longer be used to pay for such campaigns. Moreover, we believe that all issue advocacy activity—both the source of the funds and the spending of those funds—should be fully disclosed to the FEC, regardless of the way the sponsoring committee is organized for tax purposes.

We think that incentives should be structured (1) to encourage interest groups to concentrate on raising money from individuals and contributing it to candidates and parties and (2) to engage less in issue advocacy and independent expenditure campaigns. The development of incentives will likely be an ongoing process, but one way to begin might be to allow candidates who are attacked by major issue advocacy or independent expenditure campaigns to have additional time from the broadcast bank to answer such advertising. Another option is to require that stations that accept issue advocacy ads in the period before an election allow candidates to purchase rebuttal time at a steep discount.

Finally, we favor restructuring and strengthening the FEC. The commission is designed to be a weak regulatory body: three Republican and three Democratic commissioners frequently (though not inevitably) result in stalemate. The FEC greatly weakened BCRA through its rulemaking. For example, as mentioned earlier, BCRA bans federal officials from asking citizens to contribute to nonprofit associations that might engage in political activity. The FEC guidelines, however, allow federal officials to host fundraising events, to appear as keynote speakers and to praise the efforts of the group, and to suggest that the group would be more effective if it had more money—as long as these officials do not explicitly ask for the contributions.

It might seem as though partisanship in interpreting electoral rules is inevitable, but other countries, and even cities within the United States (most notably New York City), have managed to create less partisan implementing agencies. For example, Elections Canada has widespread support across the political parties in Canada. Moreover, the agency has the necessary powers to adapt to new fund-raising practices, to issue rules, to investigate potential violations of the rules, and to prosecute those who violate them (Wilcox 2004). There are many proposals for restructuring the FEC, including one by John McCain (Mann 2005). The reformed agency would need the resources to enforce the law, including a significant increase in the number of auditors and lawyers, and also the ability to conduct random audits and other fact-finding exercises.

Taken together, the reforms we support would not place undue limits on the ability of interest groups to play an active role in campaigns. Instead, the reforms would accomplish three goals: (1) encourage interest groups to undertake activities that are disclosed, (2) encourage them to undertake activities that are funded by voluntary contributions from individual group members, and (3) channel money to candidates and parties—in other words, to entities that can be held responsible for the content of communications. Compelling interest groups to rely more heavily on voluntary contributions would likely strengthen them. To raise the money necessary to participate fully in elections, interest groups would have to develop more actively politicized members.

However, money does not ensure election. Indeed, many well-funded candidates have lost to candidates with less money but broader public support. Helping challengers raise money will make elections more competitive, but reforming the redistricting process would go much further toward that end. Allowing state legislators and governors to draw district boundaries has created many districts in which one party is assured of victory. Moreover, the boundaries often make little political or cultural sense, except as vehicles to protect incumbents or to maximize the number of seats that can be won by one party or the other. A more fair, less partisan way to draw district lines might go further toward increasing competition in elections than would campaign finance reform.

SUMMARY

Interest groups are, and always have been, controversial yet necessary players in the American electoral process. According to their critics, interest groups distort the political process in favor of the better organized and better funded, subverting true democracy. In the eyes of their defenders, interest groups are a bulwark of our democracy, embodying the Madisonian notion of a competitive pluralist system.

Although we are often dismayed by many campaign practices of various interest groups in American elections, we believe that such groups are essential to American democracy. Interest groups deserve much of the credit for stimulating voter turnout in campaigns, and they serve essential functions in the political process.

List of References

Adams, Greg D. 1996. "Times of tumult: Abortion and the transformation of American political parties." Ph.D. diss., University of Iowa.

Alaska Democratic Party. 2004. "Platform." www.alaskademocrats.org/docs/adp_platform_2004.pdf.

Allen, Mike. 2005. "GOP abandons ethics changes." *Washington Post*, January 4.

American Federation of Labor–Congress of Industrial Organizations. 2004. "Union members voted overwhelmingly for Kerry," November 3. www.aflcio.org/mediacenter/prsptm/pr11032004.cfm.

———. 2005. "Electing union members to public office." www.aflcio.org/issuespolitics/politics/ppp_electing.cfm.

Associated Press. 2002. "AFL–CIO endorses Fran Ulmer for governor." June 25. alaskalegislature.com/stories/062502/ulmer.shtml.

Babington, Charles, and Juliet Eilperin. 2004. "Democratic leaders call for DeLay's ouster." *Washington Post*, October 8.

Baer, Denise L., and David A. Bositis. 1993. *Elite cadres and party coalitions*. New York: Greenwood Press.

Baida, Peter. 1992. "The legacy of Dollar Mark Hanna." In *The quest for national office*, ed. Stephen J. Wayne and Clyde Wilcox. New York: St. Martin's.

Banfield, Edward C. 1980. "In defense of the party system." In *Political parties in the eighties*, ed. Robert A. Goldwin. Washington, D.C.: American Enterprise Institute.

Bedlington, Anne. 1994. "The National Association of Realtors PAC: Rules or rationality?" In *Risky business: PAC decisionmaking in congressional elections*, ed. Robert Biersack, Paul S. Herrnson, and Clyde Wilcox. Armonk, N.Y.: M. E. Sharpe.

———. 1999. "The realtors, political action committee: Covering all contingencies." In *After the revolution: PACs and lobbies in the new Republican Congress*, ed. Robert Biersack, Paul Herrnson, and Clyde Wilcox. New York: Allyn & Bacon.

Berry, Jeffrey. 2000. *The new liberalism: The rising power of citizen groups*. Washington, D.C.: Brookings Institution Press.

Biersack, Robert, Paul S. Herrnson, and Clyde Wilcox. 1993. "Seeds for success: Early money in congressional elections." *Legislative Studies Quarterly* 18: 535–552.

Biersack, Robert, and Marianne H. Viray. 2004. "Interest groups and federal campaign finance: The beginning of a new era." In *The interest group connection*, 2d ed., ed. Paul S. Herrnson, Ronald G. Shaiko, and Clyde Wilcox. Washington, D.C.: CQ Press.

BIPAC (Business-Industry Political Action Committee). 1996. *Rising to the challenge in 1996: What business groups must do to protect free enterprise majorities in Congress*. Washington, D.C.: BIPAC.

Birnbaum, Jeffrey H., and Thomas B. Edsall. 2004. "For lobbyists, big spending means big presence." *Washington Post*, July 28.

Broder, David. 1972. *The party's over*. New York: Harper & Row.

Brown, Clifford, Lynda Powell, and Clyde Wilcox. 1995. *Serious money: Fundraising and contributing in presidential nomination campaigns*. New York: Cambridge University Press.

Bruce, John. 1997. "Texas: A success story, at least for now." In *God at the grass roots, 1996: The Christian Right in American elections*, ed. Mark J. Rozell and Clyde Wilcox. Lanham, Md.: Rowman & Littlefield.

Bruce, John, and Clyde Wilcox. 1998. "Introduction." In *The changing politics of gun control*, ed. John Bruce and Clyde Wilcox. Lanham, Md.: Rowman & Littlefield.

Campaign Finance Institute. 2004a. "Introduction." In *The $100 million dollar exemption: Soft money and the national party conventions*, www.cfinst.org/eguide /partyconventions/financing/cfistudy_intro.html.

———. 2004b. "Part III: Major donors: The political contributions of host committee donors." In *The $100 million dollar exemption: Soft money and the national party conventions*, www.cfinst.org/eguide/partyconventions/financing/cfistudy _partiii.html.

———. 2004c. "CFI's post-election analysis of the 2004 battle for Congress." www.cfinst.org/pr/110504a.html.

Cantor, David. 1999. "The Sierra Club Political Committee." In *After the revolution: PACs and lobbies in the new Republican Congress*, ed. Robert Biersack, Paul S. Herrnson, and Clyde Wilcox. New York: Allyn & Bacon.

Ceaser, James. 1979. *Presidential selection*. Princeton: Princeton University Press.

———. 1982. *Reforming the reforms*. Cambridge, Mass.: Ballinger.

Center for Public Integrity. 2004. "The Republican Convention: The party begins in New York City, paid for by special interests." www.public-i.org/report .aspx?aid=367&sid=200.

Center for Responsive Politics. 2005a. "Campaign contributions summary for Rep. Bill Thomas, R-Calif.." www.crp.org/politicians/summary.asp?cycle =2004&cid=N00007256.

———. 2005b. "Tracking the payback." www.crp.org/payback/issue.asp?issueid =EN4&CongNo=109.

———. 2005c. "Donor profiles: Independent expenditures and communications costs, 1989–2004." www.opensecrets.org/orgs/indexp.asp.

———. n.d. "The major players: Active advocacy groups in the 2004 election cycle." www.opensecrets.org/527s/527grps.asp.

Center for Voting and Democracy. "Voting and democracy report: 1995." www.fairvote.org/reports/1995/index.html.

Chapell, Henry W. 1982. "Campaign contributions and congressional voting: A simultaneous probit-tobit model." *Review of Economics and Statistics* 62: 77–83.

Common Cause. 1998. *Return on investment: The hidden story of soft money, corporate welfare, and the 1997 budget and tax deal.* Washington, D.C.: Common Cause.

Conger, Kimberly, and John C. Green. 2002. "Christian conservatives and state Republican Parties." *Campaigns and Elections* (February): 58.

Connecticut Democrats. 2004. "Platform." dems.info/ConnecticutDemocrats Platform.htm.

Cook, Elizabeth Adell, Ted Jelen, and Clyde Wilcox. 1992. *Between two absolutes: Public opinion and the politics of abortion.* Boulder: Westview.

Cooperman, Alan, and Thomas B. Edsall. 2004. "Evangelicals say they led charge for the GOP." *Washington Post*, November 8.

Copelin, Laylan. 2004. "2 DeLay Aides Booked, Freed." *Austin-American Statesman*, October 13.

Corrado, Anthony, Jr. 1992. *Creative campaigning: PACs and the presidential selection.* Boulder: Westview.

Danforth, John. 2005. "In the name of politics." *New York Times*, March 30. www.nytimes.com/2005/03/30/opinion/30danforth.html?ex=1113105600 &en=f035ec536d789831&ei=5070.

Democratic National Convention Committee. 2004a. "Calendar of public events." www.dems2004.org/site/pp.asp?c=luI2LaPYG&b=130913.

———. 2004b. "Youth to be center stage at Democratic convention." www.dems2004.org/site/apps/nl/content2.asp?c=luI2LaPYG&b=116434&ct =151112.

Drew, Elizabeth. 1997. *Whatever it takes: The real struggle for political power in America.* New York: Viking.

Duerst-Lahti, Georgia. 1998. "Introduction: Women and elective office." In *Women and elective office*, ed. Sue Thomas and Clyde Wilcox. New York: Cambridge University Press.

Edsall, Thomas. 1995. "Robertson urges Christian activists to take over GOP." *Washington Post*, September 10.

Eismeier, Theodore J., and Philip H. Pollock III. 1984. "Political action committees: Varieties of organization and strategy." In *Money and politics in the United States*, ed. Michael Malbin. Chatham, N.J.: Chatham House.

———. 1985. "An organizational analysis of political action committees." *Political Behavior* 7: 192–216.

Epstein, Edwin. 1980. "Business and labor under the Federal Election Campaign Act of 1971." In *Parties, interest groups, and campaign finance laws*, ed. Michael Malbin. Washington, D.C.: American Enterprise Institute.

Family Research Council. 2004. "Vote scorecard 108th Congress U.S. House of Representatives." congress.cwfa.org/cwfa/scorecard/?chamber=H&session =108&x=13&y=8.

Ferrara, Joseph. 1994. "The Eaton Corporation Public Policy Association: Ideology, pragmatism, and big business." In *Risky business: PAC decisionmaking in con-*

gressional elections, ed. Robert Biersack, Paul S. Herrnson, and Clyde Wilcox. Armonk, N.Y.: M. E. Sharpe.

Fisher, William L., Ralph Reed, Jr., and Richard L. Weinhold. 1990. Christian Coalition leadership manual. Chesapeake, Va.: Christian Coalition.

Fowler, Linda L., and Robert D. McClure. 1989. Political ambition: Who decides to run for Congress? New Haven: Yale University Press.

Francia, Peter L., Paul S. Herrnson, John C. Green, Lynda W. Powell, and Clyde Wilcox. 2003. The financiers of congressional elections: Investors, ideologues, and intimates. New York: Columbia University Press.

Gallup Organization. 1984. The presidential election: Exit poll, November 7. Princeton, N.J.: Gallup Organization.

Gerber, Alan, and Donald P. Green. 2000. "The effects of personal canvassing, telephone calls, and direct mail on voter turnout: A field experiment." American Political Science Review 94: 653–664.

Gerber, Robin. 1999. "Building to win, building to last: The AFL-CIO COPE takes on the Republican Congress." In After the revolution: PACs and lobbies in the new Republican Congress, ed. Robert Biersack, Paul S. Herrnson, and Clyde Wilcox. New York: Allyn & Bacon.

Getter, Lisa. 2004. "The Republican Convention; energy industry, the party animals." Los Angeles Times, September 2.

Goldberg, Carey. 1996a. "In abortion war, high-tech arms." New York Times, August 9.

———. 1996b. "In rockets' red glare, it's party, party, party." New York Times, August 12.

GOPAC. 2004. Money: A step-by-step guide to raise the necessary capital for your winning campaign. Washington, D.C.: GOPAC.

Green, Donald P. 2004. "Mobilizing African-Americans using direct mail and commercial phone banks: A field experiment." Political Research Quarterly 57: 245–255.

Green, John C., Mark J. Rozell, and Clyde Wilcox. 1995. "Faith, hope, and conflict: The Christian right in state Republican politics." Paper presented at the annual meeting of the American Sociological Association, Washington, D.C., August 19–23.

Greenhouse, Steven, and Rachel L. Swarns. 2003. "Gephardt won't get early backing of labor." New York Times, October 1.

Grenzke, Janet. 1989. "Shopping at the congressional supermarket: The currency is complex." American Journal of Political Science 33: 1–24.

Gugliotta, Guy. 1996. "Interest groups' spending had varied success." Washington Post, November 7.

Gugliotta, Guy, and Ira Chinoy. 1997. "Outsiders made Erie ballot a national battle." Washington Post, February 10.

Gusmano, Michael. 1999. "The doctors' lobby." In After the revolution: PACs and lobbies in the new Republican Congress, ed. Robert Biersack, Paul S. Herrnson, and Clyde Wilcox. New York: Allyn & Bacon.

Herrnson, Paul S. 1994. "The National Committee for an Effective Congress: Liberalism, partisanship, and electoral innovation." In *Risky business: PAC decisionmaking in congressional elections*, ed. Robert Biersack, Paul S. Herrnson, and Clyde Wilcox. Armonk, N.Y.: M. E. Sharpe.

————. 1997. *Congressional elections: Campaigning at home and in Washington*. Washington, D.C.: CQ Press.

Hertzke, Allen D. 1988. *Representing God in Washington: The role of religious lobbies in the American polity*. Knoxville: University of Tennessee Press.

————. 1993. *Echoes of discontent: Jesse Jackson, Pat Robertson, and the resurgence of populism*. Washington, D.C.: CQ Press.

Howe, Daniel Walker. 1980. "Religion and politics in the antebellum North." In *Religion and American politics*, ed. Mark A. Noll. New York: Oxford University Press.

Hrebenar, Ronald J. 1997. *Interest group politics in America*, 3d ed. Armonk, N.Y.: M. E. Sharpe.

Human Rights Campaign. 2004. "HRC scorecard rates Congress on GLBT issues." www.hrc.org/Template.cfm?Section=Press_Room&CONTENTID=23457&TEMPLATE=/ContentManagement/ContentDisplay.cfm.

Idaho Democratic Party. 2004. "Platform." www.idaho-democrats.org.

Jackson, Brooks. 1996a. "Business helps bankroll GOP, Democratic conventions." CNN transcript, AllPolitics.com, August 6.

————. 1996b. "Religious right, convention might." CNN transcript, AllPolitics.com, August 8.

Jacoby, Mary. 2004. "The gospel according to Karl." Salon.com, July 6.

Jurkowitz, Mark. 2004. "Media buzz aided anti-Kerry effort." *Boston Globe*, August 21.

Justice, Glen, and Marian Burros. 2004. "Parties are big business at New York convention." *New York Times*, August 28.

Labaton, Stephen. 1996. "A new arena for ads and political influence." *New York Times*, August 13.

Ladd, Everett Carll. 1978. *Where have all the voters gone? The fracturing of America's political parties*. New York: Norton.

Larson, Carin. 2005. "Not moving mountains: The Christian Right in Colorado." In *The values vote?: The Christian Right in the 2004 elections*, ed. John C. Green, Mark J. Rozell, and Clyde Wilcox. Washington, D.C.: Georgetown University Press.

Lengle, James I., and Byron Shafer. 1976. "Primary rules, political power, and social change." *American Political Science Review* 70: 25–40.

Levick-Segnatelli, Barbara. 1994. "The Washington PAC: One man can make a difference." In *Risky business: PAC decisionmaking in congressional elections*, ed. Robert Biersack, Paul S. Herrnson, and Clyde Wilcox. Armonk, N.Y.: M. E. Sharpe.

Lopez, Kathryn Jean. 2004. "A Kerry-league play: Tom Daschle tries to have it both ways on abortion and marriage." *National Review*, October 22, www.nationalreview.com/lopez/lopez200410221133.asp.

Lovenduski, Joni. 1997. "Gender politics." In *Britain votes*, ed. Pippa Norris and Neil Gavin. Oxford: Oxford University Press.

Maine Democratic Party. 2004. "Platform." www.mainedems.org/party _platform.asp.

Maisel, Sandy. 1996. "The platform-writing process: Candidate-centered platforms in 1992." In *Understanding presidential elections: Trends and developments*, ed. Robert Y. Shapiro. New York: Academy of Political Science.

Malbin, Michael, Robert Boatright, Mark J. Rozell, and Clyde Wilcox. 2005. "Adaptations and alliances: Strategic decisions by ongoing interest groups and advocacy organizations." In *One election later: Politics after the Bipartisan Campaign Reform Act*, ed. Michael Malbin. Lanham, Md.: Rowman & Littlefield.

Malbin, Michael, Mark J. Rozell, Clyde Wilcox, and Richard Skinner. 2002. "Interest groups adaptations in the elections of 2000." Presented at the annual meeting of the Southern Political Science Association, Atlanta, Georgia, November.

Mann, Thomas E. 2005. "The FEC: Administering and enforcing campaign finance law." In *The new campaign finance sourcebook*, ed. Anthony Corrado, Thomas E. Mann, Daniel R. Ortiz, and Trevor Potter. Washington, D.C.: Brookings Institution, www.brookings.edu/gs/cf/newsourcebk.htm.

Marcus, Ruth. 1997a. "GOP's issue conferences coincided with Hill action." *Washington Post*, July 24.

———. 1997b. "RNC steered funds to outside groups." *Washington Post*, October 23.

McBurnett, Michael, Christopher Kenny, and David J. Bordua. 1996. "The impact of political interests in the 1994 elections: The role of the National Rifle Association." Paper presented at the annual meeting of the Midwest Political Science Association, Chicago.

Miller, John J. 2005. "High caliber advocacy: How the NRA won the fight over gun rights." *National Review*, February 14.

Mississippi Center for Public Policy. 2004. "Supreme Court judicial voter guide for Mississippi." www.mspolicy.org/legislature/voterguide.htm.

Mississippi Republican Party. 2004. "Platform." www.msgop.org/platform.asp.

Morello, Carol. 2004. "W. VA Supreme Court justice defeated in rancorous contest," *Washington Post*, November 4.

Moss, Jennings. 1994. "Promises, promises: A Clinton report card at the one year mark." *Washington Times*, January 20.

Moss, Michael, and Ford Fessenden. 2004. "Interest groups mounting costly push to get out the vote." *New York Times*, October 24, A1.

Mundo, Phillip. 1999. "League of Conservation Voters." In *After the revolution: PACs and lobbies in the new Republican Congress*, ed. Robert Biersack, Paul S. Herrnson, and Clyde Wilcox. New York: Allyn & Bacon.

Mutch, Robert. 1994. "AT&T PAC: A pragmatic giant." In *Risky business: PAC decisionmaking in congressional elections*, ed. Robert Biersack, Paul S. Herrnson, and Clyde Wilcox. Armonk, N.Y.: M. E. Sharpe.

————. 1999. "AT&T PAC: The perils of pragmatism." In *After the revolution: PACs and lobbies in the new Republican Congress*, ed. Robert Biersack, Paul S. Herrnson, and Clyde Wilcox. New York: Allyn & Bacon.

Nagourney, Adam. 2004. "'Moral values' carried Bush, Rove says." *New York Times*, November 10.

National Rifle Association Political Victory Fund. 2004. "Your tools for victory; victory report: Election 2004." December 6. www.nrapvf.org/News/Article .aspx?ID=154.

National Women's Political Caucus (NWPC). 1997a. *Campaigning to win: The NWPC guide to running a winning campaign.* Washington, D.C.: NWPC.

————. 1997b. *Candidate recruitment guide for state and local caucus leaders (NWPC).* Washington, D.C.: NWPC.

————. 2005. "National Women's Political Caucus training program." www .nwpc.org/index.php?display=programdetails&id=464.

Nelson, Candice. 1994. "BIPAC: Trying to lead in an uncertain political climate." In *Risky business: PAC decisionmaking in congressional elections*, ed. Robert Biersack, Paul S. Herrnson, and Clyde Wilcox. Armonk, N.Y.: M. E. Sharpe.

Nelson, Candice, and Robert Biersack. 1999. "BIPAC: Working to keep a pro-business Congress." In *After the revolution: PACs and lobbies in the new Republican Congress*, ed. Robert Biersack, Paul S. Herrnson, and Clyde Wilcox. New York: Allyn & Bacon.

Newsweek. 2003. Poll conducted by Princeton Survey Research Associates, October 11.

Norrander, Barbara. 1992. *Super Tuesday: Regional politics and presidential primaries.* Lexington: University Press of Kentucky.

Oklahoma Republican Party. 2004. "Platform." www.okgop.com/documents /state_platform.doc.

Palmetto Family Council. 2004. "Issues guide 2004." www.palmettofamily.org /Legacy/Voter%20Guide.pdf.

Patterson, Samuel C., and Keith R. Eakins. 1998. "Congress and gun control." In *The changing politics of gun control*, ed. John Bruce and Clyde Wilcox. Lanham, Md.: Rowman & Littlefield.

Polsby, Nelson. 1983. *Consequences of party reform.* New York: Oxford University Press.

Pomper, Gerald, with Susan Lederman. 1980. *Elections in America.* New York: Longman.

Potter, John. 1997. "Where are we now? The current state of campaign finance law." In *Abridged campaign finance reform: A sourcebook*, ed. Anthony J. Corrado et al. Washington, D.C.: Brookings Institution.

Powell, Michael, and Michelle Garcia. 2004. "Arrests at GOP Convention Are Criticized." *Washington Post*, September 20.

Public Citizen. 2004a. "Study: Top U.S. air polluters are closely tied to Bush fundraising, pollution policymaking process." May 5. www.citizen.org /pressroom/release.cfm?ID=1706.

————. "Tom DeLay: Unfit to lead." November 15. www.citizen.org/documents/ACF178.pdf.

————. 2005. "Issue advocacy: Electioneering issue advocacy vs. genuine issue advocacy." www.citizen.org/congress/campaign/issues/issue_ads/index.cfm.

Republicans for Choice. 1996. *On the 1996 GOP platform committee hearings and the Republican National Convention.* Alexandria, Va.: Republicans for Choice.

Rimmerman, Craig. 1994. "When women run against women: Double standards and vitriol in the New York primary." In *The year of the woman,* ed. Elizabeth Cook, Sue Thomas, and Clyde Wilcox. Boulder: Westview.

Rosenbaum, David E., and Janet Elder. 2004. "Delegates lean left and oppose the war." *New York Times,* July 25.

Rosenstone, Steven J., and John Mark Hansen. 1993. *Mobilization, participation, and democracy in America.* New York: Macmillan.

Rozell, Mark J. 1999. "The WISH List: Moderate women in the GOP Congress." In *After the revolution: PACs and lobbies in the new Republican Congress,* ed. Robert Biersack, Paul S. Herrnson, and Clyde Wilcox. New York: Allyn & Bacon.

Rozell, Mark J., and Clyde Wilcox, eds. 1995. *God at the grass roots: The Christian Right in the 1994 elections.* Lanham, Md.: Rowman & Littlefield.

————. 1996. *Second coming: The new Christian Right in Virginia politics.* Baltimore: Johns Hopkins University Press.

————. 1997. *God at the grass roots, 1996: The Christian Right in American elections.* Lanham, Md.: Rowman & Littlefield.

Sabato, Larry J. 1984. *PAC power.* New York: Norton.

Sack, Kevin. 1996. "Differences aside, labor embraces the Democrats." *New York Times,* August 26.

Schlozman, Kay Lehman, and John T. Tierney. 1986. *Organized interests and American democracy.* New York: Harper & Row.

Seelye, Katherine Q., and Marjorie Connelly. 2004. "Delegates leaning to right of G.O.P. and the nation." *New York Times,* August 29.

Shaiko, Ron, and Marc A. Wallace. 1999. "From Wall Street to Main Street: The National Federation of Independent Businesses and the Republican majority." In *After the revolution: PACs and lobbies in the new Republican Congress,* ed. Robert Biersack, Paul S. Herrnson, and Clyde Wilcox. New York: Allyn & Bacon.

Shapiro, Robert Y. 2003. "Public attitudes toward campaign finance practice and reform." In *Inside the Campaign Finance Battle,* ed. Anthony Corrado, Thomas E. Mann, and Trevor Potter. Washington, D.C.: Brookings Institution.

Sinclair, Barbara. 1997. *Unorthodox lawmaking: New legislative processes in the U.S. Congress.* Washington, D.C.: CQ Press.

Smith, Bradley A. 2003. *UnFreeSpeech.* Princeton: Princeton University Press.

Sorauf, Frank. 1984. *What price PACs?* New York: Twentieth Century Fund.

————. 1988. *Money in American elections.* San Francisco: Scott Foresman.

Stern, Philip. 1988. *The best Congress money can buy*. New York: Pantheon.

Stone, Peter H. 1997. "GOP jousts with Business Roundtable." *National Journal*, January 11, 75.

Stronks, Julia. 1994. "The American Association of Publishers PAC." In *Risky business: PAC decisionmaking in congressional elections*, ed. Robert Biersack, Paul S. Herrnson, and Clyde Wilcox. Armonk, N.Y.: M. E. Sharpe.

Swierenga, Robert P. 1980. "Ethnoreligious political behavior in the mid-nineteenth century: Voting, values, cultures." In *Religion and American politics*, ed. Mark A. Noll. New York: Oxford University Press.

Thomas, Sue. 1999. "NARAL PAC: Battling for women's reproductive rights." In *After the revolution: PACs and lobbies in the new Republican Congress*, ed. Robert Biersack, Paul S. Herrnson, and Clyde Wilcox. New York: Allyn & Bacon.

Toedtman, James. 2004. "Where the money is." *Newsday*, September 2.

Tollerson, Ernest. 1996. "Hired hands carrying democracy's petitions." *New York Times*, July 9.

Truman, David. 1951. *The governmental process*. New York: Knopf.

VandeHei, Jim. 2005. "Business sees gain in GOP takeover." *Washington Post*, March 27, A1.

Verba, Sidney, Kay Lehman Schlozman, and Henry Brady. 1995. *Voice and equality: Civic voluntarism in American politics*. Cambridge: Harvard University Press.

Virginia Democratic Party. 2004. "Platform." www.vademocrats.org/who_we_are /platform.asp.

Walker, Jack. 1983. "The origins and maintenance of interest groups in America." *American Political Science Review* 77: 390–406.

Washington State Republican Party. 2004. "Platform." www.wsrp.org/platform.htm.

Wayne, Leslie. 1996. "Like other television shows, convention had sponsors." *New York Times*, September 1.

———. 2004. "G.O.P. club supports conservative races." *New York Times*, April 11.

Welch, Susan, et al. 1998. *American government*, 6th ed. Belmont, Calif.: West/ Wadsworth.

Welch, William P. 1982. "Campaign contributions and legislative voting: Milk money and dairy price supports." *Western Political Quarterly* 35: 478–495.

Wilcox, Clyde. 1988. "I owe it all to me: Candidates' investments in their own campaigns." *American Politics Quarterly* 16: 266–279.

———. 1989. "Organizational variables and contribution behavior of large PACs: A longitudinal analysis." *Political Behavior* 11: 157–173.

———. 1990. "Member to member giving." In *Money, elections, and democracy*, ed. M. Nugent and John Johannes. Boulder: Westview.

———. 1992. *God's warriors: The Christian Right in twentieth-century America*. Baltimore: Johns Hopkins University Press.

———. 1994. "Coping with increasing business influence: The AFL-CIO's Committee on Political Education." In *Risky business: PAC decisionmaking in congressional elections*, ed. Robert Biersack, Paul S. Herrnson, and Clyde Wilcox. Armonk, N.Y.: M. E. Sharpe.

———. 2000. "They did it their way: Campaign finance principles and realities clash in Wisconsin 1998." In *Campaigns & elections: Contemporary case studies*, ed. Michael Bailey, Ronald Fauchaux, Paul S. Herrnson, and Clyde Wilcox. Washington, D.C.: Congressional Quarterly Press.

———. 2004. "Campaign finance law enforcement in Canada and the US." Presented at Organization of American States session on campaign finance in the Americas, Cartegena, Columbia.

Wilcox, Clyde, and Carin Larson. 2005. "Prayers, parties and preachers: The evolving nature of political and religious mobilization." In *American religion and political mobilization*, ed. Matthew Wilson. Washington, D.C.: Georgetown University Press.

Wilson, James Q. 1962. *The amateur democrat: Club politics in three cities*. Chicago: University of Chicago Press.

Wolf, Richard. 1996. "Labor unions are back and packing some power." *USA Today*, October 15.

Wright, John R. 1985. "PACs, contributions, and roll calls: An organizational perspective." *American Political Science Review* 79: 400–414.

———. 1996. *Interest groups and Congress: Lobbying, contributions, and influence*. Boston: Allyn & Bacon.

Index

A31 Coalition, 35
Abortion issue, 3, 4, 7, 10, 25, 30, 31, 35, 40, 56–57, 67, 123
Access strategy, 23, 27–28, 89
Advertisements
  by 527 committees, 78, 116
  independent expenditure, 139–140
  Internet, 8
  issue advocacy, 77, 116, 142–147, 150
  radio and television, 1, 78, 118
  and treasury funds, 22
AFL-CIO. *See* American Federation of Labor-Congress of Industrial Organizations
African Americans, 10, 19, 35, 38, 134, 140
Air Traffic Controllers' Union, 125
Altria, 61
Amalgamated Lithographers Local 1 PAC, 87
America-Israel Public Affairs Committee (AIPAC), 55
American Association of Publishers PAC, 100
American Association of Retired Persons, 137–138
American Bar Association (ABA), 8, 9
American Chiropractic Association, 141 (table)
American Civil Liberties Union (ACLU), 76, 167
American Conservative Union (ACU), 76, 128
American Defense Institute, 137
American Federation of Labor-Congress of Industrial Organizations (AFL-CIO). *See also* Committee on Political Education
  delegate selection, 51–52
  endorsements, 121–122, 126
  hit lists, 126
  issue advocacy, 143
  membership, 8
  recruitment, 37
  resources, 24
  voter mobilization, 24, 116, 134, 136
American Gas Association, 63, 64
American Jewish Committee, 53
American Medical Association (AMA), 8, 9, 36, 73, 82, 93, 140
American Petroleum Institute, 55
American Political Science Association (APSA), 8
American political system, 13–20
Americans Coming Together (ACT), 8, 80, 135
Americans for a Republican Majority, 106
Americans for Democratic Action (ADA), 55, 128
Americans for Tax Reform, 11, 19, 137
American Trucking Association, 107

American Watercraft Association, 141 (table)
America Votes, 8
Amitay, Morris, 100
AMPAC, 93
Amway Corporation, 158
And For the Sake of the Kids, 144
Anheuser-Busch, 61
Annenberg Center, 164
Anti-abortion groups, 2, 21, 24, 25, 30, 142
Antiwar movement, 5
Arctic National Wildlife Refuge, 2, 158
Associated Builders and Contractors, 141 (table)
AT&T, 60
AT&T PAC, 86, 102
Ave Maria List PAC, 141 (table), 142

Barbee, Walter, 105
Barton, Joe, 63
Bauer, Gary, 50
Billionaires for Bush, 53
Bipartisan Campaign Reform Act (BCRA), 78, 147, 169, 176
Bipartisan strategies, 23, 96, 122
Black, Clint, 63
Blankenship, Don, 146
Blogging, 163
Bond, Rich, 56
Bonilla, Henry, 52
Boren, David, 105
Boxer, Barbara, 77
Brookings Institution Working Group, 175
Brown, Ron, 55
Brownback, Sam, 17
Bryan, William Jennings, 5
Buchanan, Pat, 50, 138
Buckley v. Valeo, 76, 116
Bundling, 103–105, 157
Bush, George H. W.
  abortion stance, 35
  as candidate, 50, 51, 167
  as centrist, 155
Bush, George W.
  attacks on opposition, 7
  as candidate, 1, 50, 56, 104, 166, 167
  and Christian conservatives, 1, 9, 16, 115, 138–139
  conservative support for, 8–9, 50, 135
  corporate support, 2, 7
  election results, 4
  and issue ads, 143, 144, 146
  as moderate, 155
  PAC contributions to, 104

189